HYDROPONIC TOMATO PRODUCTION
A PRACTICAL GUIDE TO GROWING TOMATOES IN CONTAINERS

JACK ROSS

Casper
Pty Ltd
publications

AUTHORS ACKNOWLEDGEMENTS

This book is based on information and data from a wide range of sources and in particular on my own involvement, initially as a commercial grower, in the cultivation of tomatoes extending over more than 60 years. This experience has included at least 16 years research into tomato production employing hydroponics technology, with emphasis on the use of containers for growing the plants.

Many organisations and individuals have been helpful in providing material for the book, with special thanks to Adelaide and Wallaroo Fertilisers Ltd; Agromatic Corporation Pty Ltd; Arthur Yates and Co. Ltd; Australian Hydroponic Association Inc.; Australian Nutrition Foundation; Australian Perlite; Auto-Pot Pty Ltd; Colemans Plumbing Supplies; Commonwealth Department of Health; CSIRO Division of Food Research; Erica Vale Aust. Pty Ltd; Growool Horticultural Systems Pty Ltd; Hydroponic Society of America; Hydroponic Society of South Australia; Hydroponic Sales and Service; International Society of Soilless Culture; Living Shade Pty Ltd; New Gippsland Seed Farm; Quantum Science; R and D Aquaponics Pty Ltd; Seed Savers Network; Simple Grow; TPS Pty Ltd.

Of the many individuals who have been especially helpful in many different ways, I thank Steven Carruthers, Jude Fanton, Jim Fah, Alan Ferris, Roger Fox, John Gwalter, Bruce Hall, Duncan Herbert, Chris King, Dr Barry McGlasson, Bruce Retallick, Dr Ben Robinson, Ray Rogers, John Ross, Greg Seymour and Allen Sinclair.

A large number of books, brochures, magazines and Government publications listed under *References* have been consulted and I acknowledge help from the authors and publishers of these sources.

In no way is the use of trade names mentioned in the text intended to imply approval of any particular brand name over other similar products not mentioned in the book.

The Author.

Published by
Casper Publications Pty Ltd
(A.C.N. 064 029 303)
PO Box 225
Narrabeen
NSW 2101 AUSTRALIA
Email: casper@hydroponics.com.au
Internet: http://www.hydroponics.com.au

© Jack Ross 1998

ISBN 0-9586735-1-9

Edited by Roger Fox
Design & Layout by Leon Wilson

CONTENTS

LIST OF TABLES

LIST OF FIGURES

Chapter 1. THE REAL TOMATO

Chapter 1. THE REAL TOMATO

What have they done to the tomato?

Where are those delicious rich red tomatoes with a zesty sweet taste and smooth fleshy texture that Grandpa grew in his back garden 50 years ago? It is almost impossible to purchase a real tomato these days in a supermarket or even at the local fruit and vegetable shop.

Most tomatoes on sale today are tasteless, squashy, tough skinned and definitely uninteresting. They certainly do not excite an appetite or tingle the taste buds. Most are almost a total gastronomical failure.

One well known nurseryman writing in the gardening column of a metropolitan newspaper recently said:

"I agree that some of the hybrid tomatoes that have hit the market in recent times look so magnificent, but taste so dreadfully wishy-washy that I would never give them garden space.

Indeed it is a fact that the original wild, smaller than a cherry sized tomato of the Andes mountains, in which many modern hybrids had their origin, has about 50 times the nutritional value, gram for gram, of vitamin C and pro-vitamin A of some of their modern descendants which may be 100 times the weight. There has to be a lesson in that!

Even the State Minister for Agriculture in New South Wales was quoted as saying at a Tomato Tasting Trial that "the modern tomato was more suited for use in cricket practice than for the table". Nevertheless, tomatoes are the most widely grown glasshouse crop in the world. There are many reasons for this, but the two main reasons are the high demand by the consuming public and the high yielding capability of the plant.

From the steady flow of adverse comments in the newspapers, on talk-back radio etc, it is evident that the consumer is far from happy about the flavour of commercially grown tomatoes. The results of many sensory experiments that the CSIRO Food Research Laboratory has conducted, confirms that the majority of cultivars are poor in flavour. Our sense of flavour is affected by how things smell and taste, and the aroma of most commercially grown tomatoes leaves much to be desired.

Flavour and texture are high on the list of the tomato connoisseur. The tomato grown for the supermarket is picked green, before flavour has had a chance to develop, and what results is a bland puffy flesh encased in a rubber-like skin, or in the other extreme, a red cannon ball with an unyielding rocklike consistency. The old fashioned delicious tomato flavour has been lost in the quest for other characteristics.

Tomato breeders are under intense pressure from commercial growers to develop new strains which will produce earlier and longer, are heavier, mature faster, can be harvested by machines, can travel better and are more resistant to disease and insect attack. While the plant breeders are being pushed to develop new strains, the advertisers are at the same time trying to convince the public that all this is being done for the good of the consumer. They fill the air waves, the newspapers and the glossy cookery books with claims that modern tomatoes "taste better than natural" - "are chock full of essential vitamins" - "supermarket tomatoes are super good foods" etc. It has almost reached the stage where many people have never sampled the taste of a real tomato. They don't know what it is like to eat a fresh, vine ripened tomato that is a delight to the eye and the palate.

It was recently reported in a television program, that developments in the food industry in the USA are moving so rapidly that by the year 2000, tomatoes will be totally square, 90 per cent solid, with skin like leather and colour like a candy apple! It was also claimed that many children, 16 years of age, have never tasted a home grown tomato. This is a pity because there are few dishes which cannot be enhanced by the rich flavour of a vine ripened tomato, grown under good conditions with the correct nutrients.

Scientists have been talking about producing better tomatoes through genetic engineering ever since the technology became available in the 1970's. In 1994, a number of magazines carried reports of work undertaken by the America Californian-based Calgene company in producing a tomato cultivar which it named 'Flavr Savr', and which the company claimed would produce tomatoes with 'summertime taste all year round'. Calgene

1: Inner Wall of the Pericarp. 2: Placental Tissue. 3: Radial Wall of the Pericarp.
4: Epidermis. 5: Outer Wall of the Pericarp. 6: Locular Cavity with Seeds.
Transverse section of OX Heart a typical home grown tomato. The body of the fruit which surrounds and encloses the seed is the pericarp and consists of outer, radial and inner walls.

specialises in horticultural genetic engineering.

It was produced via a process of gene modification and was greeted with some concern by environmentalist groups as 'tampering with nature'.

The process involved removing the gene that governs a hormone, that in turn causes the tomato to ripen. Trials indicated that the result of the action was that ripening, and eventually, rotting of the fruit, slowed down immediately the tomato was picked for market. It was reported that the project took 10 years to bring it to its present stage, at a cost of some $25 million.

Companies in Europe and Israel have been undertaking work along similar lines in an effort to develop a tomato with top class taste and which can be produced on a large scale by commercial growers.

In Australia, the CSIRO's horticultural section under Dr Jim Speirs was also engaged on a project at North Ryde (in Sydney) in 1994, to develop a tomato that 'remains hard long enough to be transported, then softens releasing flavour, about the time the customer takes the fruit home for the table'. The approach taken by CSIRO was to transpose a single purpose gene, known for its ability to induce softness, into a firm commercial variety. This was a different approach to the Calgene project, which modified a tasty tomato to slow down its softening.

Although the USA Food and Drug Administration endorsed the genetically altered fruit, as safe for sale to customers in May 1994, and supermarkets were supplied from June 1994, very little has been reported on customer reaction to the fruit. A reported comment by a group opposed to the production of tomatoes through genetic engineering was 'The middle class is moving in the direction of organic, healthy, sustainable foods and the last thing they want to hear about is gene spliced tomatoes'.

One of the few published comments by a business person who uses tomatoes was made by the Chef and Owner of Berkley's famous Chez Panisse Restaurant, a well known tomato connoisseur who sampled the Flavr Savr and said, 'Not bad, but not good enough for diners at Chez Panisse'.

However, we should not despair. It is still possible to produce that elusive 'real tomato' for the home table, by employing one of the earliest known techniques in agriculture, called hydroponics or soilless culture. Seeds of old fashioned varieties are readily available from Seed Saver Clubs but even so, some of the modern hybrids are also capable of producing good results if suitably cultivated.

A home grown, vine-ripened savoury tomato has few culinary rivals. Nothing can compare with a thick slab of rich red tomato, sprinkled with fresh chopped basil and a sprinkling of black pepper on a slice of buttered wholemeal bread.

The tomato has become an important component of the diet of most Australians. Its importance lies in the fact that it provides vitamins, mineral salts and fibre, in addition to some carbohydrate and protein. Fat content is negligible.

Origin of the tomato

The wild tomato is thought to have originated in South America, and Spanish priests probably brought it to Europe from Mexico in the mid sixteenth century. Wild tomato plants can still be found today in Peru, Ecuador and some other South American countries. The fruit is small, somewhat like the modern cherry variety. Botanists classify the tomato as a fruit, however most people consider it to be a vegetable because it is used mostly with vegetable dishes. The botanists gave the tomato the Latin name *Lycopersicon* which means 'wolf peach'. The reason is somewhat obscure. The modern scientific name is *Lycopersicon esculentum* which means edible wolf peach. The English word 'tomato' probably derived from the seventeenth century Spanish 'tomate' which in turn was derived from 'xitomate' the name given by the Aztecs to identify the plant.

When the tomato reached England, people thought it to be poisonous as it belonged to the same family of plants as the deadly nightshade. The French assumed it was an aphrodisiac and called it pomme d'amour or 'apple of love'.

In the United States, it was not until 1820 that the tomato was accepted as something useful. In that year, a fearless tomato lover named Johnson ate a whole tomato in public. People gasped in awe but when Johnson survived this daredevil feat, the tomato quickly gained a place in the diet of Americans. Tomatoes were grown commercially in the USA from about 1870. One of the noteworthy growers was Joseph Campbell whose name is still associated with the Campbell Soup Company.

The home gardener came into the act of cultivating tomatoes before the turn of the century, when Seedsmen began to include tomato seeds in their catalogues. W. Atlee Burpee and Co. of Philadelphia and London, in their 1888 seed catalogue, listed a range of seeds including varieties such as Extra Early Advance, Early Optimus, Livingston's Beauty, Essex Early Hybrid, The Cardinal, Mayflower, Burpee's Climax, Trophy and Golden Queen. There was also a range of small fruit tomatoes, including White Apple, Wonder of Italy, King Humbert, Nesbit's Victoria, Red Cherry, and Small Round Cherry.

Seeds of some early varieties are still available from some sources, particularly Seed Savers Clubs. The Diggers Club of Victoria, in 1992, marketed a range of heirloom tomatoes, including Green Zebra, an apricot size fruit with yellow markings; Red Peach, apricot size with soft skins; Peruvian Bush, a red large cherry-size tomato; Verna Orange, similar shape to Oxheart but tastier; White Beauty, a white tomato; Thompson's Seedless Grape, a plum size fruit; Purple Calabash, an unusual coloured tomato with a delicious taste; Tigerella, apricot size with yellow and orange flecks; Tommy Toe, with up to 100 tasty tomatoes of apricot size, and many others.

It is not known when tomatoes were first introduced into Australia, but they were relatively unknown prior to about 1870. There are in the country, many growers who have had a long association with the cultivation of tomatoes, with some being able to trace family involvement back nearly 100 years. In South Australia for example, tomatoes were first grown commercially in 1900, following a visit to England by a vegetable grower who saw tomatoes growing in glasshouses and brought back some seeds. He grew them in pits covered with glass frames, which were raised as the plants grew. Gradually they were grown in proper glasshouses. By 1910, production had increased considerably and tomatoes had become a favourite vegetable with many families in Adelaide.

By the 1940's, tomato growing had reached the big business stage, with breeders actively engaged in producing varieties with specific characteristics. Today, some 54 million tonnes are grown throughout the world annually. In Australia, the consumption per capita rose from 15 kg to 17 kg during the five year period 1990 to 1995, indicating the high level of popularity. Although the major supply comes from soil grown crops, hydroponics installations are rapidly becoming a source of supply, particularly for high quality table tomatoes. In 1990, there were some 300 commercial hydroponic growers located throughout Australia with about 30 specialising in tomatoes. Eleven of the growers were in New South Wales, and they had about 9 ha under cultivation.

Figure 1.1 shows the main features of a staked tomato plant at the ripe fruit bearing stage and *Figure 1.2* shows the growing and flowering characteristics of the two principal varieties of plants.

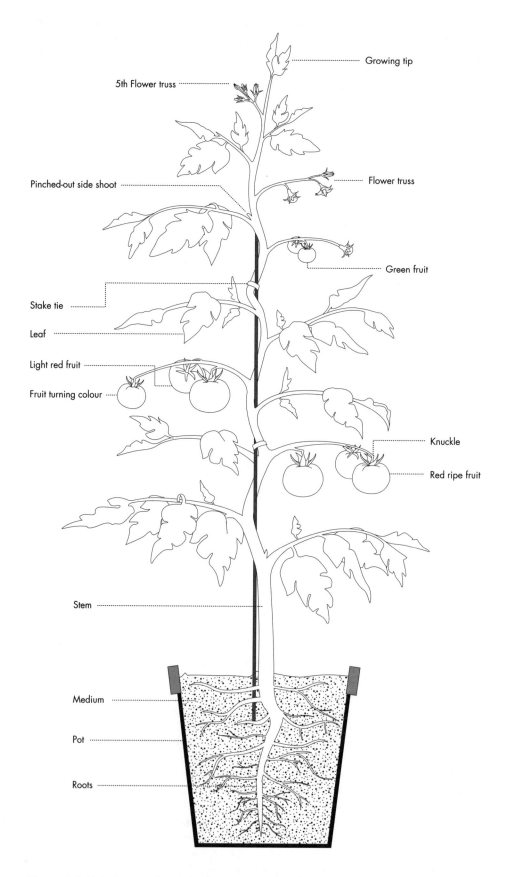

Growing tip

5th Flower truss

Pinched-out side shoot

Flower truss

Green fruit

Stake tie

Leaf

Light red fruit

Fruit turning colour

Knuckle

Red ripe fruit

Stem

Medium

Pot

Roots

Figure 1.1 Main features of typical indeterminate tomato plant

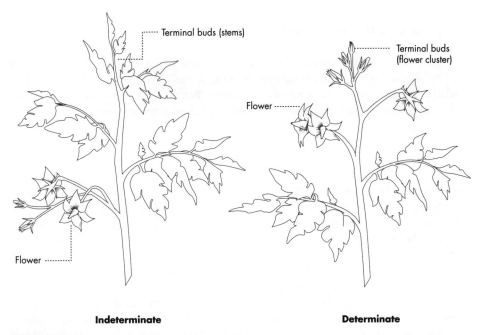

Terminal buds (stems)

Terminal buds
(flower cluster)

Flower

Flower

Indeterminate

Determinate

Figure 1.2 Indeterminate and determinate varieties

What went wrong?

Before the outbreak of the Second World War, those who can remember, are adamant that tomato quality had reached a high standard. What has happened in the intervening 50 odd years that has resulted in the present inferior product being offered in the supermarkets? Marketing experts say that the breeders and growers simply reacted to consumer demand. They say that the consumer wants every type of fruit and vegetable to be available 365 days in the year. The consumer is apparently not concerned with the fact that most produce has a limited growing time span within a certain temperature range, for optimum results.

To meet the year-round demand situation; marketers put pressure on breeders to develop strains which would crop earlier or later than normally available varieties, and where a full yearly production cycle could not be achieved locally, products were transported from distant places where the temperature enabled a crop to be produced.

A typical example of this is the production shift of the frost sensitive tomato from southern states to Queensland during winter months. Tomatoes are produced in that State for at least six months of the year. New technology, particularly in new varieties and transport, has enabled this to occur. About 70 per cent of more than 3 million 10 kg cartons of tomatoes which arrive at Sydney markets each year, are grown in Bundaberg and Bowen in Queensland.

In producing varieties which will crop out of season, can be mechanically harvested, can withstand the rigours of high speed semi-trailer transport, and yet arrive at the market in a saleable condition, the breeders and growers have met the criteria but unfortunately in the process flavour, texture and other desirable attributes have suffered.

Marketing factors also require that the fruit be picked green with the barest showing of colour, enabling the fruit to ripen during transport enroute, instead of on the vine in the field. Fruit are also picked green and gas ripened. Although gas ripening using ethylene - a natural ripening agent - is harmless, it is only *part* of the ripening process which takes place with a vine ripened tomato. On the plant, there is a slow production of acids, sugars and aromatic oils, which all combine to give a tomato that exquisite flavour that cannot be duplicated by artificial means. Perhaps it was because the change took place over a long period of time, without the consumer being aware of it, that there was no outcry for return to the earlier more flavoursome fruit.

In quest of a better tomato

Fortunately, with the proliferation of health food shops and a greater awareness of food quality, people are now seeking out products of high quality and value, grown under controlled conditions and free from harmful substances. We are in an age when the subtle distinctions between various foods are being recognised and appreciated. People's palates are becoming more sophisticated.

The tomato has become so staple an article of modern diet, that there would be very few people who would not enjoy its virtues in many forms. The rich tang and succulence of a well ripened tomato is highly prized. The different varieties have their characteristics and some tomato lovers seek out particular varieties at the market. The taste peculiar to a variety results from a combination of acids, sugars and volatile oils, which form and blend when the fruit ripens slowly in the sunshine.

Connoisseurs claim tomato varieties can be classified under a number of characteristic features, such as aromatic, sugary, acid, sharp, tangy, dry, full flavoured and bland. Compounds which contribute to good flavour are the glucose and fructose sugars and malic and citric acids and the aroma.

The flavour may be influenced by the nutrient feed mixture, the season, different stages of growth, the length of time after harvest and the environment in which the tomato is grown. Some judges are of the opinion that the flavour is enhanced if the calyx is not removed until the fruit is ready to be eaten.

Some business leaders are now beginning to recognise the need for improvement in quality of the tomato. Coles New World Supermarkets gave a grant of $10 000 to the CSIRO Tomato Project Team, whose aim is to assist in the selection of new varieties with better flavour. Part of the Team's effort is directed towards identification and measurement of the compounds which give good flavour and to find out how growing conditions influence firmness and texture. Success will mean tastier tomatoes with better keeping qualities, compared with products currently available.

Sensory evaluation

Researchers, particularly CSIRO staff, have done a great deal of work on components of tomato fruit which influence taste and flavour, but simple measurement of such factors as total soluble solids, pH, titratable acidity and electrical conductivity do not provide an adequate measure of sensory quality.

Quality is evaluated on the basis of composition and assessment by taste tests. Sensory quality is generally evaluated by an experienced panel which may comprise 20 or more people who are asked to rate colour, flavour, sweetness, texture, acidity/sourness and general acceptability on a nine point hedonic scale i.e. 9 = very good, 5 = satisfactory and 1 = very poor.

One survey conducted in 1995 at a large fruit and vegetable shop in a New South Wales country town, found that many consumers complained about poor texture in tomatoes. By texture, they meant how the fruit felt in the mouth while being eaten. Those questioned considered the most desirable attributes were absence of woodiness and mealiness, mild taste, full flavoured and the presence of a 'real tomato aroma'.

In early 1996, Arthur Yates and Co. Ltd, who market a range of tomato seeds and who have produced Yates Garden Guide for over 100 years, brought a group of food and garden experts together for a tomato tasting exercise.

The tasting was divided into four sections, comprising cherry and cocktail tomatoes; Italian and cooking tomatoes; home garden tomatoes and commercial tomatoes.

Growers Pride Sweet 100 was judged best in the cherry and cocktail section; Yates Y3423 won the Italian and cooking tomato section; Costoluto di Marmande was first in the home garden tomato section followed by Mortage Lifter, and Summertaste was judged, best in the commercial tomato section.

Chapter 2. THE NUTRITIOUS TOMATO

Chapter 2. THE NUTRITIOUS TOMATO

Composition

If we categorise the tomato as a vegetable, it is one of the most popular vegetables used in the kitchen. In considering a group comprising beans, peas, cabbages, cauliflowers, carrots, onions, potatoes and tomatoes, only peas and potatoes exceed tomatoes in total area under cultivation in Australia. Tomatoes account for up to 10% of the total area under cultivation. In terms of crop weight, some 225,000 tonnes are consumed each year.

The tomato is an important source of vitamins, minerals and fibre. One hundred grams of ripe tomato will provide nearly all the daily allowance of Vitamin A, 73% of Vitamin C, 5% of Vitamin B1, 3% of Vitamin B2 and B3, as well as many essential minerals required by the body. Canned puree tomatoes are even better in some respects. Vitamin content, especially Vitamin C, vary more with growing condition, particularly the daylight time, than with variety. Composition details are shown in *Table 2.1*.

Item	Unit	Raw red	Canned ripe	Canned puree	Canned juice
Edible portion	%	94	100	100	100
Water	g	93.7	93.9	88	93.8
Protein	g	1.0	1.0	1.8	1.0
Fat	g	0.3	0.2	0.4	0.2
Carbohydrate	g	4.1	4.1	7.1	4.1
Energy	kJ	88	84	146	84
Calcium	mg	14	9	12	7
Phosphorus	mg	25	23	35	18
Iron	mg	0.5	0.6	1.3	0.5
Sodium	mg	4	130	399	200
Potassium	mg	252	217	426	227
ß-Carotene equiv.	µg	715	646	1553	598
Retinol	µg	0	0	0	0
Thiamine	µg	60	57	90	50
Riboflavin	mg	0.04	0.03	0.06	0.03
Niacin	mg	0.6	0.6	1.7	0.8
Ascorbic acid	mg	22	18	27	17

Table 2.1 *Composition of tomato per 100 g of edible portion (Source Commonwealth Dept of Health leaflet)*

Concern with nutrition

Nearly everyone today is concerned about nutrition. Some people have access to all the food they need while sadly, in this so called enlightened world, others are starving.
Where there is an abundance of food, people are more selective in what they eat. The proliferation of health food shops bears witness to this. Many consumers are no longer prepared to accept advertisement in the media extolling the benefits of certain products. They want to know why some foods are good for the body and why others are not. They want facts on such factors as fibre, sugar, sodium, vitamins, energy, minerals, proteins, preservatives, colouring and many others. There is also an increasing number of vegetarians whose diets include vegetables, cereals and fruit, but which exclude most foods of animal origin.

All foods contain varying amounts of nutrients and it is by measuring these, that experts can determine if the recommended intake is being reached. Whatever the diet, good nutrition is achieved most easily when the diet contains a wide variety of foods.

Protein

Nutritionists recommend that about one tenth of a person's diet should be protein. This is a concentration that is found in the staple food of most countries. Proteins are built up from amino acids and the nutritional quality of the proteins vary according to the amino acids they contain, and the digestibility of this protein in the human gut.

In general, food from animal sources provides proteins of high nutritional quality, with the amino acids in correct proportions, while plant proteins are often deficient in one or more amino acids. However, those people who prefer not to eat foods of animal origin, can get the right combination of amino acids for the production of a complete human protein, by eating the right plant foods. A 100 gram portion of ripe tomato contains about one gram of protein and is about the same as an equivalent weight of celery, onion, carrot, radish or pumpkin.

Minerals

The Australian Nutrition Foundation publications indicate that the mineral elements sodium, potassium, chlorine, calcium, and magnesium are important in maintaining a normal body fluid environment, with calcium, phosphorus and magnesium being important in bone growth.

Deficiencies are unlikely in a varied diet, but where the diet is restricted to an all plant food diet, there may be some difficulty in meeting the dietary allowance for calcium. Iron is a key mineral in the formation of blood and is a common deficiency in some human diets. Meat is the best source of iron, but for those on basic vegetable diets the human body has many mechanisms of adjustment. It is believed that the higher level of Vitamin C in vegetable diets, is a key in making iron available from these diets. Tomatoes are a good source of Vitamin C.

The percentage of elements in tomatoes varies with the variety and maturity of the fruit, but typical percentages are phosphorus 0.55, potassium 4.8, calcium 0.24, magnesium 0.3 and sulphur 0.32, with iron 200 ppm.

Vitamins

A good diet consists of a wide variety of foods which provide all essential nutrients such as minerals, vitamins, protein, carbohydrates and fats, required by the body in order to stay healthy. If the right foods are eaten there is usually no need to take vitamin supplements, which are expensive and may in some cases have undesirable side effects.

In the 1930's the League of Nations Health Organisation compiled a list of the amounts of various vitamins required in the diet to maintain good health. It has remained, with little change to the present day, the basis for similar guidelines in tables of Recommended Daily Allowances.

These quantities of vitamins are not meant to be taken as supplements to a good diet, nor as supplements to compensate for a bad diet. They are meant to be the amount we should find in our food each day. The inclusion of tomatoes in the diet will go a long way towards maintaining a healthy body. The tomato as a source of vitamins is illustrated in *Table 2.2.*

Fibre

Fibre is found in most vegetables. The body does not absorb it, but it provides bulk for bowel movement.
Modern food refining has reduced the fibre content by 40% in two generations, increasing many health hazards. People are also eating less bread and starchy vegetables such as potatoes, carrots and turnips.
Statistics reveal that the consumption in Australia per capita of leafy and green vegetables has fallen 25% over the last five years. Fortunately, over the same period, the consumption of tomatoes rose by 23%.

Nutritionists recommend that people eat more fibre, preferably in natural food such as wholemeal bread, fresh fruit, nuts, seeds and vegetables including of course, tomatoes.

Vitamin	Source	Daily Req'ment	Per 100 grams of edible tomato			
			Raw Red % of Daily Req'ment	Canned Ripe % of Daily Req'ment	Canned Puree % of Daily Req'ment	Canned Juice % of Daily Req'ment
Vitamin A	Found as ß-Carotene in orange coloured fruit and vegetables including tomatoes	750µg	715µg/**95%**	647µg/**86%**	1553µg/**207%**	598µg/**80%**
Vitamin C (Ascorbic Acid)	Fruits and vegetables including tomatoes	30mg	22mg/**73%**	18mg/**60%**	27mg/**90%**	17mg/**56%**
Thiamine (B₁)	Vegetables including tomatoes	1.2mg	60µg/**5%**	57µg/**5%**	90µg/**7%**	50µg/**4%**
Riboflavin (B₂)	Vegetables including tomatoes	1.4mg	0.04mg/**3%**	0.03mg/**2%**	0.06mg/**4%**	0.03mg/**2%**
Niacin (B₃)	Vegetables including tomatoes	18mg	0.6mg/**3%**	0.6mg/**3%**	1.7mg/**9%**	0.8mg/**4%**

Table 2.2 *The tomato as a vitamin source*

Salt

With the increasing awareness of good health and fitness, people are becoming more conscious of the need to reduce salt (sodium) intake. Most Australians eat between 5 and 15 grams of salt per day, compared with a recommended daily level of 1 to 3 grams.

Excess salt in the diet adds to the risk of high blood pressure. About one in six Australians have blood pressure above normal. People susceptible to high blood pressure will lower the risk if the intake of salt and salty foods is reduced, especially from an early age.

Raw tomatoes have a salt level of about 4 mg for a 100 gm portion, but the level will rise significantly for canned tomatoes, canned puree and canned juice if salt is added during the canning process. In the case of a typical can of tomato juice, the sodium level is about 4 mg per 100 gm of juice if no salt is added, whereas the same product with added salt may have a level of about 200 mg of sodium for the same 100 gm of juice. The same order of magnitude applies for most other canned vegetables.

Nutritionists concerned with the amount of salt used, even with uncooked food, recommend that the salt shaker be thrown away and herbs and spices be substituted. With the use of the right herbs or spices, the flavour of many foods can be enhanced.

For tomato soup, the experts recommend basil or allspice, for salads use basil or cinnamon, for fresh sliced tomatoes or stewed tomatoes use basil, fennel herbs or cloves.

Acidity

Most of the food we eat contains acids. They may occur naturally, by the action of microorganisms, or they may be added during processing, for example in making tomato sauce. It is these acids which give the tomato its tart flavour. The extent of the tartness can be measured by determining total acidity. The predominant acid with tomatoes is citric acid.

The acidity of a substance can be measured using a pH meter. Although pH can be measured by the colorimetric method, whereby the colour of the substance being measured, after adding an appropriate indicator, is compared with a coded colour chart, the arrangement is not reliable when used with a highly coloured substance like red tomato. The natural colour of the tomato obscures the colour of the indicator.

In order to measure the pH of a tomato, it is necessary to reduce the fruit to liquid form. A hand operated juice extractor, usually found in the kitchen, is suitable for extracting the liquid. The liquid is placed in a small beaker and a pH meter electrode inserted in the beaker. The pH value is then read from the meter in the usual way.

In pure solutions of an acid or base, pH is proportional to the concentration of the acid or base, but this is not always the case in measuring a tomato solution, or in fact any fruit or vegetable solution, because of colloids and buffer salts which have an influence on the pH reading. This means that two solutions may give similar pH readings, whereas in fact they have significantly different total acid concentrations.

However, it is the pH value of the solution which is of most importance when the tomatoes are to be processed, requiring a sterilization process.

Cultivar	Average pH
Pixie	3.9
Flora Dade	4.0
Rouge de Marmande	4.1
Grosse Lisse	4.25
Tiny Tim	4.25
Apollo	4.3
Longkeeper	4.3
Redlands Summertaste	4.3
Sweet 100	4.3
Yellow Pear	4.35
Mighty Red	4.4
Burnley Bounty	4.45
Tropic	4.5
Sunray	4.6
Ox Heart	4.7
Ponderosa	4.7

Table 2.3 *Typical average pH readings for hydroponically grown vine ripened tomatoes*

Cherry tomatoes with large clusters of small size fruit are easy to grow hydroponically in containers and produce high yields over a long period. Sweet Bite is flavoured with a fine balance of sweetness and acidity.

There are a number of factors which can influence the pH value as indicated by a meter. These include:

- the acidity
- the degree of ripeness
- the growing environment, such as temperature variations
- storage conditions
- processing variables, such as sterilization, temperature, added salt etc.

The pH of tomatoes usually falls within the range 3.8 to 4.9 and it is because of the range factor that some varieties are marketed as being "low acidity types", where they are in the high end of the pH scale. The majority of varieties give a reading close to 4.3 when fully ripe. *Table 2.3* shows measured average pH values of some cultivars grown in containers in an unheated glasshouse, with measurements being taken at various times throughout the year. Measurements indicate that pH is influenced by a number of factors, including cultivar, seasonal variations during the growing period, maturity of the fruit, stage of ripeness, length of storage period prior to taking measurement, technique in producing the juice/flesh for assessment and the conductivity of the nutrient solution fed to the plant.

Food technologists consider that titratable acidity gives the best measure of the free acids which affect taste. They consider that pH does not give a good measure. *Table 2.4* assembled by the CSIRO Food Research Laboratory, shows the levels generally found. Acidity has to be balanced with sugars. The table also indicates the firmness and taste test scores of some varieties of tomatoes grown in the field in New South Wales and harvested in

Selection of small cocktail/cherry tomatoes in 250g clear plastic marketing punnets. Average diameter, average number of fruit per punnet and sugar Brix level measurements - clockwise from top (L) - yellow pear cocktail 20mm, 50 and 7.4%; small red cherry, 25mm, 38 and 4.1%; medium orange/red cherry, 28.5mm, 16 and 4.0%; and large dark red cherry, 38.5mm, 11 and 5.0%.

March 1986. With some cultivars, the lowest pH is found to occur when the fruit is harvested at the breaker stage, that is, with first colour at the blossom end of the fruit, followed by the light red stage harvest, when 75% of the fruit surface shows pinkish-red. Tests by some workers have shown that tomatoes harvested at the coloured stages, are high in titratable acidity, but others disagree with these results, so much more research needs to be carried out in this area.

Processors who are concerned with cooking and preservation of tomato products, have preferred characteristics for ripe tomatoes. They look for a pH in the range 4.1 to 4.3, ascorbic acid above 18 mg per 100 grams of puree, total solids as high as possible but preferably over 6%, and acidity between 5.5 and 7.0. The fruit must be a good red colour with the absence of white tissue or green jelly, and above all, it must be an acceptable tomato flavour.

Sugars

The soluble carbohydrates of the tomato fruit are almost entirely reducing sugars. Sugars contained in a red ripe tomato are typically in the range 2.4 to 3.6 grams per 100 grams fresh weight, with components being glucose 1.1 to 1.6 g/100 g; fructose 1.2 to 1.9 g/100 g and sucrose less than 0.1 g/100 g. Because they constitute such a high percentage of the total soluble solids, they have an important effect on the taste of a ripe tomato.

In the case of two varieties, Grosse Lisse and Rouge de Marmande (widely grown in home hydroponics systems), fructose concentration (%w/v) was measured at 1.13 for Grosse Lisse and 1.12 for Rouge de Marmande, while glucose was 1.08 and 0.86 respectively.

	Astragale (French)	Dombito (Dutch)	Flora Dade	Grosse Lisse	Inra F1 (French)	Ohmiya (Japanese)	Rouge de Marmande	Rutgers (Old US)	79T248 (New US)
pH	4.10	4.20	4.00	4.20	4.10	4.00	4.10	4.10	4.20
Titratable Acidity	8.30	7.50	8.70	6.30	7.60	6.70	6.40	7.60	7.10
Citric Acid Concentration (%w/v)	0.64	0.54	0.63	0.42	0.62	0.52	0.41	0.65	0.58
Malic Acid Concentration (%w/v)	0.13	0.16	0.15	0.21	0.13	0.10	0.22	0.11	0.17
Malic + Citric (%w/v)	0.77	0.70	0.78	0.63	0.75	0.62	0.63	0.76	0.75
Acidity/Sourness (Scale 0-15 cm)	7.30	6.50	7.40	6.60	7.40	7.30	5.70	7.60	7.30
Fructose Concentration (%w/v)	1.11	1.21	0.79	1.13	1.115	1.36	1.12	1.26	1.19
Glucose Concentration (%w/v)	0.94	1.07	0.75	1.08	0.98	1.19	0.86	1.09	0.98
Fructose + Glucose (%w/v)	2.05	2.28	1.54	2.39	2.13	2.55	1.98	2.35	2.17
Total Soluble Solids (°Brix)	3.80	4.50	3.60	4.40	3.80	4.30	4.10	4.80	4.20
Firmness (Compression mm)	1.96	1.42	1.25	2.05	1.97	1.51	2.01	1.92	1.76
Sweetness (Scale 0-15 cm)	6.70	6.60	5.90	6.60	6.70	6.90	6.30	6.60	6.50
Flavour (Scale 0-15 cm)	7.40	5.60	5.30	5.90	7.00	7.20	5.40	6.40	6.40
Texture (Scale 0-15 cm)	7.60	5.60	6.00	5.60	6.70	6.80	6.00	6.30	6.20
Acceptability (Scale 0-15 cm)	7.50	5.80	5.40	5.80	6.90	7.20	5.50	6.60	6.20

Table 2.4 Chemical composition, firmness and taste test scores of field grown tomatoes (Courtesy CSIRO Food Research Laboratory)

The concentration and density of sugar in a tomato, are measured by a refractometer employing the Brix scale, named after a German scientist of the 19th century. The scale on which the percentage by weight of sugar in a solution at a specified temperature is given, is in degrees or percentage. Portable units are used by many tomato growers with an interest in assessing the quality of the fruit. A temperature correction table is provided, to enable the exact level to be determined. Hydrometer types are also available.

The extent of sugar entering a developing fruit on the vine is not a fixed proportion of the total quantity available to the plant. It varies as the truss develops and the fruit production can be severely affected if the growing environment changes, particularly during periods of low light level. When light is below the optimum requirement of the growing plant, the inadequate sugar supply sustains the growth of the leaves, stem and root system at the expense of the developing flower clusters. This may result in flower abortion.

This situation is a particular problem with varieties with large root systems at the early growth stage, such as Mighty Red, Beefsteak and Burnley Bounty, when grown during late autumn, winter and early spring when the light level is low. It is practice by some growers producing top quality tomatoes for high class hotels during these seasons, to cut back part of the fast growing root system and to remove some of the lower level leaves.

However, as the fruit begins to develop beyond about marble size, the developing fruit becomes the major user of sugars, so affecting the development of the rest of the plant. In addition to a slow down in leaf, stem and root growth, flower clusters on the upper trusses are affected. Above about the fourth truss, the number of fruit which set may fall off considerably.

During off-season growing, some truss pruning is desirable to improve the size and sugar content of the remaining fruit. For Grosse Lisse and Burnley Bounty, growing in an unheated glasshouse during autumn/winter, pruning trusses to 4/5 fruit will result in a good yield of marketable fruit with high sugar content.

In measuring the sugar content of tomatoes, it will be found that the sugar Brix level of fruit nearer the stem is higher than for fruit further out on the truss.

Restricted irrigation cycles and increased conductivity of the nutrient solution, will influence the amount of sugar in the fruit for most varieties. The reason for this is that about 85% of the water accumulated by the fruit comes via the phloem, one of the main conducting tissues of the stem, and restriction of water and increased nutrient concentration reduces the quality of phloem sap entering the fruit, yet the quantity of sugars entering the fruit is not changed. This results in a higher sugar concentration in the fruit.

In a trial of Grosse Lisse grown in containers with nutrient concentration of CF25, the sugar Brix level was 4.8% and increased to 6.0% for a solution with a concentration of CF35. One cherry tomato variety grown as a group of three and fed with a nutrient solution of CF45, produced an average sugar Brix level of 6.0%. However, the yield was poor compared with others grown in a solution of CF25.

There is a limit to which the nutrient concentration can be taken to increase the sugar Brix level, as too high a concentration will reduce plant growth, reduce the total yield, and produce a high level of unmarketable fruit, mainly with blossom-end rot.

The sugar content varies considerably during the ripening stage and is one of the reasons why a tomato at the Red Ripe colour stage, where the entire fruit surface has reached the maximum red colour characteristic of the cultivar, has superior taste to one which has not reached the Red Ripe colour stage. Sugar content increases progressively throughout maturation and ripening.

There is also some difference in the amount of reducing sugars when measured for the whole fruit compared with substance in the locules. A fruit with a reducing sugar level in g/100 ml of 3.6 for whole fruit at the Red Ripe colour stage, would typically be 3.0 at Green colour and 3.4 at the Light Red colour stages. Measurement of the substance in the locule would be about 2.1 for Green, 2.7 for Light Red and 3.2 for Red Ripe colour stages.

The sugar/acid ratio is one of a number of factors which have an influence of the taste of a tomato fruit. Acid content does not vary greatly between cultivars grown at

Box of Grosse Lisse tomatoes harvested from first and second trusses of plants grown in a hydroponics installation employing 150mm square rockwool slabs in a gully system. Grosse Lisse is a very popular variety with home gardeners with a well balanced acidity/sourness characteristic. These fruits gave average measurements of pH 4.25 and sugar Brix level 4.4%.

Sweet 100 or Sweet Bite cherry size tomatoes are popular with salads and are prolific bearers in hydroponic installations. They are a very old variety with seed being sold over 100 years ago by Australian seed merchants.

the same time and under the same environmental growing conditions, but there can be significant difference in reducing sugar levels. In an examination of nine cultivars, the concentration of malic plus citric acids varied from 0.63 to 0.78 %w/v, with Grosse Lisse being 0.63 and Rouge de Marmande also 0.63. With the same cultivars, concentration of glucose plus fructose varied from 1.54 to 2.39 %w/v, with Grosse Lisse being 2.39 and Rouge de Marmande being 1.98.

Acidity is usually highest for early grown fruit and lowest for the warm/hot mid season fruit. The level rises again for fruit harvested late in the growing season. There is not a great deal of difference in sugar concentrations for the same cultivars, provided measurements are made when the fruit is at the full Red Ripe colour stage. However, some cultivars with restricted growing periods do not follow this pattern.

Chapter 3. SOILLESS GARDENING

Chapter 3. SOILLESS GARDENING

How it began

The term soilless gardening or soilless culture as it is defined by The International Society for Soilless Culture, is "the growth of non-aquatic plants with their roots in a completely inorganic medium, where the roots are supplied with a nutrient solution". An alternative name "hydroponics", meaning "water working", is more popular in many countries, is widely used in literature and is internationally accepted. It is the preferred name in Australia.

The growing of plants without soil is not new. It has been practiced since the first century AD, but as a studied science it had its origin in 1699 as a result of work by John Woodward, a Fellow of the Royal Society in England. Woodward carried out experiments to try to find out how plants obtained their food supplies. The technique remained a laboratory curiosity until 1929, when Professor William F. Gericke of the University of California took it out of the hands of the laboratory experimentalists and transformed it into practical crop growing without soil. The Professor's trials using water culture were an outstanding success, so much so, that his soilless cultivated tomato plants grew to a height of some eight metres and the fruit had to be harvested using a step ladder. He named the new science "hydroponics".

Hydroponics spread rapidly throughout Europe, India and the United States and received a boost during the Second World War. Its ability to provide great quantities of fast growing vegetables to large numbers of Servicemen on isolated islands, where soil conditions were unsuitable for soil grown crops, and also for the Occupation Troops in Japan immediately after the cessation of hostilities, was put to good use. The systems installed for feeding the troops were of enormous proportions and required skilled people to operate and maintain them.

After the War, investigations were commenced in several countries to develop systems which could be set up and operated by unskilled people and which would meet or supplement the food needs of only a few people. One such centre was established in Darjeeling in India in 1946.

Now, hundreds of thousands of householders and flat dwellers throughout the world raise tomatoes and other foods in simple hydroponic units on rooftops, on balconies or in backyards. In the commercial world, it has been taken up with considerable enthusiasm. In England, for example, the time honoured method of growing tomatoes in soil is no longer viable in many areas. Growers have switched to hydroponics.

It is recognised that hydroponics is the most economical way of supplying water and nutrients to plants, with the opportunity of maximising results. The costly operation of acquiring land with the right soil, soil preparation, channelling, and disease and pest control are very much minimised. Also, the intensive and continuous cropping of tomatoes on one site, has in some cases introduced problems which require steam or gas sterilization of the soil. Many growers have therefore been compelled to make radical changes to their traditional methods of growing tomatoes. Every technical advance in crop nutrition, energy and chemical saving, environmental control, crop protection and plant breeding, has had to be exploited to the full. As a result, there has been an increasing swing away from soil culture in some areas, to hydroponic cultivation.

There has been rapid development of hydroponic systems, employing several techniques, suitable for economic commercial application. Combined with advances in electronic control equipment, plastics technology and analytical services, present day growers have the opportunity to control the growing environment of their crops more precisely than ever before.

Advantages and disadvantages

There are many advantages of hydroponic gardening. The most important include:
- The nutrient solution, unlike soil, is homogeneous and easy to sample, test and adjust to maintain optimum mineral levels.

- Uniform results are more easily obtainable.
- Yields are as good as crops grown in the best soil, making the system economically feasible in expensive land areas.
- No weeding, digging or hoeing.
- Simple to operate.
- Crop rotation is not necessary.
- No soil borne diseases or pests, unless introduced.
- Less water stress on plants during hot weather conditions.
- Greater planting density may be possible for some plants.
- More efficient utilisation of fertiliser, particularly with static feed and recirculating systems. With soil cultivation of tomatoes, about 50% of applied fertiliser is not taken up by the plant.
- Reduced water loss.
- Complete control of nutrient supply to plants.
- Produces delicious and clean products.
- Sterilization process simplified.
- Crops can be grown on a site where the soil has been contaminated or otherwise unsuitable.
- Potential to grow crops where no soil exists.
- Rapid turn around of crops.

There are of course some disadvantages and these include:
- Higher cost to establish, compared with a typical soil garden.
- Plants need to be more closely watched for changes in growth habits.
- Supporting some plants may be more difficult compared with soil.
- Regular mixing and application of nutrients is necessary.
- Introduced soil borne diseases may spread rapidly to other plants via the nutrient solution if recirculated.
- Incorrect solution formula may cause nutritional disturbances.
- The medium must be regularly flushed.
- Cost of pre-mixed nutrients may be expensive.
- Less margin for error than soil based cropping.

Although hydroponic gardening has many advantages compared with soil gardening, there are a number of things that it does not do. For instance it:
- Rarely produces crop yields better than good soil crops, but it is more consistent with high yields.
- Does not change the nutritional quality of the product.
- Does not alter the growth characteristics of the plant.
- Does not substitute for poor light, low or high temperature, or bad management.
- Does not reduce the water requirement of the plant.
- Does not alter the plants susceptibility to disease or insect attack.

Figure 3.1 illustrates a typical commercial installation using pots for growing tomatoes. The length of each double row would be dictated by the space available. A polyhouse 10 m wide and 60 m long would accommodate 1000 plants, allowing adequate service lanes and light. The design can also be used for an installation using vertical or lay-flat plastic bags.

Although many hydroponics installations in past years were designed on the basis of allowing excess nutrient solution to go to waste in the soil, this practice has in more recent

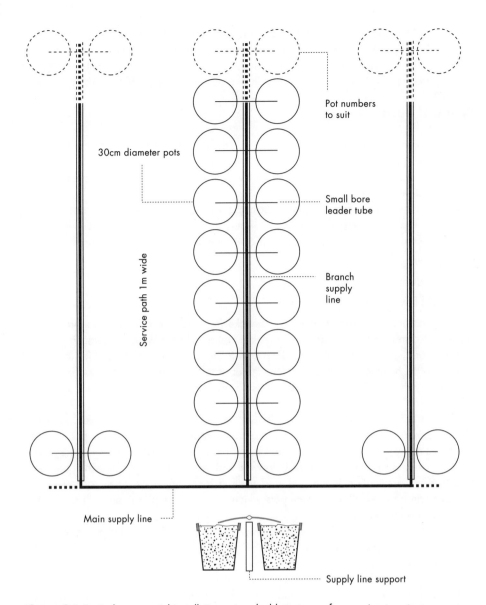

Pot numbers to suit

30cm diameter pots

Small bore leader tube

Branch supply line

Service path 1m wide

Main supply line

Supply line support

Figure 3.1 *Typical commercial installation using double pot rows for growing tomatoes.*

times been abandoned by the majority of growers, for a number of reasons. In some countries, the practice of allowing nutrient solutions to enter the soil and consequently find their way into underground water tables, is prohibited by law.

Return of surplus solution to the main storage tank is relatively straight forward with systems employing containers. The most popular arrangements include:

• Linking each container with a flexible tube to a return pipe of appropriate diameter, installed at a level below the bottom of all containers. This pipe slopes towards a collection tank which in most cases, will be the main supply tank.

• In the case of pots, placing a number of pots (usually three) in a polystyrene container, with the solution draining from the pots being collected in the container and draining back to the storage tank, via a return pipe which caters for a group of containers. This arrangement is widely used in installations where pots stand in a reservoir of solution to a predetermined depth (usually 50 mm), with the solution above the 50 mm level being drained off.

• Placing containers in a channel with a fall towards the collection tank. This usually takes the form of a cast concrete channel in the floor, or simply a plastic sheet laid in a channel scooped out of the soil. A third arrangement is to place the containers on corrugated fibre cement or plastic roofing sheets.

The disadvantage of exposed return systems, is that water losses due to evaporation are high during periods of high temperature in the growing area, a build up of algae often occurs, consuming valuable nutrients, and dust, dirt and dead leaf material may be carried down to the storage tank. However, a mesh filter screen will solve the rubbish problem.

Types of systems

Hydroponics involves growing plants in a nutrient solution, with or without an inert medium (such as gravel, sand, perlite, scoria, vermiculite, rockwool etc) to provide anchorage for the root system. The plants flourish when they receive optimum nutrition and are grown in a suitable environment.

Although there are three basic types of hydroponics culture, they are all based on the same principals and employ solutions of water and fertiliser chemicals for feeding the plants. The chief differences occur in the growing medium. They may be classified as:

- Water culture systems.
- Aggregate culture systems.
- Nutrient flow systems.

Water culture was used by Professor Gericke in his tomato growing experiments. It is somewhat cumbersome and difficult to master, but still has a wide following in the commercial world, particularly using the deep flow technique. It is seldom used for tomato cultivation by the home gardener. One of the major problems is the need to support seedlings, immediately they are put in the system. Another is the requirement to regularly aerate the solution.

The aggregate culture system is widely used by both commercial and home growers. It uses solid inert media such as sand etc, in a container ranging from a small pot, to a very large bed many cubic metres in volume. The nutrients are applied on the surface by watering can, drip, spray, or jet feed, or below the surface by sub-irrigation techniques. With pots, surface application is the preferred method for tomato cultivation, although other methods can be used, such as small pots which sit in a large plastic pipe, through which the solution is circulated.

Nutrient film systems employ a continuously running pump to pass a film of nutrient solution through the roots of the plant. The technique is employed extensively in the commercial production of tomatoes, as well as other vegetables, but is not appropriate for the home gardener using only a few pots or containers.

Figure 3.2 shows the choices available in terms of nutrient application, media and the feeding arrangements for the cultivation of tomatoes in pots.

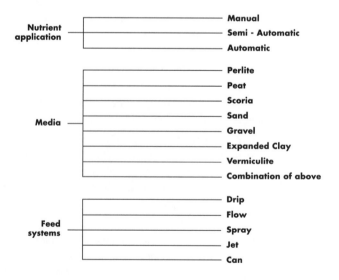

Figure 3.2 Pot culture choices.

Although great emphasis was placed on the development of hydroponic crop production during and immediately after the War, to meet food requirements in areas where soil cultivation was not practicable, the commercial growing of tomatoes using soilless techniques had been practised in Australia many years before the War. Those farmers growing crops without soil were not aware that they were employing a new technology, which years later would become wide spread.

In 1936, a grower about 20 km out from Brisbane with a property which butted onto a fresh water creek, grew tomatoes for the Brisbane market using a soilless arrangement.

The installation comprised 24 rows, each about 20 m long, with each row being provided with a trellis for supporting indeterminate tomatoes. The soil had a nematode problem, so the grower devised a scheme whereby he could grow tomatoes without the plant roots making contact with the soil, and without using any soil whatsoever except for the seedlings, which were grown in potting mix obtained from a nursery.

He set up a series of overlapping sheets of galvanised roofing iron, folded to form a U shaped channel. Wooden pegs about 30 cm high kept the sheets in position. The property had a slight slope towards the creek, so that solution fed in at the top end would work its way down to the far end, where surplus flowed into the creek.

The farmer had an arrangement with a horse trainer to take away straw and manure from the stables, and with a sawmill operator for the supply of sawdust and shavings. The straw was put through a motor-driven chaff cutter, so the end product was basically a chaff-like material.

The chaff and sawdust were mixed together in a 50/50 ratio and some lime added during the mixing process.

The medium was placed in the channels and the seedlings planted in it at about 50 cm spacing. The seedlings had been grown in small bottomless paper tubes treated with paraffin. The seedlings were placed in their growing position still in the paper tubes. With this procedure, the plant received no shock and seedlings could be transplanted during the hottest period of the day without any set back.

The plants were irrigated with two solutions mixed with creek water. The grower had a number of old raised-up black iron ship's water tanks, about 1.2 m cube size, in which he hung bags of horse or cow manure. The hessian bags and the contents were suspended in the water in the tank for 2-3 days before use. He referred to the tanks as 'liquor tanks.'

A large concrete tank contained a second mixture. This tank was referred to as the 'fertiliser tank' and contained a complete fertiliser obtained from a commercial supplier of agricultural materials. It was made to a ratio of 10% nitrogen, 4% phosphorus and 6% potash. Added to this was a trace element mixture, details of which are no longer available. He employed a special boiler made from a 44 gallon (200 l) drum and heated by a high pressure kerosene burner to heat the water, so that the fertiliser material dissolved more easily, before being transferred to the concrete tank.

The liquor and fertiliser tanks were connected by hoses to a 4000 litre irrigating tank, into which water was pumped from the creek. Pre-determined quantities of liquor and fertiliser were fed into the irrigating tank before the pump was started up.

The irrigating tank was linked to the growing channels by a series of main and branch hoses. A branch hose with tap fed into a chamber at the head of each channel, where the rate of nutrient supply was controlled so that the solution drained down through the medium, without backing up to overflow point.

The growing medium was topped up from time to time, to take account of settlement or breakdown during the growing season.

Following a problem with magnesium deficiency during the first year of using the system, a foliar spray was applied at intervals as recommended by the agricultural adviser.

The whole nutrient feed arrangements were handled on a manual basis, with the farmer going from row to row three times a day controlling solution feeds to the channels and supervising the entire operation. His son was responsible for preparing the nutrient solution and filling the irrigating tank. The farmer grew two indeterminate varieties. One was a mid-season variety with an extended cropping period, with mature fruit being slightly pointed in the longitudinal section and deep red colour when ripe. The other was a late variety producing medium to large fruit, globe to deep globe in shape and orange/red in colour when ripe.

"BURNLEY BOUNTY"

Jet Feed
188g

Flow Feed
168g

Drip Feed
158g

Selection of fruit from four trusses of three groups of Burnley Bounty plants fed by different feed systems from a common nutrient supply yank. Three plants comprised each group making a total of nine plants in the trial. Medium was 50% perlite, 25% scoria and 25% peat. Average weight of fruit taken over the total yield of four trusses harvested during October/November was 188g for plants fed by jet feed system, 168g for flow feed and 158g for drip feed.

"MIGHTY RED"

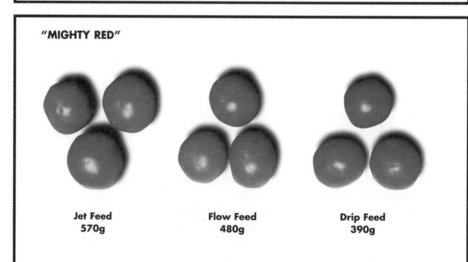

Jet Feed
570g

Flow Feed
480g

Drip Feed
390g

Selection of three best fruit from first truss of three Mighty Red plants fed by different feed systems from a common nutrient supply tank. Each group comprised three plants making a total of nine in the trial. Medium was 75% perlite, 20% scoria and 5% peat. The three best fruit from plants fed by jet system weighed 570g followed by flow feed of 480g and drip feed of 390g. Harvested during September/October, the total yields followed the same ratio pattern.

Secondary supply tank with cover removed. The float ensured a 50mm reservoir of nutrient solution was maintained throughout the entire installation during the hottest of days with tomatoes in full crop. Individual containers could be taken out of the network for maintenance without affecting others in the group.

Three 200 litre nutrient storage tanks elevated to provide gravity feed to an unheated glasshouse research installation. Three identical storage tanks were located below floor level inside the glasshouse. Each tank was provided with separate pump/motor, pipework and manually operated interchange valves so arranged that systems could be operated independantly, enabling nutrient solutions of different mixtures to be provided for three concurrent test bed trials.

Two parallel primary nutrient solution tanks, part of a static feed system for 12 large polystyrene containers filled with perlite over a 50mm scoria base. The installation catered for a few vegetables but mainly tomatoes tied to the wire fence behind the containers. Tomatoes grown included Burnley Bounty, Celebrity, Apollo, Ox Heart and Sydney Giants. The two small tanks were subsequently replaced by a single 200 L tank.

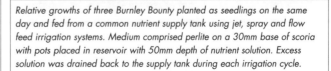

A group of electric solenoids associated with an automatic nutrient feed installation providing drip feed supply to plants in two large polyhouses. Plants were grown in rockwool slabs in plastic bags with irrigation cycles being determined by the amount of solution remaining in selected containers by a monitoring system specially developed for the purpose.

Relative growths of three Burnley Bounty planted as seedlings on the same day and fed from a common nutrient supply tank using jet, spray and flow feed irrigation systems. Medium comprised perlite on a 30mm base of scoria with pots placed in reservoir with 50mm depth of nutrient solution. Excess solution was drained back to the supply tank during each irrigation cycle.

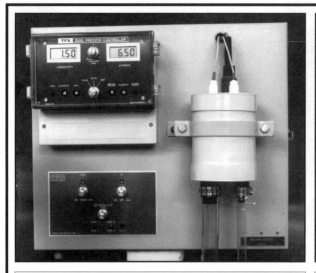

TPS Hydroponics Dosing System HP2 - DS. Features include purpose designed dosing pumps which eliminate the common problems found with some other control systems where solenoid valves malfunction; Ratio Control which allows the ratio of A and B nutrients to be easily adjusted as required during the plant growing cycle; HP2 Dual Controller designed for pH and conductivity control with each channel having independent settings for the control points.

TPS Dual Process Controller, a pH and conductivity control unit with control point in each independent channel operating a seperate relay providing control of solenoid valves and feed pumps. The unit also includes a timed addition function which uses an adjustable timer to limit the addition of nutrients or pH correction solution.

This latter variety had a bush which was very brittle and wind gusts often broke many stems.

At the stage when the fruit on about 75% of the plants had reached the point of harvest from the first truss, the grower applied ammonium sulphate dissolved in water along each channel, at the rate of about two kilograms per row. The application of this additional nitrogen at this stage stimulated the growth of the plants and assisted in the production of fruit of marketable quality and size from the higher level trusses.

Harvesting of the mid season variety extended over a period of 6-8 weeks, while the late variety extended over a period of 7-10 weeks.

Details of yields per plant are not available, but from the market agent payments it appears that marketable yields per plant would have been at least 4.8 kg for mid-season plants, and 4.3 kg for the late season plants.

Automatic feed systems

With large installations, it is normal practice to provide facilities to continuously monitor the state of the nutrient solution in terms of pH and conductivity, and to automatically make corrections as required.

The equipment used is generally referred to as proportioners, although other names are also used. When preparing concentrated solutions for proportioners, two separate mixtures are required to avoid problems with precipitates. One contains calcium nitrate and the other contains the rest of the minerals, although some growers mix the iron concentrate with the calcium nitrate. A twin head proportioner is fitted to the system and when activated, the proportioner draws equal volumes from each tank and mixes them with an appropriate amount of water, to provide the dilute nutrient solution.

There is no need to provide large storage tanks for the mixtures, as the amounts injected are relatively small. Accurate control is necessary because of the highly concentrated nature of the mixture. The proportioner can increase the conductivity of the system solution, but it cannot reduce it if the proportioner malfunctions and injects too much concentrate.

Temperature has an important bearing on the conductivity, and temperature sensing circuits are usually built-in to maintain conductivity at the desired level. Where large storage tanks are provided and bed flooding is practiced, the temperature variations of the solution may fluctuate widely, causing difficulty in the conductivity correcting process.

Experience has shown that even the best automatic systems can malfunction, and the wise grower will carry out a regular nutrient checking operation. One method is to implement a series of spot checks at various points, using portable meters as part of the normal management practices.

In addition to automatically correcting conductivity, the system will correct for pH variations. A third container is provided and is filled with appropriate solution. In the majority of installations, the pH will rise with time and nitric acid or phosphoric acid is used. If it is necessary to regularly increase pH, then potassium hydroxide solution may be used.

Probes used for monitoring purposes maybe placed either in the main holding tank, or in a sample container.

The principles and operation of automatic systems are quite simple, but it is important to keep all equipment clean, paying particular attention to probes. Appropriate piping material and fittings should be installed and there should be no leaks. Leaking nitric acid in particular, will result in considerable damage if allowed to fall on equipment. With most systems, the pH testing probe will need to be buffered once a week and the conductivity meter cleaned with detergent every two or three weeks.

Many control systems are available for the commercial grower, including the TPS Model 2082HP, which was widely used during the 1980's. Some are still in operation. It is a three channel controller developed for the commercial grower, with channels for pH, conductivity and temperature monitoring. Each channel has an adjustment to allow setting of the pH, conductivity and temperature control points. Each control point operates a separate relay, providing for control of solenoid valves, feed pumps or whatever additional method is required. The system incorporates an alarm device. If any one of the three channels deviates from its normal control setting by a pre-set amount, a common alarm relay contact closes and the corresponding alarm light on the control panel comes on.

In this way, the controller is continuously checking on all the functions for correct operation, and immediately alarms if anything malfunctions, well before any crop damage occurs.

In its original standard form, the device had meter displays, but digital readout units were later available. Also available, was a timed option function which used a pre-set timer to add nutrients, then waited to confirm that the addition was correct, and that full mixing had taken place, before further addition was made.

The TPS Hydroponics Dosing System HP2-DS is the latest AC powered version. Improved technology has enabled the production of a highly reliable control system providing accurate control, easy installation and low maintenance. The unit incorporates specially purpose-designed dosing pumps, which lift the A and B nutrient solutions and the pH solution from the storage drums and add them into the main nutrient storage tanks in controlled doses. Another feature is the Ratio Control, which allows the ratio of A and B nutrients to be easily adjusted, to cater for changes in feed requirements to plants during the growing cycle.

The system uses a HP2 Dual Controller designed for nutrient, pH and conductivity control. Each channel of the controller has independent settings for the control points. Each control point operates a separate relay, providing for control of the dosing pumps. Liquid crystal digital displays are employed for ease of reading, accuracy and reliability.

The controller has signal outputs for remote recording. These can be used for either remote display of the pH and conductivity levels, or for data logging by computer.

The complete facility which is easy to install, comprises dose-system mounting panel, dose-system electronics plus three dosing pumps, assortment of air and drain hoses, sample flow adjustment tap, flow-through sample chamber with flow sensor, controller with conductivity probe, pH probe and two pH buffer solutions, conductivity standard solution and an installation handbook.

Other automatic dosing systems available for the commercial grower include NZ Hydroponics, The Dosetronic 'L' employing stainless steel valves; Autogrow Systems, Nutri-Dose, a microprocessor based combined CF/pH controller; and others.

Computer technology is making inroads into automatic feed systems. Software permits continuous monitoring and control of almost all operations. Because of increasing application, units are becoming cheaper and more versatile. Models that form the heart of software designs are becoming more complete and dynamic and allow better predictions.

Simple automatic feeders, requiring no power for operation, are available for home

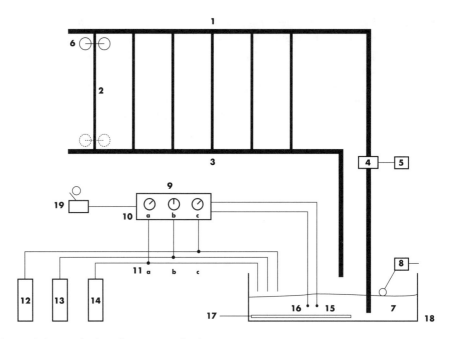

Figure 3.3 *Basic facilities for automatic feed system.*

installations. Typical is the Auto-Pot Fertigation Unit, manufactured by Agromatic Corporation Pty Ltd, in Melbourne. It uses three bottles. Two contain nutrients as Part A and Part B mixes, and the third acts as a mixer and sedimentor. An injector in the cap of each nutrient bottle adds a minute dose of fertiliser to the water as it passes to the plant.

Figure 3.3 illustrates the basic features of an automatic system designed to operate with a commercial installation. Details are as follows:

1. Main delivery pipe of size suitable to provide correct feed rate to all pots in the installation.

2. Branch feed pipes to feed each double row of pots.

3. Return pipe for return of solution to the storage tank. The pipe is terminated above the water level to give aeration of returning water.

4. Electrically driven pump.

5. Timer for operation of the pump in accordance with predetermined feed cycle.

6. The growing pots. Each pot is fed by either drip, flow, spray or jet feed arrangement.

7. Nutrient solution in storage tank.

8. Float valve for control of top-up water.

9. Automatic control equipment.

10. Meters indicating Temperature, pH and Conductivity of the nutrient solution.

11. Electrically operated solenoids.

12. Nutrient concentrate A.

13. Nutrient concentrate B.

14. pH correction solution.

15. pH probe.

16. Conductivity probe.

17. Solution heater.

18. Storage tank.

19. Alarm bell.

Not all automatic systems operate on a recirculating basis. Many large installations provide just sufficient solution to meet the plant needs, plus a small excess amount, about 5 to 10% of which is discarded. With this latter arrangement, pathogens are prevented from entering the solution and affecting other plants. It also simplifies the control of the correct conductivity and pH levels. *Figure 3.4* shows the two basic systems in simplified diagrammatic form.

Supply tanks

Supply tanks used for the storage of the nutrient solution can take many forms, and the type chosen will be influenced by the type of feed system in operation. The most popular tanks include:

• Large plastic drums.

Drums of 200 litre capacity are readily available from second hand sources, as they are used for shipment of orange juice, tomato pulp, olives and other products. The drums are lightweight, long lasting, cheap and easily worked for fitting pipes, taps etc. They should be thoroughly washed out before use, to remove all traces of previous content. For the home gardener, 20 litre drums may be more convenient.

• Fibreglass tanks.

Regular sizes in square or other shapes are readily available, or can be made to order by fibreglass fabricators. The tanks should be painted black or made with black pigments, if mounted outside, to prevent algae formation problems. Both plastic and fibreglass containers are ideal where above ground mounting is required to provide for gravity feed.

• Concrete formed tanks.

This is usually poured concrete construction using formwork, concrete blocks or bricks rendered and painted with several coats of epoxy resin paint. A suitable lid is necessary to keep out rubbish and light.

• Plastic lined excavation.

One of the cheapest below ground tanks can be made by digging an excavation and lining it with a thick black polythene sheet. If there are pebbles in the soil, the bottom should have a layer of sand and sacks hung on the sides to prevent puncture of the plastic when the tank is filled with water. Tanks located below ground level should be so constructed, that water cannot flow into the tank from an outside source and that rubbish is not able to enter. A sump should be provided to ensure that the tank can be completely emptied.

A very important aspect of successful cultivation of tomatoes is to ensure that the water supplied with the nutrient solution contains adequate dissolved oxygen. Whether the nutrient solution is supplied as a drip feed arrangement with the excess going to waste, or as a recirculating system, the supply tank has a major role in assisting in the diffusion of atmospheric oxygen into the water. The extent of the oxygen which can diffuse into the water depends upon a number of factors, including the area of the water exposed to the atmosphere and the temperature of the water.

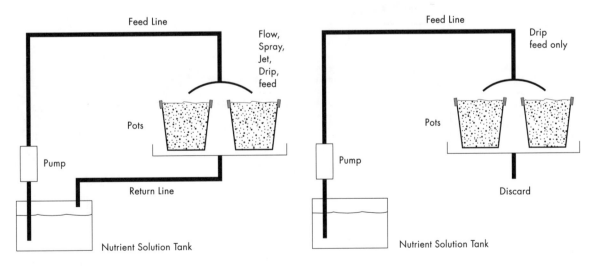

a. Recirculating system

b. Waste system

Figure 3.4 Two basic systems using pots.

The amount of oxygen required by a well developed plant will increase as the temperature rises. Unfortunately, with increasing temperature the amount of oxygen in the water decreases, so every effort should be made to see that in the design of the installation, maximum diffusion of oxygen into the water is possible at all times to meet the plant requirements. The design of the supply tank or drum, and nutrient return feed lines, need careful attention. Many growers who use the 200 litre plastic drums, mount the drum vertically, fill the drum with water and nutrients through the plug hole, and then replace the plug. A better practice as far as aeration or oxygen diffusion is concerned, is to mount the drum horizontally and make a cut-out on the top about 25 cm square, with the cut-out being perforated and hinged to keep out rubbish. The exposed surface is greatly increased. This is illustrated in *Figure 3.5*.

Where recirculation of the nutrient solution is involved, there are a number of ways of increasing the surface area of the water for aeration purposes. These include branched outlet, spray, venturi, high fall and exposed return. Other techniques include feeding compressed air into the tank, or agitating the solution with paddles.

A venturi system which can be fitted to a submersible pump in the nutrient solution tank, is also available. It can be so installed as to direct a stream of air bubbles vertically through the solution, or horizontally towards one wall, providing a longer path for the bubbles before passing to the atmosphere.

Typical aeration techniques are illustrated in *Figure 3.6* and although aeration has only a small effect on dissolved oxygen concentration, it is nevertheless important. An additional feature is that it also reduces the temperature of the nutrient solution in hot weather, an important factor in dissolved oxygen level.

The hydroponic process

Plants have certain requirements for growth and production of fruit. These include oxygen, carbon dioxide, light, water, favourable temperature, support for roots, and certain minerals. The fundamental difference between soil culture and hydroponics, is in the way the essential minerals are supplied to the roots.

Oxygen, carbon dioxide and light are Nature's gift and normally are freely available. The same may be said about water, except that it will have to be delivered to the plant by some means by the grower. Support for the roots and supply of minerals have to be undertaken by the grower.

In hydroponics, the supply of nutrients is a controlled and balanced procedure. This is a

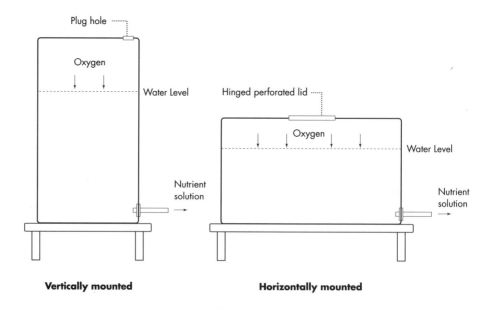

Vertically mounted   **Horizontally mounted**

Figure 3.5 *Typical methods of mounting 200 litre drums.*

major point of difference compared with soil culture. In soil cultivation, many fertilisers are applied in the form of organic materials, but plants cannot use these directly. The fertilisers have to be broken down to inorganic forms. Even then, the grower generally has little idea just how much plant food is readily available to the plant at any given time.

A number of mineral elements are required by the plant for growth and fruit production. Some elements are required in large quantities while others are required as a trace only. Nitrogen, phosphorus, potassium, calcium, magnesium, and sulphur are taken up in relatively large amounts, while iron, manganese, boron, zinc and copper are needed in only small quantities. Those required as a trace only are sometimes available in the form of impurities in other added elements.

Figure 3.7 shows typical reduction in the nutrient solution strength, as the minerals are extracted by the plants. The data was obtained from a glasshouse crop of tomatoes, grown in pots and fed by a flow system automatically for four half hourly periods, between 5 am and 4 pm daily. The tomatoes were cherry varieties.

Root support for plants growing in soil is generally no problem. Even a huge forest giant of a tree can be safely anchored. In a hydroponics system however, the types of media employed do not lend themselves to good root support or anchorage. For tomato plants, separate systems such as wire cages, frames, stakes, pipes, nets etc must be provided for many varieties. Stakes and the like have to be anchored to the growing bed or container by external means.

The nutrient solution used in hydroponics consists of suitable water and added mineral salts. Highly saline water is not suitable without special treatment. The best concentration and ratio of various elements depends on the plant, its stage of growth, quality of the water, the season and the amount of light. No single best formula can be recommended for all conditions likely to be encountered during the growing life of a plant.

Tomato plants can tolerate a wide range of strengths of some of the minerals, but care must be exercised to ensure that they are available in proportions that avoid deficiencies and toxicities. Minerals in the mixture should contain no injurious substances which, while harmless in the soil, may be toxic in hydroponics.

The rate of nutrient uptake by the plant's root system is not a linear process. The rate of

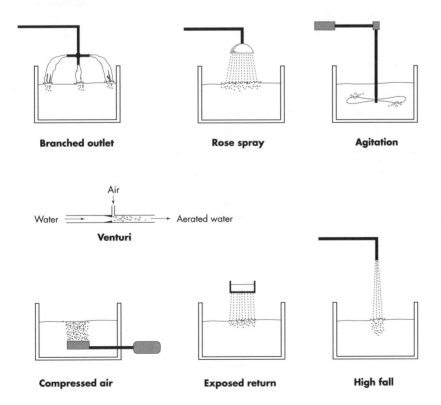

Figure 3.6 *Ways of aerating the nutrient solution.*

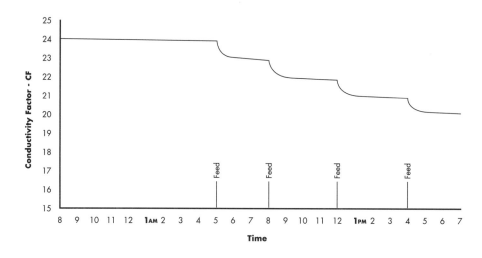

Figure 3.7 *Change in conductivity of nutrient solution over a 24 hour period.*

uptake increases rapidly at low concentration and becomes progressively slower as the concentration increases to a point, called the cut-off point, where no further uptake increase takes place.

With a properly balanced nutrient mixture, the plant should be able to take up just what it wants for its proper growth and development. However, situations sometimes occur, for a number of reasons, where there is an imbalance in one or more elements, in which case the insufficiency will be reflected in the behaviour of the plant. For example, there may be a deficiency in iron availability because the pH of the solution was allowed to rise too high. The plant would probably show symptoms of chlorosis on terminal leaves and stunted growth.

Once a particular element deficiency has been identified, a quick fix solution can often be effected by application of a foliar spray in accordance with *Table 3.1*, but the nutrient solution should be replaced as soon as possible. Proper plant growth is possible only when all elements are adequately supplied and are in proper balance with one another. The absorption rates of nutrients applied as foliar sprays may be a matter of hours, but some take days.

There is no evidence to suggest that the mineral and vitamin contents differ between hydroponics and soil grown crops, provided in each case the plant has access to sufficient water and air and the correct amount of minerals to satisfy its needs. However, in either case, it is possible to raise or lower the mineral content of the fruit, and so affect the taste, by making appropriate adjustments in the feed solution.

Element to be supplied	Fertiliser source	Spray strength as %
Iron Fe	Chelated iron Fe EDTA	0.02
Calcium Ca	Calcium nitrate	1.0
Zinc Zn	Zinc sulphate	0.1
Manganese Ma	Manganese sulphate	0.1
Copper Cu	Copper sulphate	0.1
Molybdenum Mo	Ammonium molybdate	0.08
Nitrogen N	Urea	0.25
Potassium K	Potassium sulphate	2.0
Magnesium Mg	Magnesium sulphate	2.0

Table 3.1 *Foliar sprays*

Nutrient solution reticulation

In a large installation involving thousands or even hundreds of pots, careful consideration needs to be given to the design of the nutrient solution reticulation system. Each pot has to be fed separately, using any one of a number of feed arrangements, including drip, flow, spray or jet systems.

The reticulation network involves basically main supply lines, branch supply lines, small bore leader tubes or plastic emitters, pumps and storage tanks.

In designing the main and branch supply lines, it is important that the water carrying capacity of these lines be adequate to provide the correct amount of solution during each feed cycle, and that each leader tube or emitter gives the same output, or at least approximately the same output. For each device to give the same quantity during each cycle, the water pressure must be constant at the point where each leader tube or emitter enters the branch line. Constant pressure along the complete length of a pipe is not possible in practice, due to pipe wall resistance and other factors. A 10% differential is usually taken as being acceptable. The length and diameter of the leader tube have a bearing on the amount of solution supplied at the pot and these factors need to be taken into account.

For a flow, spray or jet feed arrangement, the water requirements would naturally be greater than that required for a drip system operating over the same period of time. In typical installations with absorbent media, flow, spray or jet systems may operate at say, 10 minute intervals every hour, or four-hourly intervals with a reservoir during peak summer growth whereas a dripper system may operate continuously during daylight hours.

Micro tubing is widely used for leader tubes. It is readily available in diameters of 0.5, 0.76, 0.89 and 1.00 mm. The rate of discharge from the tubing is governed by the pressure of the liquid at the point where the tubing is inserted into the branch feeder pipe, the length of the micro tubing, and its diameter.

By reference to graphs showing head-discharge relationships, the correct tubing diameter, pressure and length can be determined for a required discharge rate. For example, a 30 cm length of 0.5 mm tubing, will provide a discharge rate of 1 litre per hour for a branch line with a 3.5 m head (5 psi). With small diameter micro tubing, the blockage rate is high and line filtering equipment needs to be provided.

Plastic fittings are readily available for flow, spray and jet-feed systems to operate with low pressure, for example, from gravity feed tanks, but drippers generally require high pressure water for proper operation. The manufacturers usually recommend a minimum pressure, typically l00 kPa (14.5 psi), for correct functioning. There are several brands on the market which will provide outputs of 2 or 4 litres per hour.

The most widely employed branch feed lines are black polythene tubing of diameters 16, 20 or 25 mm. These diameters may also be suitable as main supply lines for small installations up to about 50 pots, but above that, larger pipes would be required in most cases. For a very large installation, pipes of 100 mm diameter or more may be necessary. The larger pipes are usually unplasticised polyvinyl chloride material, with solvent weld joints. Temperature has an important influence on pipe performance, particularly at the solvent weld points. Where possible, pipes should be protected from direct sunlight and the temperature of the nutrient solution should be kept at an acceptable temperature.

Figure 3.8 shows recommended maximum lengths of black polythene branch feeder lines, giving 2 or 4 litres per hour outputs for various dripper or pot spacings. *Figure 3.9* shows flow rate and head loss for various main PVC feeder pipes up to 100 mm diameter.

Many types of pumps are on the market to meet the needs of all sizes of installations. Most manufacturers recommend the use of pumps employing plastic parts, for movement of hydroponics nutrient solutions, although some growers have reported no problems with cast iron impellers. The majority of pumps used in hydroponics are electrically powered from commercial electric mains. Diesel, petrol or battery driven units are costly to purchase and maintain and are seldom employed. Pump types are mainly single stage centrifugal, multi-stage centrifugal or helical rotor designs. However, other types have been observed to operate successfully on commercial hydroponics installations.

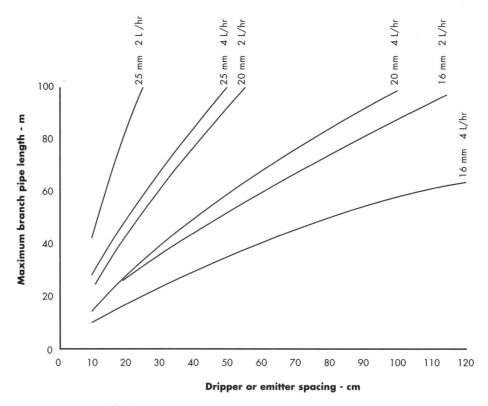

Figure 3.8 *Branch feed pipe sizes.*

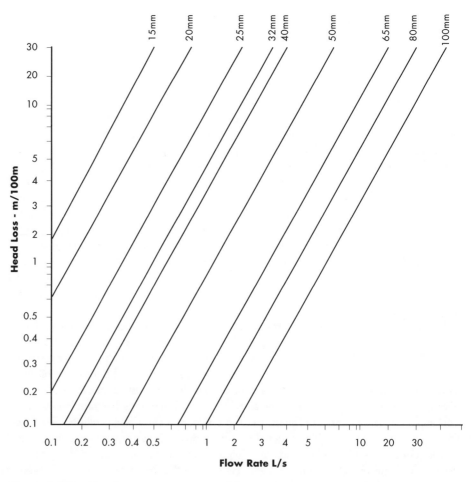

Figure 3.9 *Head loss for various pipe sizes and flow rates.*

The motor power required to drive a pump is found from the formula:

$$P_m = P_p/e_m \text{ kilowatts}$$

$$\text{where} \quad P_p = \frac{9.8Qp}{1000e_p}$$

Q = flow rate (litres per second)
p = (pressure) head (metres)
e_p = pump efficiency (typically 0.7)
e_m = motor efficiency (typically 0.8)
P_p = pump power (kilowatts)

For large installations, the selection of the correct size and type of pump is important from an economic point of view. Large motors consume large amounts of electric power and consequently operating costs can be a major factor in the overall expenses of the hydroponic installation.

Nearly all hydroponic installations require water to be lifted, and in selecting a pump it is necessary to determine the pump duty. This is a relationship involving the quantity of water to be shifted and the head to which the water has to be delivered. The determination of the head is illustrated in *Figure 3.10*.

It is necessary to consider:

• the static delivery head, or height that the water has to be lifted to the highest drip or emitter.

• resistance to water flow caused by piping, fittings etc, particularly the filter system.

• dripper or emitter operating pressure.

The static lift height can be readily determined from the physical layout of the pump and the dripper or emitter points; the total friction or resistance is determined by reference to graphs or tables for various pipes and fittings and the dripper or emitter operating pressures are available from manufacturer's data sheets. The quantity of water to be shifted is governed by the number of outlets and the feed rate. For example, an installation of say 500 drippers or emitters delivering 2 litres per hour, would require a flow of 1000 litres per hour or 0.28 litres per second.

The pump would therefore be required to give an output of 0.28 1/s against the calculated head. Tables and graphs supplied by manufacturers simplify selection of the correct size pump to meet the requirements.

In the overall design of the system, an arrangement which would provide a flow to each plant of 500-600 ml per minute is desirable. Trials with many tomato cultivars extending over a long period, indicated 750-1000 ml per minute produced the best yields in terms of weight and marketable fruit. Increasing the flow to 2 litres per minute per plant, had a negative effect with some varieties. Growth rates were reduced, even though the higher flow rate presented more nutrients per unit of time to the root zone. With a jet feed arrangement, some physical root damage was noted if water pressure was excessive.

Several small and medium-sized systems are available with some novel means of recirculating the nutrient solution.

One system in operation in South Australia was based on a design manufactured commercially in the USA, but adapted to employ Growool cubes as a medium rather than perlite.

The installation was used to grow Tiny Tim tomatoes, for supply on a contract basis, to restaurants and motels in the Barossa Valley. It comprised five separate units, each unit comprising a 6 metre length of 150 mm x 75 mm plastic gully fitted with end caps and designated the growing gully. The top of the gulley had 20 cut-outs of a size to accommodate a 75 mm latticed nursery pot. A similar size gully, also fitted with end-caps, was attached to the bottom of the growing gulley and designated the storage gully. It was so mounted, that the 75 mm side of the storage gully was attached to the 150 mm base of the growing gully. They were kept together by self-tapping screws and glue. A 25 mm hole was drilled in the two gullys, so that water could flow from one to the other. A small air compressor unit was part of the installation.

The medium employed was 75 mm Growool cubes, inserted into the latticed nursery pots.

The bottom storage gully was almost filled with nutrient solution, which was forced up into the growing gully under air pressure, on operation of the compressor. A water level switch caused electric power to the compressor-drive motor to be disconnected, once water dropped to a predetermined level. When the air pressure dropped back to normal atmospheric pressure via a bleed valve, the nutrient solution drained back into the storage gully.

A timer clock caused the compressor to operate every hour, between 6 am and 6 pm daily.

The grower found he obtained the highest numbers of tomatoes with a nutrient solution of CF20 . He found he could harvest ripe fruit in 6-7 weeks after planting, by increasing conductivity to CF28, compared with 8-10 weeks when using solution of CF20. However, yield fell by 10-15% when employing the CF28 solution.

With the CF28 nutrient solution, fruit size was mostly in the range 1.5-2.0 cm diameter, compared with up to 3 cm diameter for the lower CF level. The Chefs at the restaurants expressed preference for the smaller sized fruit. They were of the opinion that these fruit had better texture and flavour.

To prevent the plants from falling over when in fruit, the grower placed small frames similar to those used to support carnations, over each plant, with the frames tied to the gully by cord.

To meet the demand for his high quality cherry tomatoes, the installation accommodated 100 plants at various stages of growth. Five units, each one with its own compressor, were employed. Each unit was mounted on 150 mm square wooden posts, set in the ground and spaced 90 cm between rows. Solution level in each storage gulley was maintained by a float valve in a secondary tank, which in turn was linked by a feed line to the main storage system, comprising two 200 litre plastic drums in parallel. The feed solution was dumped every six weeks throughout the year.

The compact installation was enclosed in a small polyhouse, about 7 m square with roll-up sides. This allowed tomatoes to be produced throughout most of the year.

Before deciding on the permanent system to be employed with his small business, the grower set up an installation along the lines of the USA-designed system. This used two 100 mm pipes with the growing pipe filled with perlite. A drilled 25 mm pipe inside the growing pipe, allowed the solution from the storage pipe to be forced by pressure into the growing pipe. However, he had so much trouble with the swirling perlite damaging the plant roots, that he abandoned the proposal in favour of one using no solid medium material.

Growing tomatoes in space

In recent years, a great deal of effort has been placed in the development of new technology to enable people to exist on long space flights and on possible Lunar and Mars bases. Some of this work has been associated with plants for providing food, including tomato plants grown using suitable hydroponic systems which could function in a space environment.

In 1991, a crop of tomatoes was harvested from seeds which spent six years in orbit, on board one of the NASA orbiting facilities.

At Houston in the US, there is a very large complex which for at least six years has been growing at least 30 different types of plants. In a press release, it was reported that scientists were using the facilities to produce hydroponically grown 'lunar lettuce', 'cosmic carrots' and 'extra-terrestrial tomatoes'.

The scientists were endeavouring to have the plant growth cycle assist in regeneration of the atmosphere and purification of water. Major problems which need to be overcome include light and volume requirements.

There were some 12 million tomato seeds recovered from the orbiting satellite, when it returned to earth after its long journey. These seeds and other untreated control seeds were distributed to schools and organisations throughout the US.

Recovered seeds planted at the Houston facility site produced their first seedlings in just over 66% of the time which seeds normally take to sprout. Growth patterns of the plants were about the same as plants grown from the control seeds. No chemical analysis data of the tomatoes has been made available but in a taste test, the public voted the space tomatoes as 'very tasty'.

Ongoing work at Houston includes development of aeroponics systems. In 1991, one drum-aeroponics installation used to extend growth, had tomato plants going into their sixteenth

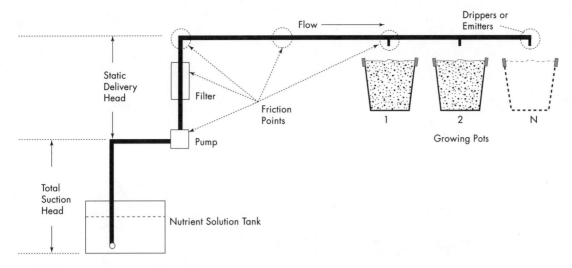

Figure 3.10 *Head factors in pumping solution.*

cycle of production.

Aeroponics techniques are of course not confined to space requirements. The principle is many years old and a number of successful installations are in operation throughout the world, particularly in Italy. However, there are very few installations in Australia and none is involved in commercial production of tomatoes.

In a typical system, the plant roots are suspended in a closed container, chamber, or trough in which the roots are sprayed with hydroponic nutrient solution periodically by jets, to maintain 100% relative humidity. Because of the size to which roots of some tomato varieties grow, 'A'-frame mist chambers have been used with some installations.

A small trial installation in Adelaide in 1986 was designed to accommodate six indeterminate tomato plants, using a fibreglass chamber 20 cm wide, 45 cm deep and 2 metres long, with removable end-caps. The container was made deep, because of experience with root systems produced by some varieties when grown in pots. Cut-outs were made in the top to accommodate 100 mm plastic pots, spaced 30 cm apart. Jets were fitted into a high pressure 25 mm plastic pipe located on one of the walls, 20 cm below the top and beneath each cut-out. The jets were located on the wall, so as to be clear of the large root system during its growth cycle. Flow rate from each nozzle when operational, was approximately 4 litres per hour.

Six Grosse Lisse tomatoes were used in the first trial. Seedlings were grown separately in a static feed system, after being planted in 75 mm Growool cubes placed in 75 mm latticed nursery pots. When roots emerged from the latticed pots, the pots were transferred to the cut-out in the chamber and the facility started up.

The nutrient solution was set at a concentration of CF15 and pH at 6.2. A pulsed irrigation feed cycle, to provide nutrient solution atomised at the roots, was initially set at 7 seconds operation every 15 minutes, with surplus nutrient being returned to a 200 litre holding tank. As the plants grew, and root systems reached a length of about 15 cm, the irrigation cycle was changed to provide 15 seconds operation every 10 minutes during hours 5 am to 8 pm, and 20 seconds operation every 60 minutes outside these hours.

When the six plants were in full production with fruit on all trusses, the amount of solution returned to the holding tank was calculated as approximately 98.2% of that supplied over a 24 hour period.

The plants grew more vigourously than a control group grown in 30 cm pots in perlite medium and fed the same nutrient solution. Good quality fruit was produced by both groups, but the yield from the aeroponics group was very much higher than that produced by the control group. Average per plant to the fourth truss, for the aeroponics group, was 8.8 kg compared with 6.2 kg for the control group. Yields from Grosse Lisse in perlite would frequently be much higher than 6.2 kg, if grown in a nutrient solution higher than the CF15 used in the trial.

The root system of the plants in the aeroponics system grew to a large size. Roots were 10-15 cm in diameter in the vertical mode and after reaching the bottom of the chamber they formed a dense mat for the full 2 metre length of the chamber, and about 20 cm deep.

Chapter 4. NUTRIENTS

Chapter 4. NUTRIENTS

Essential elements

A tomato plant has often been compared with a biochemical factory. A number of materials are used in manufacturing the all important foods, enzymes, hormones, vitamins and fibres. These materials exist in a form which the plant in a normal growing environment, can absorb and use. They contain elements essential for the growth and development of the plant and the production of fruit.

Essential elements for proper growth and development include oxygen, hydrogen, nitrogen, carbon, phosphorus, calcium, sulphur, magnesium, manganese, iron, copper, zinc, boron and molybdenum. Some of these elements are required in only small amounts but nevertheless any one of them may become a limiting factor in plant welfare. The elements are found in enzymes and co-enzymes which regulate the rate of biochemical reactions, while others are important in food storage. Deficiencies in any element may cause the plant to exhibit certain symptoms or characteristics, which give a clue as to which element is deficient.

Carbon and oxygen are supplied by the atmosphere in the form of carbon dioxide gas. Although the concentration of carbon dioxide gas is low - of the order of 3 parts in 10,000 parts by volume - the total amount available in the atmosphere is enormous. Even though plant life consumes a large amount, the amount remains relatively constant.

The carbon dioxide is taken up by the plant by diffusion through the stomata, mainly on the underside of the leaves, into the intercellular spaces of the cells containing chlorophyll. Carbon dioxide gas also enters into solution with water, which is drawn up via the root system and stem to the leaves. Through a complex chemical process, the initial food substances and related compounds are made. In some commercial glasshouses, additional carbon dioxide is released into the enclosed growing area to substantially increase the crop yield. A concentration increase of 10 times that normally available in the atmosphere will, in some controlled situations, result in a yield increase of 50%.

The roles of various elements are as follows:

Oxygen

Oxygen plays an important role in the welfare and development of a plant, by virtue of the part it plays in the process of respiration.

Life functions would cease should there be a failure of respiration. The plant obtains its oxygen from the atmosphere, via the leaf, and from water, via the root system. There is usually no problem in oxygen uptake through the stomata in the leaves, but uptake via the root system can be deficient if roots are grown in water which is not well aerated, or in media such as fine compacted sand through which air cannot penetrate.

Hydrogen

The plant obtains most of its hydrogen from the water, absorbed through the roots. It is important, in that fats and carbohydrates are composed of hydrogen, together with oxygen and carbon. The hydroponicist will soon realise the importance of hydrogen, when measuring the pH of the nutrient solution. It has to be within defined limits, the values being determined by the needs of the particular plant being cultivated. The acidity of the solution is due to hydrogen ions and its alkalinity is due to hydroxyl ions.

Nitrogen

Nitrogen is required to perform many functions. It is involved in the formation of protein, the production of chlorophyll, protoplasm, hormones and certain acids. If the plant is fed an amount of nitrogen excessive to its needs, it will be soft and spindly and flowers may fail to set. If however, it does not receive sufficient for its needs, it will become hard, due to the deposition of excessive amounts of cellulose and lignin in the cell walls.

The plant receives its nitrogen from the nutrient solution and the atmosphere. Because the season has a considerable influence on the amount of nitrogen taken up by the plant, it is practice by some growers to use different concentrations of nitrogen for winter and summer crops.

In the growing situation, tomato production is best when only sufficient nitrogen is available, during the first two or three months after planting, to allow a good sturdy vine to develop, but not enough to produce soft growth. Once the plant reaches the stage where it has a heavy crop and the fruit begins to ripen, then the nitrogen requirement is high.

Nitrogen is unique among the major elements, in that it can be taken up by the plant root system either as an anion or cation. Many nutrient mixes contain a large amount of nitrate and a small amount of ammonium nitrogen source. With the ammonium nitrogen, H^+ ions are released from the roots causing the solution to become increasingly acid. For nitrogen supplied in nitrate form, the nutrient solution becomes alkaline, as OH^- ions are released from the roots to maintain electrostatic equilibrium.

Since the tomato plants reduce the nutrient solution pH when an ammonium source is used, and increase the pH when an all nitrate solution is used, the pH will remain fairly constant when the grower adjusts the nitrogen sources to appropriate levels. However, care must be taken to ensure a correct balance between the nitrate form and the ammonium form. A 50/50 ratio will probably result in ammonium toxicity. A ratio of 75% nitrate to 25% ammonium is adopted by many growers, while others prefer a much greater ratio of about 90% nitrate to 10% ammonium. Success with growing tomatoes depends to a large extent on the good management of the nitrogen forms and levels.

Figure 4.1 shows the effects of three ammonium nitrate levels on the pH of a nutrient solution with perlite medium. A 10% ammonium nitrate level resulted in minimum pH change, over a 60 day trial with Whopper variety.

Phosphorus

Phosphorus is very important for the production of high quality tomatoes. It stimulates the production of flowers and fruit, encourages healthy root growth and expedites the process of ripening. In ripe tomatoes, the jelly-like mass of tissue in which the seeds are formed, contains a large amount of phosphorus. Phosphorus also influences the hydrolysis of starch to sugar, as well as the synthesis of starch from sugar.

Typical nutrient mixtures provide phosphorus at a concentration of 30 to 100 ppm. Care has to be taken not to use a concentration too high, as an iron deficiency situation may develop. If excessive iron is added in order to correct the imbalance, it may influence the availability of phosphorus to the plant. Hence it is important to maintain a correct iron/phosphorus ratio in the solution. Because phosphorus is translocated quickly, deficiency usually shows up in mature growth.

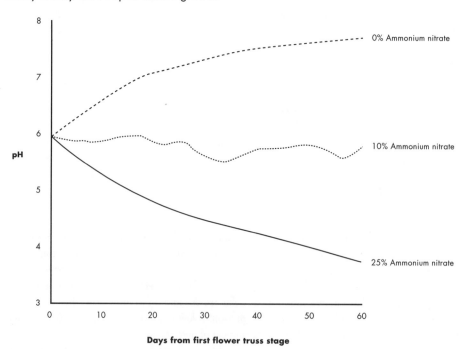

Figure 4.1 Variations in pH with various levels of ammonium nitrate.

Potassium

Potassium is absolutely essential for good growth and it vastly improves the keeping quality of the fruit. Tomatoes with a high potassium feed will maintain firm, solid flesh for a long period, even when picked at the red ripe stage. Some varieties grown in pots, with potassium levels of around 300 ppm, will result in a shelf life of up to 25 days. With a level of 200 ppm, a shelf life of up to 20 days is typical. Loss of firmness is the main criterion used for determining the end of shelf life.

Potassium differs from most other essential elements, in that it is not a constituent of the manufactured compounds, or a part of any living tissue. Its role is basically regulatory, and has little impact on crop yield. Trials indicate that under controlled conditions, the yield will remain about the same, for potassium levels over a range 50 to 400 ppm. However, increased potassium levels reduce ripening disorders, increase the dry matter content of the fruit, the potassium level in the fruit and the electrical conductivity of the juice, all of which enhance the flavour improvement.

There is a problem, nevertheless, in using increasing levels of potassium, in that it adversely affects the magnesium uptake. If potassium is too high, it may be necessary to resort to foliar spraying with magnesium sulphate. The most widely used source of potassium in a nutrient mixture is potassium nitrate, although potassium sulphate may be used where it is desired to keep down the nitrogen level. It is employed in a range of concentrations, but most favoured mixtures contain levels in the range 100 to 450 ppm.

During southern winters, when there are long periods of cloud, potassium can be applied at a higher strength than for summer. However, if using potassium nitrate, the extra nitrogen introduced needs to be taken into account. If too much nitrogen is available, the sugar level will fall and the fruit will be watery. Also, some reports indicate that if there is an excess of potassium, the acid level of the fruit will rise with some varieties. Sydney Giants is one case.

A major problem resulting from potassium deficiency is 'tomato greenback' a physiological disorder in which the top of the fruit nearest the stalk fails to colour properly. This disorder is prevalent in pot culture of tomatoes, where the root system is subjected to alternately wet and dry conditions. To prevent this situation with large pots during the summer period, a reservoir is necessary, or the frequency of the nutrient feed should be increased to three times during the day. With the reservoir, care should be exercised to ensure that the liquid is kept well aerated, as the root oxygen level has a major effect on the potassium uptake by the plant.

Calcium

Calcium is required in large quantities for the stem and the roots. It is also required to assist with the absorption of nitrogen. Calcium does not move about like some of the other elements and any deficiency quickly shows up in the new leaves.

A shortage of calcium may lead to blossom-end rot of the fruit. This can have a major effect on the marketable fruit from the crop. Low levels of calcium also affect the size of the fruit. The crop yield will decrease significantly if the calcium level falls much below 100 ppm. Concentrations above 100 ppm do not appear to be an advantage from a yield point of view.

Calcium is usually provided in the form of calcium nitrate, with calcium concentration being in the range 250 to 500 ppm. One of its important properties is that it reduces the toxic effects of certain other salts.

Magnesium

Magnesium has a major role in the formation of chlorophyll. If there is a deficiency of magnesium, there will be a transfer of magnesium from the bottom older leaves to new top leaves. This results in the older leaves taking on a light green to yellow appearance This reduction in dark green colouring reduces the amount of photosynthesis, and so affects growth aspects. Leaves will also be brittle and may curl up and turn yellow in colour.

The magnesium level should be closely watched if the potassium concentration is increased much above 300 ppm. If this occurs, the magnesium level should be maintained or increased to 75 ppm. If this is not practicable, then a 1% foliar spray of magnesium sulphate will be beneficial.

Sulphur

Sulphur is usually supplied in the nutrient solution through sulphates of the main salts. In the plant, it is incorporated into a number of organic compounds, including proteins and amino acids. It is necessary for the manufacture of new cells and for the liberation of energy. Sulphur is not very mobile and deficiency generally shows up on the upper leaves of the plant.

Iron

Iron is very important in the cultivation of tomatoes. A deficiency will quickly show up in the leaves and will inhibit growth and development. A shortage of iron frequently results in acute chlorosis, an unhealthy condition due to deficiency in chlorophyll. Iron is not very mobile within the plant and the effects of a shortage will show up as a yellowing in new leaf growth.

Iron is added to the nutrient mixture in the form of iron sulphate, an inorganic compound, or as chelates containing iron. Many hydroponicists prefer the chelate form, since it remains in solution and is readily available even under a relatively wide range of pH values. The most popular compound is EDTA (ethylene diamine tetra acetic acid) giving about 13.2% Fe. Other chelated forms can be as low as 7%.

Close control of pH is necessary to ensure stability of iron in the nutrient solution. The content of soluble iron decreases rapidly for a pH above about 6.5. In fact, in a system where the nutrient is circulated for one hour per day, the iron will almost disappear after four weeks of operation. If the pH is down to 5.5, there will still be a significant amount of iron in the solution after four weeks, although it will have fallen to about 15% of the original start-up value.

An iron deficiency frequently shows up when the fourth or fifth cluster is developing, and nutrients are being diverted from the rest of the crop. Field trials indicate that with a concentration of about 10 ppm, a good crop will be produced up to the stage where the fruit is ready for harvesting, but after the first picking takes place, the plants will provide an improved response if the level is dropped to a normal concentration of about 5 ppm.

Iron deficiency in the nutrient solution is one of the most common problems encountered in growing tomatoes in containers, and the grower needs to keep a close watch on the plants. The effect develops slowly and the first sign of trouble is usually when the plants lose their dark green colour and begin to become chlorotic. The symptoms appear first on the young leaves, gradually working their way down to the older leaves. Frequently, blossom drop will occur.

Iron drops out of the nutrient solution fairly quickly, compared with most of the other elements in the solution. This occurs for a number of reasons including:

- Oxidisation of iron by UV light (sunlight), where the solution is fed to the top of the container with drip, flow, spray or jet systems.
- Oxidisation of iron resulting from aeration, more so with the jet feed system than flow or spray systems, and rarely with static feed system.
- A rise in the pH of the nutrient solution above about 6.5.
- Normal uptake by the plants for their growth and development.
- Insolubilisation by other nutrient components.

The use of a medium which causes a rise in pH, has also an important influence on the availability of iron. The employment of calcareous material can be a major problem for the unwary.

One Australian cherry tomato grower obtained a supply of crushed material from a quarry near Mt Gambier, in South Australia, for use with his installation comprising some 150 pots and 50 large polystyrene containers. The quarry produced sawn blocks of mined material known as Mt Gambier Stone, for houses and industrial buildings. The material comprised tiny compressed shells, which had excellent water holding properties. An analysis showed the material comprised mainly calcium carbonate, with traces of phosphorus, magnesium, sodium, potassium, zinc and manganese.

However, if used untreated for hydroponics purposes, the calcium carbonate will raise the pH of the solution, causing precipitation of phosphates, iron and manganese from the nutrient solution.

When first employed, the grower was not aware of potential problems in using the material untreated. The crop was a failure, so he called in an Industrial Chemist who treated the medium with a superphosphate solution.

The grower commented that the yield after treatment was at least 20% above the previous year's crop, when he employed a gravel/peat mixture as medium.

Manganese

Manganese affects tomatoes in much the same way as iron, except that chlorosis is not confined to the younger leaves, as is the case with iron. There is some evidence of interaction with varying amounts of manganese and iron and it is a wise precaution to ensure that the proportion of manganese to iron is maintained within certain limits for healthy growth of plants.

Other elements

Elements such as copper, boron, zinc, and molybdenum are essential but are required in only small amounts. Various other elements are believed to have some influence on the growth and development of tomato plants, but there is very little information readily available in the literature on their individual effects or functions.

Table 4.1 shows the roles of various elements in growth.

Deficiency and toxicity

Table 4.2 summarises element deficiency and toxicity symptoms in a nutrient mixture. Tolerance ranges vary for different elements and for different growth stages of the plant. The water supply has an influence on element availability and toxicity. For instance, excessive calcium in the supply will increase the pH and so influence the availability of individual elements. The water may also introduce sodium and chlorine, both of which may have a deleterious effect on the plant.

Some water sources contain elements that the plant does not require for its welfare. These may accumulate in the nutrient solution and probably in the plant tissue. However, not a great deal is known about the tolerance of tomato plants to high concentrations of non-nutrient elements in the feed solution, or in the plant tissue. First indications of nutrient deficiencies will usually come from observations of plant symptoms. Tests available to pinpoint the trouble, include pH analysis of the nutrient solution, conductivity measurement which measures the total salt concentration in the solution, nutrient solution analysis and plant tissue analysis.

Some of these tests require expensive and sophisticated laboratory apparatus and would only be undertaken by a commercial grower with a large investment in the crop.

Where test and analysis facilities are available, it is good management to sample the solution every week for the first month after the facility has been commissioned, in order to test for likely problems with the installation. In one large installation, the contractor interposed a 20 m run of water and nutrient feed pipes, so that the nutrient mixture passed down the galvanised pipes. At the end of the first month after commencement of operations, a full nutrient analysis showed a rising level of zinc and enabled quick action to be taken to trace the source of the trouble.

Where large crops are involved, many growers include a regular program of tissue analysis, when the plants are at an advanced stage. Tissue analysis is the best method to evaluate the nutritional status of the plants and the success of the fertilisation program being practised. The technique is to select a random sample of leaves, about fifth or sixth from the top of the plant. The leaves are dried, but before drying, the blades are separated from

PLANT MATTER	ELEMENT
Chlorophyll	Nitrogen, Magnesium
Cell walls	Calcium
Protein	Nitrogen, Sulphur, Phosphorus
METABOLIC REGULATORS	**ELEMENT**
Photosynthesis	Phosphorus, Manganese, Magnesium, Copper
Root development	Phosphorus, Calcium
Carbohydrate in fruit	Potassium
Chlorophyll synthesis	Potassium, Iron, Manganese, Zinc
Protein synthesis	Potassium, Manganese, Magnesium

Table 4.1 The role of elements in growth.

ELEMENT	AVERAGE LEVEL
NO_3^-N	13000ppm
PO_4^-P	7000ppm
K	7%
Ca	2.5%
Mg	0.7%
Mn	37ppm
B	40ppm
Mo	2ppm
Zn	70ppm
Cu	6ppm

Table 4.3 Average nutrient levels in tomato tissues

the petioles. Analysis for NO_3^-N, PO_4^-P, K, Ca and Mg are usually made on the petioles and the minor elements on the blades.

Growers with large installations may carry out a full analysis four times during the growing season. One test is made at the seedling stage, just after the plants are transferred to the main hydroponic installation, two tests are made about mid-season, and one when the crop has reached the stage where the first picking is to take place.

A minimum of 5 grams dry weight is required for test purposes, and as the leaves are picked when green, it is necessary to harvest a minimum of 35 grams of leaf weight. Leaves should not be dispatched in sealed plastic bags, as they will sweat. Plain paper bags are more satisfactory.

The level of elements in the plant tissue covers a wide range, but average figures for healthy tomato plants are shown in Table 4.3.

The nutrient solution

As the medium makes no contribution to the growth and yield of the plant, all the nutrient elements must be added to the water. The water supply itself may contain some dissolved minerals which are useful to the plant, but most will have to be added to the water in a soluble form. Adding substances which cannot be dissolved by the water, is of no use to the plant. The plant cannot take solids directly into its system.

The process whereby the water and nutrients are taken up together, into the living cells of the plant, is called absorption. When the nutrients are dissolved in water, the elements lose their chemical bond with other elements and divide into separately charged units, called ions. It is the movement of these ions (they may be positive ions {cations} or negative ions {anions}) through the cell membranes, that makes up the process of absorption.

The movement of nutrient ions through the cell membranes is quite complicated, but because of the size, shape, strength and nature of their electric charge, plant cells are able to selectively distinguish between the different ions. The process is, however, only marginal in selectivity and if the nutrient mixture is such that high concentrations occur, they may become toxic to the plant. While some individual cells may be marginally selective, it is important that the plant be provided with a properly balanced solution of nutrient ions. This is one of the fundamentals, upon which the successful application of hydroponics is based.

Tomato plants are gross feeders and need an adequate and balanced supply to develop good quality fruit and a high yield. The balance of nutrient levels, and in particular the relative content of nitrogen, phosphorus and potassium, has a considerable influence on the growth and quality of the fruit. The proper balance between nitrogen and potassium is

ELEMENT	DEFICIENCY SYMPTOMS	TOXICITY SYMPTOMS
Nitrogen	Leaves pale green; stems thin; leaves small with lower ones yellowish; fruit small; flower buds fall off	Excessive stem and leaf growth; leaves very dark green; few blossoms and fruit; root system much smaller than normal
Phosphorus	Foliage dark green with lower leaves often purplish; plant stunted; hard stems; poor root system; deficiency first shows in mature leaves; leaves drop prematurely; fruit setting will be delayed	Unknown
Potassium	Symptoms like leaf burn; leaves roll and frequently drop; growth restricted; uneven ripening of fruit-blotchy; soft stems	Excessive potassium may upset availability of other elements
Magnesium	Yellowing between veins with veins remaining green; curling of leaf margins; fruit production reduced if deficiency is severe	Large light coloured leaves
Iron	Young leaves chlorotic (yellow); symptoms work down to older leaves; stunted growth; blossom drop	Not known
Manganese	Mottled yellowing of leaves; chlorosis less severe than in iron deficiency; leaf has net like appearance; very few flowers will form	Reduced growth and spindly
Sulphur	Yellowing of leaves; veins lighter than surrounding areas; upper leaves curled downwards	Reduced leaf size and growth
Calcium	Young leaves hooked, finally dying back at tips and in margins; growing point dies; fruit subject to blossom end rot; stems thick and woody; roots brownish and poorly developed	Not known
Boron	Young leaves light green; stalk dies back; upper leaves remain small and curl inwards; stem cracks and corky areas develop; fruit may darken and dry out	Progressive necrosis of leaf beginning at tip and moving towards leaf centre
Zinc	Small leaf size; leaf margins distorted; stalks have shortened internodes	Produces iron chlorosis; plant spindly and stunted
Copper	Young leaves wilted without spotting or marked chlorosis; leaves bluish-green in colour; stalk may bend over; very few flowers will form	Reduced growth; thick and dark rootlets
Molybdenum	Leaves curl upwards; interveinal mottling developing first on older leaves; drying or scorched leaves	Leaves turn yellow
Chloride	Not known	Severe leaf burn; ragged margin as dead tissue breaks away
Sodium	Not known	Prevents uptake of potassium

Table 4.2 Element deficiency and toxicity symptoms for tomatoes

ELEMENT	RANGE mg/1 (ppm)
Nitrogen (nitrate)	100-300
(ammonium)	0-30
Phosphorus	10-100
Potassium	100-400
Calcium	100-500
Magnesium	25-100
Manganese	0.25-5
Iron	0.5-14
Sulphur	30-400
Copper	0.05-0.75
Boron	0.05-2
Zinc	0.05-2
Molybdenum	0.01-0.1

Table 4.4 *Optimum nutrient concentration range*

PACK 1	
Potassium phosphate	18 g
Potassium sulphate	55 g
Ammonium phosphate	10 g
Magnesium sulphate	46 g
Iron EDTA	3.3 g
Boric acid	0.18 g
Manganese sulphate	0.02 g
Zinc sulphate	0.04 g
Ammonium molybdate	0.005 g

PACK 2	
Calcium nitrate	81 g

Table 4.6 *Two pack nutrient mixture*

CHEMICAL	AMOUNT
Macro elements	
Calcium nitrate	680 g
Magnesium sulphate	250 g
Potassium nitrate	350 g
Potassium chloride	170 g
Monopotassium phosphate	200 g
Micro elements	
Iron chelate (10% Fe)	15 g
Manganese sulphate (28% Mn)	1.78 g
Boron (20.5% B)	2.43 g
Zinc sulphate (36% Zn)	280 mg
Copper sulphate (25% Cu)	120 mg
Sodium molybdate (39% Mo)	128 mg

Table 4.7 *Formula for 1000 litres of nutrient solution*

ELEMENT	CONCENTRATION mg/1 (ppm)
Nitrogen (nitrate)	196
(ammonium)	-
Phosphorus	31
Potassium	279
Calcium	160
Magnesium	48
Manganese	0.25
Iron	0.8
Sulphur	64
Copper	0.02
Boron	0.06
Zinc	0.05
Molybdenum	0.04

Table 4.5 *Hoagland's solution*

an important factor in achieving good growth characteristics. A combination of low nitrogen and low potassium levels, produces soft fruit, while a high nitrogen and high potassium combination will produce firm fruit.

Experience with container culture of many different varieties of tomatoes, indicates that plants amply supplied with potassium and just sufficient nitrogen to allow steady stem growth together with fruit development, will result in production of a good crop with firm, well coloured fruit of good taste and texture. When harvesting of the crop has commenced, the nutrient balance can be modified in favour of nitrogen, in order to maintain extension growth and to enable the higher trusses to continue normal development, despite demands by developing fruit on the lower trusses.

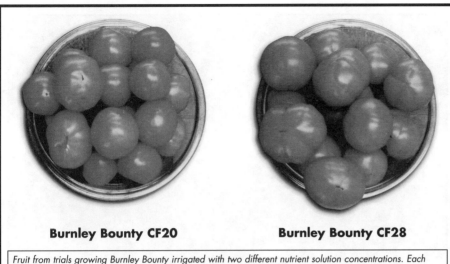

Burnley Bounty CF20   **Burnley Bounty CF28**

Fruit from trials growing Burnley Bounty irrigated with two different nutrient solution concentrations. Each group in the trial comprised three plants. Total average yield from first six trusses with solution CF20 was 7.1kg when trial was terminated in mid November compared with 7.4kg for the group fed with solution CF28. Fruit weight averaged 227g for CF20 and 232g for CF28. The average sugar Brix level was 0.2% higher for the CF28 group and the shelf life was better by several days.

The growth pattern should be closely monitored if the nitrogen component is increased during long periods of cloud coverage, or following the application of shadecloth over the growing area. The growth may become excessively vigorous, with trusses being widely separated and tending to be erect and much branched, instead of standing out strongly from the stem.

Most tomato plants are tolerant of a fairly wide range of nutrient elements, some varieties more so than others. *Table 4.4* shows typical concentration levels. A widely used nutrient formulation which fits into the range was designed by Hoagland in 1938 and is shown in *Table 4.5*. Many commercially available mixtures follow the Hoagland formula, with a few minor variations. *Table 4.6* shows the formula of one mixture available, which is sold in small containers for the home gardener and in bulk for the commercial grower. It is a two-pack mixture.

In referring to elements in a mixture, it is usual to refer to them as being in parts per million (ppm). One ppm is one part by weight, in one million parts by weight. Milligrams per litre is the same figure, since one litre of water weighs one million milligrams. The maximum figures listed in *Table 4.4* are useful when hard water is being used. They enable the grower to ensure that the total amount of any element is within the acceptable limits.

The Tables do not necessarily list the only chemicals to be used in order to arrive at the concentrations indicated. Many chemicals provide more than one element, and there are probably hundreds of different combinations which could be used. *Table 4.7* illustrates the formula developed by one grower, who ran a very successful and profitable installation of several thousand pots, using a drip feed system. Conductivity of the made-up solution was about CF28.

Nutrient uptake

A plant differs in its nutrient requirements according to the type, the stage of growth and the environmental conditions under which it is grown. Many growers develop a mixture which they consider to be best suited to a particular crop eg. tomatoes, while others use what may be considered as a general purpose mixture, to be a compromise for a number of different plants. They rely on the inherent selectivity and adaptive ability of plants to adjust themselves to a range of conditions.

If the nutrient concentration is too low for some particular plants, growth will be slow, crop yield will be low and plants will wilt during hot weather, due to the cells being bloated with water. If the mixture is taken to the other extreme, where concentration level is too high, the plants may make rapid growth, but will subsequently die prematurely. The plant

Cherry tomatoes grown in 30cm pots with a medium comprising 40% perlite/40% scoria/20% vermiculite on a 30mm gravel base. Three plants were fed with a relatively weak nutrient solution of concentration CF12 and irrigated at hourly intervals between 7am and 7pm daily for 10 minute periods. Yeilds were equal to plants grown with a solution of CF22 but sugar Brix level was lower and shelf life was also lower.

cells become very turgid and when twisting the stem around the support string, the stem will probably snap. However, tomatoes are heavy feeders and some varieties prefer solutions with a concentration approaching CF30. Work in Israel indicates some good results with CF as high as 40. The total soluble salts of fruit grown at high levels is increased, resulting in improved flavour.

The maximum concentration which plants will tolerate in a hydroponics nutrient solution, without growth reduction or other adverse effects, is not well documented, but trials indicate a wide variation with different species. Some tomato cultivars have produced good crops with concentrations as high as CF45 with no apparent adverse effects, while others have performed poorly, so it would be unwise to use strengths above about CF40 particularly for long periods.

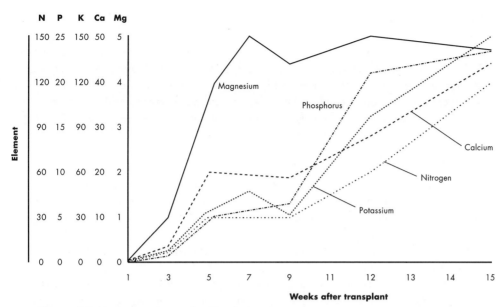

Figure 4.2 *Nutrient uptake rate kg / ha / wk.*

Weeks after transplant	N	P	K	Ca	Mg
1	0.9	0.1	0.5	0.6	0.1
3	5.2	0.9	5.3	3.4	1.0
5	35.4	5.7	34.2	21.7	4.1
7	34.9	6.2	54.9	20.8	5.0
9	31.5	6.5	35.4	19.6	4.6
12	64.5	23.1	113.2	30.6	5.2
15	135.0	24.6	159.7	48.8	4.8

Table 4.8 Nutrient uptake rate (kg/ha/wk) for Flora Dade tomato, yielding 15.8 kg fruit per plant. (David Huett).

Some successful commercial growers follow a pattern of varying the strength of the solution with plant growth. They find it important to ensure the early development of the first flower truss. One particular grower starts off by feeding the young seedlings with a solution with a conductivity of CF25, and when the fourth true leaf develops, the level is boosted to CF40 until flowering commences. Then the solution conductivity is maintained at CF30, until three weeks before harvesting. The solution concentration is then dropped to CF25 and maintained at that level until end of the crop.

Figure 4.2 and *Table 4.8*, prepared from work carried out by Dr David Huett of the New South Wales Department of Agriculture at the Tropical Research Station, Alstonville, show the great changes in nutrient uptake which occur during the growing and cropping phase. The peak nutrient demand occurs during the rapid fruit filling stage, towards the end of the crop cycle. Yields will be substantially reduced if there is inadequate nutrient supply during the fruit growth period. The amount of some elements, particularly nitrogen, potassium, phosphorus and calcium should be increased.

Whenever it is desired to change to a new mixture, particularly if it is stronger than the one being used, it is good practice to thoroughly flush out the pots with plain water before adding the new mixture. This action will remove accumulated salts. Salts in the pots may add to those being fed and result in the conductivity level being excessively high. The sudden increase in level may cause root scorch and other undesirable reactions.

Selecting a mixture

The grower has three options in selecting a mixture for the particular plant requirement. The elements can be purchased separately and accurately weighed to produce the desired concentration in the solution, a pre-mixed commercial product can be used, or the pre-mixed commercial product can be modified by the addition of other specific elements.

Although in some situations it may be more economical for the grower to purchase the chemicals separately, there is frequently a problem in ensuring the mixture is accurate, in terms of the amount of each element. This is because of the difficulty in weighing out accurately the very small amounts required as trace elements. For example, if the formula calls for 0.1 gram of a certain chemical, it is unlikely the home gardener would have equipment available to measure or weigh such a small amount. Another factor is that suppliers usually pack materials in bulk lots, which means the grower would have a stockpile large enough to last for years, in the case of some chemicals.

Very few of the recommended formulae would allow all elements to be mixed together in a concentrated form. The majority require a two pack format, while others may require five or more stock solutions. The pack or stock solutions should not be mixed together in the concentrated form.

The quality of the water used in preparing the nutrient solution should be known. Some formulae are based on the use of distilled water, but distilled water is costly and would seldom be an economical proposition for a commercial grower. If details of dissolved salts in the water are not known, there is always the possibility of the nutrient solution being very much over strength in one or more salts. This may lead to a toxicity problem and result in poor growth and low yield. There are cases on record where commercial growers found it necessary to shift operations to another area, because of unsuitable water.

After taking into account salt levels in the water supply, satisfactory mixtures may be prepared by selecting the optimum limits of concentration e.g. CF22 to CF28 and targeting for pH in the range, say, 5.5 to 6.4. But if certain elements are at significant levels in the water supply, then the amount added should be reduced accordingly. There is no single ideal mixture which will be optimum for all tomato varieties and at all growth stages. The mixtures indicated in the Tables have, however, been found to give good results with pot culture using drip, spray or flow feed installations. Most commercially produced mixtures, formulated specifically for hydroponics, will give good results throughout the year and with most tomato varieties, provided they are used in accordance with the manufacturers directions. It is certainly less fuss for a home gardener, who may have only a dozen or so pots, to purchase a ready mixed product.

It is useful to enquire from the manufacturer whether the mixture has been formulated for local mains water, or rain water. Some enthusiasts insist that rain water is superior, because it does not have large amounts of dissolved salts and flourine. However, if the mixture has been designed for local hard water, which may have a pH of say, 7 to 8, and tank water is used in lieu, then the solution will probably be outside the preferred pH range. Unless the grower has equipment for measuring and adjusting the pH, then it would be wise to use mains water.

In some cases, growers supplement the supply of nutrients to the plants by foliar sprays. This action is usually taken when it is desired to increase the level of a particular element, such as iron or calcium or magnesium etc. Contrary to popular belief, these nutrients applied as foliar sprays are not absorbed quickly. Some will take many days, with the rate depending on the size of the bush, the temperature and the substance applied. Typical absorption times for 50% absorption are, calcium 10 to 50 hours, phosphorus 5 to 7 days, potassium 10 to 20 hours, zinc 1 to 2 days, iron 10 to 20 days, magnesium 10 to 20 hours and nitrogen (as Urea) 1 to 2 hours.

Application of nutrient solutions

A number of methods of applying the nutrient solution for container culture have been found to be satisfactory. These include:

1. Manual methods　　　2. Pump methods

- Watering can.
- Gravity feed.
- Wick system.

- Drip feed.
- Flow feed.
- Spray feed.
- Pressure or jet feed.

The method chosen would be influenced by the number of plants being cultivated, cost considerations and whether unattended operation is required.

Watering can.
This is by far the simplest method of applying the nutrient solution. However, care should be taken to use a plastic can with a plastic rose. The use of galvanised can and rose may result in stripping of the zinc, which may upset the zinc balance in the solution. A major advantage of the watering can technique, is that it ensures the application of a highly aerated solution. The filling of the can from the tap and the emptying via the rose, ensures that the water is subjected to the maximum exposure to the atmospheric oxygen.

The solution can be allowed to drain away, or the surplus used to supplement a reservoir in which the pot stands. If the reservoir arrangement is adopted, the stored solution should be dumped at frequent intervals - preferably every fortnight - as the conductivity will rise due to build up of unabsorbed salts and the water will become stagnant.

The frequency of watering depends upon the size of the pot, the stage of growth of the plant, atmospheric temperature and wind. Two or three waterings a week may be sufficient for seedlings during mild weather, but for a fully grown plant with a heavy crop of tomatoes in summer, at least two applications a day may be desirable, particularly if the pot does not stand in a reservoir.

Gravity feed.
Two methods are commonly used with this arrangement. One is called the bucket method, and the other is known as the float or static feed method. The bucket method involves the use of a plastic bucket of suitable capacity, connected to the bottom of one or more pots by a length of flexible tubing. If the pots have drainage holes, these should be blocked up. The pots should be interconnected at the base by flexible tubing, so that liquid entering one pot flows freely to the others.

The bucket filled with the nutrient solution is lifted to a level just above the top of the pots and allowed to drain by gravity. A minute or so after it has emptied, the bucket is lowered to the floor and the surplus nutrient will drain back into the bucket, provided the bucket is at a lower level than the pots.

The bucket should have sufficient capacity to fill all the pots to a level just below the surface of the medium. If the bucket weight, when filled with liquid, is beyond the ability of the hydroponicist to lift, then a pulley and rope system may be required. This method has been used most successfully with a number of small patio installations, with Pixie and Sweet Bite tomatoes.

With the float or static feed method, the raising and lowering of the bucket is not required. The interconnected pots are linked by a plastic tube to a reservoir, which contains the nutrient solution. The level in the reservoir is controlled by a valve, which allows solution from a bulk storage tank to maintain the required level. The reservoir maintains a level of 5 to 6 cm of solution in the pots. The solution rises to the plant root zone by capilliary action, once the plant has grown to a height of about 15 to 25 cm.

The major advantage of the system is that it can be left unattended for relatively long periods, and is suitable for even large staked plants.

One problem is that water becomes stagnant unless air is bubbled throughout the solution at frequent intervals. The alternative is to replace the reservoir solution at about fortnightly intervals.

One successful static feed system using a multiple growing station set-up, was employed by an Adelaide hydroponicist to provide most of the family vegetable needs, including tomatoes. It used a series of 10 large polystyrene containers, in which were planted lettuce,

PLANT 1		PLANT 2	
Truss number	Fruit wt-g	Truss number	Fruit wt-g
1	250	1	190
	215		130
	200		170
	120		160
	180		140
	105		155
			80
2	252	2	230
	260		125
	130		230
	125		100
	135		250
			240
			210
3	260	3	120
	190		125
	180		153
	250		188
	240		
4	122	4	190
	200		250
	185		225
	195		120
			188
Total yield 3.794 kg		Total yield 3.969 kg	
Average weight 20 fruit - 189 g		Average weight 23 fruit - 172g	

Table 4.9 Burnley Bounty grown in static feed installation with fresh perlite medium

PLANT 3		PLANT 4	
Truss number	Fruit wt-g	Truss number	Fruit wt-g
1	135	1	250
	200		215
	230		205
	180		95
	105		
	65		
2	105	2	120
	130		152
	245		80
	175		260
			130
			110
3	95	3	195
	188		180
	255		155
	142		240
	235		122
	85		
4	130	4	110
	125		185
	188		135
	166		202
Total yield 3.179 kg		Total yield 3.141 kg	
Average weight 20 fruit - 158 g		Average weight 19 fruit - 165 g	

Table 4.10 Burnley Bounty grown in static feed installation with reused perlite medium

beetroot, carrots, onions, radishes, beans and four containers with indeterminate tomato plants.

The primary nutrient storage system comprised two parallel 20 litre plastic drums, mounted on a metal frame about 90 cm high, to provide gravity feed to a secondary storage tank, fitted with a float valve in the drop line from the primary feed tanks. In mid summer when tomatoes were in full production, three 20 litre drums were in service.

The secondary storage tank and the polystyrene growing containers were mounted on the same horizontal level, with inlet and outlet fittings so positioned that a 50 mm level of nutrient solution was maintained in the bottom of each container. An indicator float, made from a cork and coloured drinking straw inside a 20 mm vertical pipe, open at both ends, provided a continuous visual indication of the nutrient level in each container.

As the nutrient level dropped due to uptake by the plants and evaporation loss, it was replaced automatically from the secondary tank, which in turn was topped up by operation of the float valve.

Every container was fitted with a tap and push-on fitting, so any single container or groups of containers could be easily dismantled from the system, and physically removed if necessary, for maintenance work during replanting of a new crop.

After termination of each crop, the perlite was removed and put through a sieve to remove as much root material as possible. The perlite was then returned to the container and soaked in fresh water for 24 hours. Water was then drained out, the container put back into position and the new crop planted.

With plants which had small root systems, like radishes, carrots, and beetroot, the perlite was reused two or three times, but in the case of tomatoes with their dense root mat, new perlite was employed for each planting. Experience showed that reusing unsterilized perlite for a second crop of tomatoes, resulted in yield reduction of about 20% with some varieties. As an example, two Burnley Bounty plants grown in one container with new perlite, produced a crop as shown in *Table 4.9*. *Table 4.10* shows the yields to fourth truss of two plants, grown at the same time and connected to the same feed solution, but grown in perlite which had previously been used with Apollo varieties.

The result of the trial, with harvesting taking place during the April/May period, indicated that the plants in the new perlite produced a higher yield per plant and higher average yield, than those grown in the reused perlite. Average yield of the plants in the reused medium was 83% of that in the new perlite, with average weight of fruit being 161 g, compared with 180 g for the new perlite group. The leaves of the two plants grown in the reused perlite were much paler, with some showing a pale yellow colour. The fruit matured a few days earlier on the first truss, but there was no apparent difference with fruit on other trusses.

A third group of two Burnley Bounty were grown in a reused vermiculite medium, but the medium was so badly broken down after being passed through the sieve to remove roots, that it lost most of its water retention properties. The plants were removed after about eight weeks, when it became evident that the waterlogged conditions did not suit them.

Although the installation was a static feed system, with long solution distribution feed lines, no trouble was experienced with any of the crops due to aeration problems. The containers had large surfaces areas and the perlite allowed adequate oxygen to reach the plant root system.

Because of the range of different plants grown in the system, concentration in the primary feed tank was kept to CF20, with a pH of 6.0. The solution was replaced every five weeks, but before feeding it to the plants, every container was flushed out with fresh water to remove accumulated salts.

The only problem experienced was during periods of heavy rain, when the container would be filled with water. However, they could be drained easily by opening the tap at the end of each main 20 mm feed line, allowing the water to run to waste.

Simple automatic siphon systems are available which will drain excess water from the container. However, some designs have caused problems, as once activated, they keep on draining until the water level falls to the normal level, but in the process the nutrient supply tank is also drained.

A recent development in static feed technology is the self-contained mini home system, employing the patented 'Kink' valve invented by John Gwalter of Hydroponic Innovations, Port Macquarie.

A typical arrangement comprising nutrient solution holding tank, Kink valve and a four pot trough system, is shown in *Figure 4.3*. The Kink valve which is the heart of the system, is a simple, reliable valve that can be easily disassembled, or even cleaned out by blow-through. It is designed to be constrained by the bottom of the container, if a shallow depth is required. Thus a valve when so installed, would be bent at about 90 degrees and would shut off the flow in 15-20 mm of nutrient solution. Delivery rate is about 10 litres per hour.

The technology can be adapted to cater for larger size pots. The pots can be placed in standard large size polystyrene containers with removable covers, using cut-outs to suit the particular pot size. Alternatively, specially designed plastic pots can be used so that part of the base stands in the cut-out section of a plastic channel.

John Gwalter has been active in the development of facilities for hydroponics installations for many years. Besides the Kink valve, he has developed through his business Hydroponic Innovations, many other devices and systems including:

- Air splitting valve.
- Air lift system.
- Wick return.
- Self-watering pot with supply from mains.
- Mains pressure reducer.
- Automatic gravity dosing system.
- Automatic liquid ratio mixer (gravity).
- Gravity supply herb garden.
- Level control for home NFT systems.

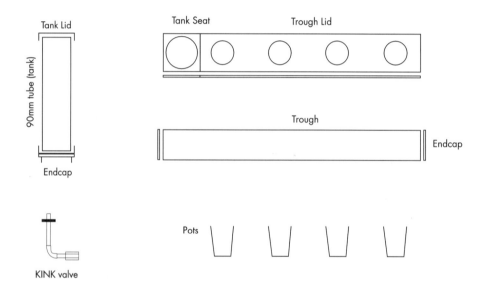

Figure 4.3 *Self contained mini home system - employing KINK valve.*

A hydroponics system which employs no electrical or mechanical devices, popular with many home growers, is the gravity/vacuum system. The main feature of the system is an air-tight nutrient storage tank. The level of solution in the growing container is controlled by an air hose, which releases the vacuum in the storage tank to allow makeup solution to pass into the growing container, to restore the correct level.

When growing pots are placed in a reservoir, where the lower part of the medium is permanently waterlogged, the effect on plant behaviour will vary with different cultivars. Some tomato plants thrive in this environment, provided there is sufficient dissolved oxygen in the nutrient solution. The root system will grow out through the holes in the pot and produce a dense mass in the reservoir. Others will react to the permanently wet environment by changing the root growth pattern. With some plants, the downward growth of the root system will stop, just above the water point, and roots will branch out horizontally to wind around the walls of the pot. Where perlite is employed as medium, downward growth will change direction about 2 cm above the water line.

One noticeable effect on plant growth with the static system, is the appearance of leaf roll with some varieties. Leaves either curl upwards, or they roll over the upper surface, starting with the older bottom leaves. The problem has been observed with Grosse Lisse and Mighty Red, particularly when grown in 20 cm pots. Although there is seldom much impact on plant growth compared with other feed systems, the yield of marketable fruit in several trials has indicated a yield fall of 1-1fi kg per plant at the maximum summer production stage, compared with flow or jet feed systems set up as drain-through systems.

Environmental temperature also has a noticeable effect on yield with static systems. For plants grown in an unheated glasshouse during winter, with fruit picking during September, the yield can be on the average, 1fi-2 kg lower than for plants grown in drain-through systems.

Even with drain-through systems, during the cooler seasons some varieties will show signs of leaf roll, but this can be easily corrected by reducing the frequency of the irrigation cycle, or reducing the period of application of the nutrient at each cycle.

Recent work with static feed systems has indicated that some tomato cultivars provide increased yield weight and fruit size, for reservoir levels other than 50 mm. However, further research work needs to be undertaken to define the mechanism of interaction between the depth of solution in the reservoir, the maturity of the plant, the medium, and the micro-climate surrounding the plant, for different cultivars.

Wick system

The wick system has been used with some success with pot culture, in growing small tomato plants, but is not suitable for the large indeterminate types.

In this system, the roots are moistened by the nutrient solution passing by capillary action, up the wick from a reservoir. A wick made from glasswool, rayon, polyester or lamp wick, is passed through a hole in the bottom of the pot. The wick must be at least 10 cm in the pot, with the end teased out to give better distribution. The other end of the wick hangs in the nutrient solution.

As water is lost by transpiration at the leaves, water moves from the medium to the plant and the solution moves up from the reservoir by capillary action, to replace that taken out of the medium. For a large plant, the amount of liquid being drawn up through the wick, is less than that lost by the leaves during high temperatures, and the plant will quickly wilt. A variety which has been satisfactorily grown with the wick system is First Prize. One enterprising grower grew eight plants on a balcony, with 20 cm pots and two wicks inserted into each pot. With a large reservoir, in which all eight pots were placed, the owner left the plants unattended for six weeks while away on holidays, and on return was welcomed by a beautiful crop of ripe tomatoes.

Highly absorbent media is essential for the wick system. Perlite is ideal, but vermiculite has also been used with success.

An alternative to the wick is a capillary mat. One system available commercially is the Auto-Pot Capillary Mat system, where the mat is kept moist by a SMART-Valve, which maintains a 35mm deep nutrient solution in a well around the base, and the edges of the mat are immersed in the solution. Water is drawn up from the well, by the capillary mat material, and into rockwool cubes or pots with either centre, or outer perimeter holes.

Drip feed

Drip feeding of tomatoes in containers is widely practiced by commercial and home growers. It is easily installed, has low maintenance requirements and is economical in the use of water. Although various types of plastic drippers are available, most clog easily with salt build-up. Spaghetti or small bore tubing is preferred by many growers.

Drip feeding depends on low application rates of nutrient solution, to develop an onion-shaped wetted zone below the surface of the medium. The diameter and depth of the wetted zone depends on characteristics of the medium, the temperature, the rate of flow of the liquid and the application time. Very porous media, such as perlite and vermiculite, give a relatively wide wetted zone, but coarse gravel has a narrower and deeper wetted zone for the same application rate.

For economical reasons, the flow rate should be adjusted to ensure minimum loss through the bottom of the pot, if no recovery is required.

As drip feeding results in the steady use of the nutrient solution, the supply tank should have sufficient capacity to meet the daily needs and any desired extended periods. Feeding does not have to be continuous, but should be effected at sufficiently short intervals to give an adequate moisture level.

Advantages of drip feeding are:

- Nutrient solution is constantly available to meet the plant needs.

- There is uniform application of nutrients to all plants.

- Requires minimum labour for operation. Timers can be employed if intermittent feeding is desired.

- The root zone area is adequately wetted for pot culture.

- Volume of nutrient to individual plants can be easily decreased or increased.

- Provides a well aerated solution, by virtue of the drops passing through the atmosphere.

Disadvantages include:

- Blockage of plastic drippers can occur.

- Salts accumulate on the extremities of the wetted zone. These need to be flushed out regularly.

- Root development may be hindered if a medium such as gravel is used, due to the restricted horizontal wetted zone.

- Feed lines must be checked at regular intervals to ensure free flow of liquid.

- It is not always a straightforward operation to vary the flow rate to meet a greater uptake of the plant.

In order to produce a satisfactory flow through small bore tubing, a gravity supply tank will need to be mounted at least one metre above the outlet. For very large installations, where hundreds of containers are involved, a pressure pump is necessary, but some means of controlling flow into branch lines has to be incorporated in the installation.

Flow feed

Instead of using a spaghetti tube of 1-1fi mm diameter, as for a drip feed installation, tubing approximately 3 mm in diameter will allow a continuous flow of nutrient. A typical feed rate is 500 to 600 ml per minute for about 10 minutes.

Two adaptations of this arrangement both result in good crops of tomatoes in pots. One allows the nutrient to flow straight through the medium back to the tank, and the other uses a siphon system. The flow-through arrangement can employ a single tube outlet, but for 30 cm diameter pots, experience has shown that there is a large dry area at the top of the perlite. To overcome this, a small plastic T-piece inserted in the tube will divert the liquid across the surface of the medium, resulting in more uniform wetting.

In the siphon arrangement, the only water outlet is via a siphon tube mounted inside the pot. When the nutrient solution fills the pot to the level corresponding to the top of the siphon tube, draining automatically commences and empties the pot. This method thoroughly saturates the medium, a beneficial action during summer when the plant is at maximum growth and production rate.

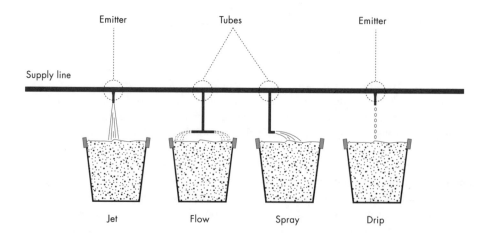

Figure 4.4 Nutrient solution feed systems.

Spray feed

This method produces a good crop of marketable fruit and can be used with all varieties.

In one installation of 70 pots, 20 mm plastic feeders were strapped across the tops of the pots and small plastic spray fittings suspended from the 20 mm feeder, to about one third distance between top and bottom of the pot. The pots stood in polystyrene boxes, so that surplus nutrient solution drained back to an underground tank. The top of the pot was covered with a masonite cover with hole and slot, so that it fitted on the pot lip after allowing the plant stem to pass through. The bottom of each pot contained 60 mm of gravel. The plants were started off using 150 mm square rockwool slabs and when they were of sufficient height, were transferred to the pot, the lid placed in position and the nutrients applied via the spray fitting. A gravity feed system using three 200 litre plastic tanks provided sufficient pressure to operate the spray devices.

The roots were drenched with the spray, and the rockwool blocks together with the matt of roots, retained sufficient moisture to meet the plant's needs for at least three hours, when the cycle was repeated. During night time periods, the spray cycle was extended to five-hourly intervals, except in mid-summer when four-hourly cycles were implemented.

Pressure or jet feed

This system uses gravity or a pump to provide pressure, and is a popular arrangement with both commercial and home growers with container installations.

Nutrient solution being provided by pressure or jet feed arrangement to plant in perlite medium. Pressure is provided by mounting the supply tank about 1.5m above the growing container and placing a 1.5mm diameter nozzle in the main feed line about 200mm above the medium. On striking the medium at high velocity, a flurry of bubbles is created, ensuring a high degree of aeration as the solution passes down to the root zone. The photograph also shows a drilled aeration pipe to further improve air supply throughout the entire medium and to facilitate the escape of gases produced by the roots.

One installation catering for 100 pots in a glasshouse, used three 200 litre aboveground tanks to provide gravity feed, with the surplus nutrient being collected by three similar tanks mounted below pot base level. The low level tanks were automatically topped up as required. The nutrient was pumped in to the high level tanks by an electric pump at preset intervals, using a programmable timer with memory. A series of 20 mm plastic pipes were branched from a 37 mm main feeder pipe and fitted across the tops of the pot lips, or raised about 150 to 200 mm above. The nutrient was applied to each plant via a small plastic nozzle, pushed into the 20 mm branch pipe, or via a small piece of tubing.

The major advantage of this system is that the liquid on being ejected from the 1fi mm diameter nozzle, strikes the medium with high velocity, creating a flurry of bubbles and ensuring a high degree of aeration as the feed passes down through the root network.

Basic principles of the drip, spray, flow and jet feed systems are shown in *Figure 4.4*.

The drip, flow and jet systems will create so-called 'onion' diagrams of wetness, with varying moisture levels radiating out from the point where the solution falls on the medium. The moisture onion diagram for each system will vary with the type of medium, the temperature, rate of solution feed and solution application time.

Moisture level measurements with a typical drip feed installation, employing 1fi mm spaghetti tubing, feeding 30 cm diameter pots irrigated on a 10 minute cycle, with perlite medium, produced a moisture level 30% at 1.5 cm from the water impact point. This dropped rapidly to about 10% at 3.5 cm, and 2% at 7 cm. For a 50/50 perlite/peat mixture, the readings were 35% at 1.5 cm, 20% at 3.5 cm and 3% at 7 cm. Readings were taken 2 minutes after irrigation cessation.

In a flow system, a T-piece in the down tube resulted in the medium being wetted by two, almost horizontal, solution streams. There was no solution falling in the centre of the pot where the plant stem was located, so the moisture level there was very low until about 5 cm out, when it reached 30% level right to the edge of the pot. Moisture levels measured at right angles to the stream, fell to about 10% at a distance of about 5 cm from the stream centre line, and to about 2% at 10.5 cm. In theory, there is a large area of the medium which would have an almost zero moisture level, but in practice capilliary action results in some moisture being maintained throughout the entire volume of the pot. An examination of the root systems after completion of cropping, showed roots being just as dense in the low moisture zones, as in those saturated with solution.

With the pressure or jet feed arrangement using 1fi mm diameter nozzle, the moisture level was about 35% at a distance 3 cm out from the jet impact point, falling to 20% at 6 cm and 2% at 10.5 cm. These figures were obtained with perlite medium, but with plants growing in 50/50 perlite/vermiculite, the results were within about 5% of those using perlite only.

Pots set up for spray feed arrangement were fitted with a 90 degree plastic spray fitting, fixed against the wall of the pot, and the top of the pot was covered with a masonite disc to confine the spray within the pot. Measurements showed that moisture content was about 35% for the entire surface area of the medium, when the solution pressure was sufficient to ensure complete surface coverage of the medium.

With systems which operate on the basis of surplus nutrient solution going to waste in the ground, in the immediate vicinity of the growing area, the water and its nutrients are usually lost. However, there are a few installations where the excess solution is taken to a large underground storage tank, or a dam, via a large pipe or channel, for subsequent reuse in an irrigation system for growing soil crops or pastures. One farmer grew potatoes successfully by making use of the runoff from a cherry tomato hydroponics system.

In the case of static feed or recirculating arrangements, it is a simple matter to gain access to the discarded solution, because a storage tank is usually available. There are two ways the discarded solution can be put to use. One is to reuse it as a nutrient-stripping facility, by feeding it to another installation which will accept a feed system with lower than normal nutrient levels. Systems with low nutrient levels have been successfully employed when using reclaimed water from sewerage treatment works. Much work has been done in this area in recent years, particularly overseas, in growing such crops as sugar beet, broad beans, sorghum and fodder crops.

The other use is to pump the solution to soil grown crops, where advantage can be taken of nutrients remaining in the discarded solution. Where the sodium chloride is high, due to salt buildup from long period use of input water (which itself may have a relatively high salt level from the start), it is common practice to dilute the discarded solution with water, before applying it to the soil grown crop or pasture.

Where the soil grown crop is another crop of tomatoes, the plants will tolerate a discarded solution which has reached a conductivity level of CF40, chloride up to 400 ppm and sodium up to 250 ppm. However, at this level, dilution by water would be good management practice.

With a large installation, the system is easier to manage if the circulating solution is regularly bled, by taking off a proportion of the circulating solution and replacing it with fresh solution, instead of the whole storage tank contents being recirculated until it has outlived its usefulness.

pH and conductivity

It is important that the hydroponicist understands the meaning of the terms 'pH' and 'conductivity'. Although it is possible to manage a successful installation without being bothered with such technical terms, it helps much more to assess just what may be the cause, if something goes wrong with the plant or the whole crop.

pH
The term pH is the symbol for hydrogen ion concentration and is derived from the words 'potential of hydrogen'.

It is a measure of acidity or alkalinity and covers a range 0 (acid) to 14 (alkaline) for

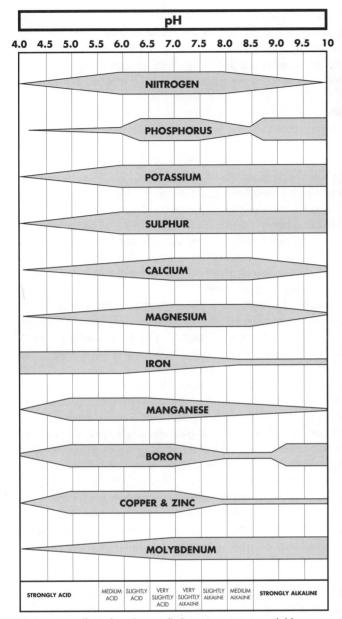

Figure 4.5 *Effect of acidity or alkalinity on nutrient availablity.*

LIQUID COLOUR	REACTION	pH VALUE
Red	Very strongly acid	2
Orange	Strongly acid	4
Yellow	Weakly acid	6
Yellow-green	Neutral	7
Green	Weakly alkaline	8
Greenish-blue	Strongly alkaline	10

Table 4.12 *Colour and pH value*

pH value	Hydrogen ion concentration	
0	10 000 000	
1	1 000 000	
2	100 000	
3	10 000	acidity
4	1 000	
5	100	
6	10	
7	0	neutral
8	10	
9	100	
10	1 000	
11	10 000	alkalinity
12	100 000	
13	1 000 000	
14	10 000 000	

Table 4.11 *Relationship of pH and hydrogen ion concentration*

almost all aqueous solutions. A pH measurement of 7 is considered to be neutral and corresponds approximately to distilled water. In hydroponic tomato culture, we are concerned with a range of just above 5.5 to just below 6.5, i.e. slightly on the acidic side. The relationship of pH and hydrogen ion concentration is shown in *Table 4.11*.

The pH value has a determining influence on the availability of the various elements to the plant. This can best be explained by reference to a chart like *Figure 4.5*, in which the width of the bands indicates the relative availability of each plant food element at various pH levels. If it is assumed that the pH of the nutrient solution is to be maintained within the range 5.5 to 6.5, then the bands give a clear indication of what is likely to happen below and above the range. Below about 5.5, the availability of phosphorus, potassium, calcium, magnesium and molybdenum fall off rapidly, whilst above 6.5 iron and manganese are not readily available.

There are three simple ways of measuring the pH of the nutrient solution. The method used would generally be governed by cost considerations, especially for the home grower. The methods are paper strip, liquid indicator and meter.

With the paper strip method, a coloured strip of paper is dipped into a sample of the solution to be measured. The specially treated paper will change colour. The colour is compared with a colour chart supplied with the pack of strips. Although not a very accurate method, it is usually sufficiently accurate for a spot check by the home gardener. Ordinary litmus paper is not very accurate with hydroponic nutrient mixtures, as the papers are intended for use with raw water and not water containing a high level of salts. Although specially buffered papers are available to provide a more accurate reading, they are light sensitive and deteriorate rapidly.

The liquid indicator method also involves the matching of colours, in order to determine the pH value. A sample of the nutrient solution is placed in a test tube and one or more drops - depending on instructions - are added. After mixing, the solution will change colour. The colour is then compared with a colour chart, usually pasted on the bottle. The colour change and reaction will generally be along the lines of *Table 4.12.*

It can be seen, therefore, that for tomatoes, we would be looking for a yellow colour after the drops had been added to the solution.

The most accurate and fastest method is to use a pH meter. This may be an instrument designed to measure pH only, or a dual function device, capable of measuring the pH and conductivity of the nutrient solution. The instrument has a probe which is placed in a sample of the solution, and the pH reading is indicated by a pointer which comes to rest above the scale. Most meters today provide a digital readout.

A typical dual function instrument is the TPS Hydroponics Analyser, Model HP80A. It has a pH range of 4 to 9, with an accuracy of ±0.05. The latest version, Model HP81, provides a digital readout with 12 mm liquid crystal display. An unusual device is the NZ Hydroponics pH Wand, a microprocessor driven device with large, easy to read printed vertical scale 4.0 to 7.6.

The pH electrode consists of a pH-sensitive glass membrane, attached to a sealed insulating tube containing a solution of fixed pH, in contact with a silver-silver chloride half cell. The potential developed across the membrane is compared with a stable reference potential e.g. the silver-silver chloride half cell in contact with an electrolyte containing chloride. Completion of the circuit is accomplished by means of a porous ceramic constriction, which allows the reference electrolyte to slowly flow into the sample, continuously flushing the constriction. *Figure 4.6* shows construction details.

There are conflicting views among growers regarding the optimum pH for hydroponically grown tomatoes in containers. Some growers operate within the range 6 to 7, some within the range 5.4 to 6.0, while others have produced best crop results with solutions with pH of 4.5 to 6.6. However, most growers operate their systems within the range 5.5 to 6.5, with solutions just above 6.0 for the majority of varieties.

It is important that the solution be controlled to prevent it becoming alkaline, as there will most likely be precipitation of calcium phosphate, which not only will result in blockage of line feed jets, but will also coat the roots of the plants.

If the pH is below 5.5, potassium hydroxide or other suitable substance should be added in sufficient quantity to raise the pH reading.

If the pH is too high, phosphoric acid or nitric acid can be used. Phosphoric acid is preferred by many, as it adds phosphorus in the process, and contributes to the mineral needs of the plants. If, however, the pH is exceptionally high because of a high level of calcium bicarbonate in the water supply, the use of nitric acid may be desirable. Should phosphoric acid be added in this situation, calcium phosphate will be produced. This is an insoluble white precipitate, which is unavailable for uptake by the plant. In the end, the decision on whether to use nitric acid or phosphoric acid usually boils down to a question of safety. Concentrated nitric acid is very corrosive, whereas phosphoric acid is milder in this regard. In all cases of adjusting pH, whether using potassium hydroxide, nitric acid or phosphoric acid, extreme care should be exercised and appropriate safety precautions adopted. Sulphuric acid is another suitable acid.

The introduction of ammonia in the nutrient solution is another way of reducing the pH. The ammonia, in being converted to nitrate, makes the solution acid. This conversion or oxidation is carried out by nitrifying bacteria in the micropopulation.

The pH changes in the nutrient solution frequently take place fairly rapidly, depending on the mass of the plant root system and the volume of nutrient solution per plant.

The growth of the plant is a factor in making the medium more acid, through the release

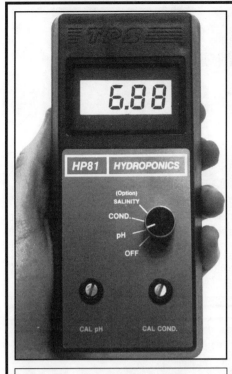

TPS Portable Hydroponic Analyser HP81 for measuring pH and conductivity with 12mm liquid crystal digital display. The pH range is 0 to 14 and conductivity 0 to 19.99 mS/cm with automatic temperature compensation. The instrument features a 'low battery' indicator

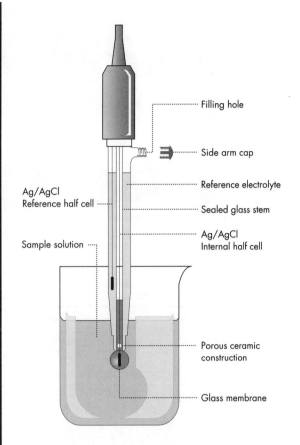

Figure 4.6 *Ionode Pty Ltd pH electrode.*

of organic acids and hydrogen ions from living roots. As the root tips move through the medium during the growth process, the outer layers of cells at the tips are scraped off against the sharp medium particles, particularly scoria, sand and gravel. Also, when the plant is removed, many small roots remain in the medium and eventually die. The longer the period the medium remains in service, the greater the accumulated organic matter and the more attention necessary to bring the pH level to the desired figure.

With fresh medium, where there has been no accumulation of root or other vegetative material from previous crops, the pH of the solution, will most likely increase when tomatoes are growing, if the solution is not acidified. With rapidly growing plants, the pH will soon rise above 6.5 and likely cause an iron deficiency problem. The pH increase is due to the rapid uptake of the nitrate ion into the growing plant, with a subsequent release of carbon dioxide into the nutrient solution. The carbon dioxide forms bicarbonate, a weak acid, which reacts with hydrogen ions in solution to form undissociated acid, resulting in a rise of pH.

Conductivity

Conductivity is a measure of the strength or amount of mineral salts dissolved in the nutrient solution. A liquid in which salts are dissolved, will allow electricity to pass through it, just as a current will pass along a piece of copper wire. The higher the concentration of salts, the greater the current that will pass through the solution for a given voltage. The solution is termed an electrolyte, and its resistance to conduction is measured in units called Ohms. Its ability to conduct is known as its 'electrical conductance' and is measured in units called Siemens. For simplicity, conductivity is often expressed as milliSiemens/centimetre (mS/cm), so that whole numbers are used. Typical meters available for hydroponic application enable conductivity to be measured in units of EC (Electrical Conductivity) with a scale reading of 0 to 5, or CF (Conductivity Factor) with a scale 10 times larger i.e. 0 to 50.

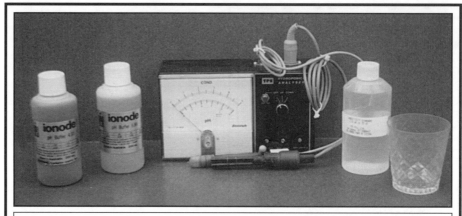

TPS Hydroponics Analyser for measurement of pH and conductivity with analogue meter. The pH range was 4 to 9 and conductivity 0 to 5mS/cm automatically temperature compensated to 25°C. Solutions were provided for calibration purposes. Although analogue meters are no longer standard devices by most manufacturers, many hydroponic operators preferred them as the pointer quickly stabilised due to inherent damping characteristics, and maximum and minimum points could be marked on the glass cover by spirit pen for easy reference purposes.

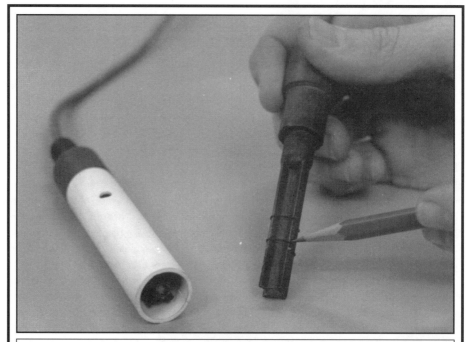

Type HK-1 Conductivity probe with plastic body employed with TPS Hydroponics Analyser. The device measures conductivity in the range 0 - 19.99 mS/cm automatically compensated to 25°C. Accuracy is + or - 0.2%. The shank of the probe is made of Rytol and the two circular conductors are platinum wires.

In addition to the abbreviation CF for Conductivity Factor, abbreviations cF and Cf have also been used in some publications.

To measure conductivity with a portable meter, the sensor is placed in a sample of the nutrient solution and the battery will cause a current to flow through the solution and the meter. The meter needle will traverse the scale, and the point where it comes to rest will be a measure of the conductivity, as indicated on a calibrated scale. Digital readout instruments are now the preferred types.

As plants remove the elements, the electrical conductivity will fall and if a recirculating system is being used, a close watch should be kept, by regular measurements to ensure that the strength does not fall below a prescribed level. An automatic system will raise an alarm.

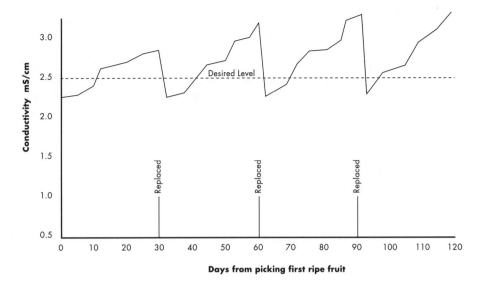

Figure 4.7 *Changes in conductivity of nutrient solution.*

In interpreting the meter reading, in relation to the condition of the nutrient supply, it is important to know the composition of the water supply used to make up the solution. Typical mains water supplies contain considerable quantities of chloride, sodium and sulphate impurities, and every time the nutrient mixture is topped up with water, these impurities will accumulate in the solution, as they may not be taken up by the plants. Hence, the situation could occur where plants have almost depleted the solution of the originally added nutrients, yet the conductivity reading is within the acceptable range, simply because of the unusable salts added via the water supply. The measured EC may even rise with time, as shown in *Figure 4.7*, if the top-up water has a high level of salts and the plants use large quantities of water during high growth and cropping periods. Although the strength of the added nutrients will fall with time, they may be replaced by salts in the top-up water at a greater rate. In the example, the desired level of EC was 2.5 and the solution was replaced every 30 days.

Because of possible problems such as this, the hydroponicist who must use a water supply with a high level of impurities, would be wise to dump the solution at regular intervals. Intervals of one month are typical practice.

As the welfare of the plant is greatly influenced by the effective conductivity (i.e. salts) which it can absorb, and not necessarily by the total as indicated by the meter, the initial conductivity or salinity of the water used to make the nutrient solution, should be measured and taken into account. For example, if the water has a measured conductivity of 0.5 mS/cm, then it is necessary to add this figure to the conductivity figure which the nutrient would have in distilled water.

It is not a simple exercise for the home gardener to measure the level of each salt in a solution, but nitrate test strips are available which will allow a check to be made on the nitrate nitrogen concentration of the solution. Hydroponic solutions should contain about 200 ppm nitrate nitrogen, and a check on the level existing in the solution can be useful in assessing the likely condition of the mixture. If the nitrate nitrogen has been excessively depleted, then it is likely that other elements are also low in concentration, even though the conductivity meter may show a reading which may tend to indicate an acceptable condition.

In addition to a meter which measures EC (Electrical Conductivity) in either milliSiemens/cm (mS/cm), or microSiemens/cm (μS/cm), there is a meter used by many hydroponicists which measures Total Dissolved Salts (TDS), and presents the readings as parts per million (ppm). The TDS is the concentration of a solution as the total weight of dissolved solids.

Although there is no direct relationship between mS/cm and ppm, the TDS figure is multiplied by 0.64 to provide a rough estimate of EC (in mS/cm). If the instrument does not have inbuilt temperature compensation, then the operator will need to refer to a

Temperature Conversion Table.

Many different instruments are available for measurement of nutrient solution conductivity, some calibrated with more than one scale. The range includes TPS Model LC81 Conductivity Meter, a multi range instrument; NZ Hydroponics Truncheon, a sophisticated microprocessor driven device without switches, provided with calibrations EC and CF or PPM; Orion portable TDS meters; Milwaukee pocket pen and table top conductivity meters with calibrations PPM or mS/cm; Eutech Cybernetics microprocessor based TDS and conductivity pocket testers, with Models TDScan 10 (PPM) and TDScan 20 (EC); Hanna Instruments microprocessor based EC meters; Australian Scientific pocket conductivity meter with automatic temperature compensation; and many others.

Conductivity can be measured by a number of electronic techniques, but the materials employed for the probe and the system design will have an important influence upon the long term consistency of the readings. NZ Hydroponics, who have made major contributions to hydroponic measuring instruments and systems over the years, have come to the conclusion that the best material for use with a probe is carbon, used in conjunction with electronic equipment based on microprocessor chip technology.

Water

Plant requirements

An adequate supply of water of acceptable quality, is critical to the growth and development of tomato plants. A large bushy plant will require a lot of water during a period of high temperature, wind and low humidity. Only a small amount is retained within the body of the plant, most of it is lost through the leaves because of the high rate of transpiration.

The plant takes in its water requirement via the roots and causes it to move up through the xylem in the stem, to the leaves. The water, and intake of salts which may be dissolved in the water, depends upon the behaviour and relationship of membranes and solutions, especially the rate of osmosis and the concentration of the nutrient ions which exists in the root zone.

When a container is filled with a highly absorbent medium such as perlite, and water is applied over the surface, some of the water will drain away if sufficient quantity is applied. The water which remains in the medium is held there against the force of gravity. The water capacity of the medium is defined as the amount held against gravity.

Substances such as crushed rock have low capacity, necessitating more frequent cycles of water compared with absorbent materials. However, not all water held by the medium against the force of gravity is available for use by the plant. Frequently, the leaves of a large plant will droop or wilt, even though there is still some water trapped in the medium. This property is associated with a phenomenon called the 'permanent wilting percentage'. The difference between the capacity of the medium and the permanent wilting percentage, is called the available water i.e. the water the plant can absorb.

The temperature of the water also plays an important role in the welfare of the plant. It influences the viscosity and the tension on the surface of the capilliary films. Thus, the water moves less rapidly when cold than when warm. This is why some growers who grow tomatoes out of doors during the colder periods, use warm water when applying the nutrient solution, particularly during the morning.

The condition of the leaves has a considerable influence on the amount of water absorbed by the plant. The water absorbing power of the root system is affected by osmotic pressure and this in turn is determined by differences in the concentration of water on each side of membranes of the absorbing cells. An important feature of these membranes is that they are permeable to minerals dissolved in the nutrient mixture, but impermeable to organic substances.

Organic substances, such as sugars, are in solution with water within the absorbing region, and generally are in greater concentration than the minerals in solution in the nutrient mixture. When there is sufficient water at the root zone, water will diffuse into the root system, because of the lower concentration of water in the absorbing cell. The sugars are produced in the leaves by photosynthesis and pass down the phloem of the stem to the roots. A plant with large healthy dark green leaves will produce more sugars, because of the higher level of photosynthesis, than a plant with pale or diseased leaves, and this will result in the absorption of more water through the root system.

In situations where a pot stands in a reservoir of nutrient solution, the pot should be regularly flushed, preferably using a rose, and the reservoir solution replaced. The plant roots constantly respire and give off carbon dioxide and take in oxygen. If the oxygen in the medium or reservoir liquid is exhausted, absorption of water will almost cease. Also, tests by researchers show that in situations where the nutrient concentration is high and the oxygen level in the water has been almost depleted, blossom-end rot may appear on a large percentage of the fruit. One grower had an 80% crop loss.

Light is another factor in water utilisation by the plant. About 80% of the incident light is absorbed by the leaf, but only a very small proportion of it is involved in the manufacture of food. The greatest proportion is changed to heat. This induced heat energy results in a rise in temperature of the leaf. The temperature rise in turn causes an increase in the rate of transpiration, and so a greater demand for water.

Plants grown in an environment sheltered from the wind, will require less water than those grown in the open. When water is exposed to wind, water vapour molecules are rapidly carried away. However, a leaf is biophysical in nature and other factors come into play.

The rate of absorption of water through the roots, and turgor of the guard cells of the leaf, have to be taken into account. If the rate of absorption is less than the rate of transpiration, the stomata will close, resulting in a decrease of the transpiration.

The factors which influence the uptake of water act together. A well aerated medium, with water at a suitable temperature and nutrient of optimum strength for the plants, promotes the rapid diffusion of water into the plant. Conversely, plants in a medium which is cold, and contains too little moisture or nutrient solution, with a conductivity which is too high, will limit the amount of water absorbed.

Similarly, those factors which influence the loss of water also act together. High light intensity, high temperature, wind and low humidity result in a high rate of transpiration. That is the reason why more water is taken up by the plants during the day compared with night, on a clear day compared with a cloudy day, on a windy day compared with a calm

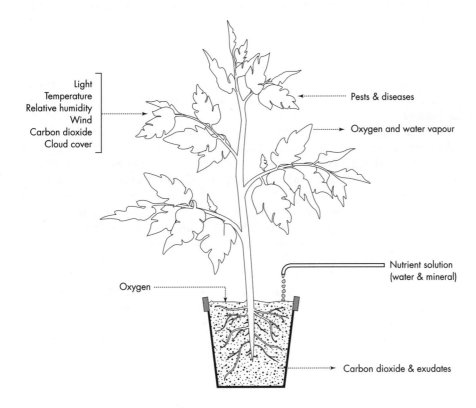

Figure 4.8 Factors influencing growth of plant.

day, on a dry day compared with a rainy day and during summer compared with the cooler seasons.

If all other factors are favourable, water availability may be the limiting factor in the growth and development of the plant. If insufficient is available over a period of time, the plant cells will be small. This produces stems with short internodes, small leaves and undersized fruit. The small leaves reduce the amount of photosynthesis, causing a drop in plant growth and fruit yield. In the extreme case, the plant will wilt, photosynthesis almost comes to a standstill due to closure of the stomata and the plant will starve and finally die. *Figure 4.8* summarises the main factors which influence plant growth.

Problems with containers

A sign of insufficient watering of a tomato plant grown in a container, becomes evident in the rate of extension of the stem, reduced leaf size and small poorly developed fruit. Leaves subjected to a high rate of transpiration and a low rate of absorption, will draw water from the fruit. This reduces the size of the fruit and blossom-end rot will occur as the fruit develops.

Too much water can also bring about problems with container culture. Where new seedlings are interspersed with well grown plants, there is often reduced light available for the seedling, because of the shadow caused by the larger plant. This may lead to leggy development of the seedling. The environment and developing root system may ensure abundant absorption of water, but the lower temperature and reduced light intensity combine to bring about a low rate of transpiration. The high absorption by the roots and low transpiration by the leaves cause elongation and stretching of the cells. The same conditions of high water absorption and low transpiration, also bring about cracking of ripe fruit.

Watering cycles

The time between watering cycles, whether carried out manually or by auto pump, depends on a number of factors, the most important of which are size of the bush, time of day, temperature and type of medium in which the plant is growing. For a 30 cm diameter pot with perlite or scoria medium, and an advanced plant at the cropping stage, feeding two or three times a day using a flow feed would result in a good crop during summer days. Once or twice a day feeding would generally be adequate in the cooler months. The flow system would need to have a feed rate of 500 to 600 ml per minute, for about 10 minutes duration, particularly during a hot day. For a drip feed system, irrigation would need to be carried out at two hourly intervals during daylight, and once about midnight during summer. During cooler months, feeding intervals may be stretched out to 5 to 6 hours. If gravel is used in the pots, then feed intervals would need to be shortened.

Extensive trials have shown that irrigating cycles should not be too frequent, particularly if the pots are standing in a reservoir. The perlite may be excessively wet, resulting in decreased fruit yield and poorly coloured fruit. The condition may delay maturity and lower the amount of soluble solids. On the other hand, if the perlite becomes excessively dry, because of insufficient cycles and no reservoir, the fruit will be well coloured, there will be an increase in soluble solids, maturity will be faster but the yield will be reduced both in terms of weight and numbers of marketable fruit. For Grosse Lisse, the yield may fall by 40% for a single-cycle mode, compared with a three-cycle mode.

Water quality

With regard to quality, a good yardstick is that if the water is suitable for human consumption, it would probably be suitable for hydroponics. Mains or bore water frequently contains a range of salts, with calcium and magnesium often present in considerable amounts in so called "hard" waters. Sulphate and sodium ions are often present and make a contribution to the conductivity. It is generally accepted that the electrical conductivity of the water, before any nutrients are added, should be less than about 500 microSiemens per centimetre (500 µS/cm), or a total concentration of less than 350 ppm. If measurements indicate that the salt levels are above 300 ppm, special treatment of the water would be necessary.

Before starting on large scale hydroponics, it would be wise to obtain details of the mineral content of the water supply to be used. An analysis may indicate a wide variation over a year. Dry seasons and rainy seasons make big differences to the amount of salts found in the water. Experienced growers recommend that artesian water be analysed every six months, and surface water sources be analysed every two or three months, where there is concern about pollution from industrial waste.

When an analysis of the water sample has been made, the results will be given as total dissolved salts (TDS). This is a good general measurement and a first approximation of water quality, but it is not of much help to the hydroponicist who wishes to monitor the water quality with equipment usually in service.

Because all salts do not respond the same to conductivity measurements. there is not an exact agreement between TDS measurement and CF measurement using the conductivity meter. The TDS, nevertheless, is a useful indicator. Since in most hydroponic installations, the general level of total nutrient salts would be 2000 to 3000 ppm, this would tend to override the much lower level of dissolved salts found in the average public water service. *Table 4.13* shows an analysis of the water supply in some Australian capital cities.

Many hydroponicists firmly believe that rainwater drained from the roof of a house or other building, is the only type which should be used. The argument is, that it is the only way in which complete knowledge of the amount of minerals fed to the plant is possible. However, this approach can have its pitfalls. Analysis has shown that rain water taken from building roof tops and stored in galvanised tanks, can frequently be more variable in mineral content than water taken from the ground. In addition to contaminants washed off the roof, there is the problem of dissolved zinc from the tank.

One hydroponic grower found that his tomatoes began to yellow at the growing points. The yellowing progressively got worse, until it affected both plant growth and crop yield. At first it was suspected that the problem was a deficiency in iron in the nutrient solution. More iron chelate was added to the solution and a leaf spraying program was also put into operation. The problem remained, and after an analysis of the nutrient solution, it was found that the zinc level was some 50 times above that which had been added. The zinc had gradually been released from the tank walls with time. The yellowing was explained by the fact that an excess in zinc can interfere with a plant's iron nutrition, and cause symptoms to develop which suggest an iron deficiency. The lesson to be learnt is that if water is to be stored for any length of time, the tank should not be constructed of untreated galvanised iron, or else the walls should be suitably treated.

The problem of excess of an element and how it affects the uptake of other elements, is important when the hydroponicist is experimenting with nutrient solutions, in order to determine a mixture for optimum fruit yield. For example, too much calcium or zinc or manganese or copper or phosphorus, can induce a deficiency of iron.

When an element interferes or prevents the uptake of another, it is described as antagonism. An element which can increase the availability and uptake of another is described as stimulation.

Capital City	Calcium	Sodium	Chloride	Bicarbonate	Magnesium	Sulphate	Electrical Conductivity µS/cm
Adelaide	15-40	60-150	100-250	65-165	13-30	2-50	250-600
Brisbane	40-80	20-50	30-110	70-100	40-90	1-85	300-600
Melbourne	2-6	3-5	5-7	NA	1-2	1-3	40-50
Perth	3-35	35-140	60-250	10-140	5-15	5-75	250-950
Sydney	2-15	10-40	15-30	NA	2-10	2-15	100-350

Table 4.13 Analysis of some capital city water supplies in ppm.

Chemical	Weight to provide 1 ppm of prime nutrient (gram)	Weight to provide 1 ppm of associate element (gram)	Typical purity %	Solubility ratio solute/water
Calcium nitrate	5.9 Ca	8.3 N	90	1:1
Potassium nitrate	7.2 N	2.7 K	95	1:4
Monopotassium phosphate	4.4 P	3.5 K	98	1:3
Potassium sulphate	2.2 K	5.4	90	1:15
EDTA iron	6.55 Fe		10.5	highly soluble
Magnesium sulphate	10.3 Mg	7.7	45	1:2
Manganese sulphate	3.07 Mn			1:2
Copper sulphate	3.91 Cu			1:5
Boric acid	5.64 B			1:20
Ammonium molybdate	4.42 Zn			1:3
Ammonium molybdate	1.84 Mo			1:3

Table 4.14 *Amounts of chemicals required to provide 1 ppm in 1000 litre of water*

Varying element concentration

It is a simple procedure to alter the amount of one or more elements in a hydroponic solution, to deal with a water problem, a nutritional problem, or to obtain optimum performance with a specific crop, e.g. tomatoes, at various stages of growth.

Table 4.14 shows the amounts of various chemicals necessary to provide a 1 ppm increase in a 1000 litre tank solution. The element is added to the normal solution used in the system, when topping up is necessary, or at other suitable times. The frequency of topping-up will be dependent upon a number of factors, including water quality, stage of growth of plants, size of the crop, the temperature, rate of application of the nutrient solution to the growing area, relative humidity, light intensity and the extent of air movement in the growing area.

The uptake of many elements is influenced by local environmental conditions, such as temperature and light intensity, so it is not possible to be definite on amounts of particular elements to be added on a universal basis. The grower needs to be guided by local conditions.

The figures shown in the Table are for amounts of pure chemicals. Where the chemicals are not pure, suitable allowance should be made to bring the concentration to the desired level.

Reclaimed wastewater

In recent years, there has been a concerted effort to find ways of making use of reclaimed wastewater from sewerage treatment works, rather than discharging the effluent into lakes, creeks, rivers or the ocean.

In 1989, the World Health Organisation advocated the reuse of sewage effluents in agriculture as a preferred means of disposal.

Since that time, considerable progress has been made in the development of projects employing reclaimed wastewater for irrigating timber plantations, for horticultural products grown in soil and for hydroponic installations, mainly using run-to-waste gravel beds, or modified NFT flow-through systems.

Effluents from sewerage treatment works frequently contain organic chemicals, pathogens and toxic metals and although these may restrict the uses of the effluent, they do not necessarily prevent utilisation in all cases. Many treatment works now incorporate methods to eliminate pathogens in the discharged water and the risk of disease can be reduced by employing methods of irrigation which prevent contamination and transmission of disease. Tomatoes on indeterminate plants in particular, are physically remote from the applied solution, and contamination of fruit is unlikely. Scientists have demonstrated the existence of a physical barrier of plant tissues, to the translocation of human viruses to sections of the plant above the root system.

Wastewater from sewerage treatment works contains many elements essential for plant growth, but for employment with a hydroponics system, the mineral concentration and other factors are far from ideal.

There are a number of important parameters associated with water quality, which need to be taken into account if wastewater is to be used for growing produce by hydroponic methods. These include nutrients, organic materials, suspended solids, salinity, toxic materials, pathogens, the irrigation system employed, media and odour.

The wastewater as discharged from detention ponds at the treatment works, usually contains considerable organic material and other suspended solids. When fed into containers holding media of the types usually used with containers, decaying material is trapped in the media, resulting in production of a sour odour and drippers are easily clogged. The decaying organic material reduces the amount of nitrogen available to the growing plants. Perlite, peat and rockwool and some other media, are difficult to clear of trapped organic material, even with back flushing. In several trials, the media could not be reused after termination of the crop experiment.

The characteristics of the wastewater vary from site to site throughout the country, but the figures shown in *Table 4.15* (obtained from the Port Macquarie Sewerage Treatment Works in 1995), is representative of a country installation, where wastewater is available for reuse in an agricultural environment.

A small trial involving a total of 12 Grosse Lisse tomatoes was undertaken, using 30 cm plastic pots fed with a spray system providing 0.8 litres of solution per minute per plant, with an irrigation cycle of 10 minutes and excess solution going to waste.

For the first six weeks of growth after plant out, the plants were irrigated at 7 am and 1 pm daily. After that period, the irrigation cycles commenced at 7 am, 1 pm and 4 pm.

The trial was set up as three Groups, each of four plants. *Group A* plants were the Control Group, with perlite medium, and fed with a commercially produced hydroponic nutrient mixture. *Group B* plants were in perlite medium and irrigated with modified wastewater and foliar sprays, while *Group C* plants were grown in granulated rockwool medium and also irrigated with modified wastewater and foliar sprays.

As indicated in *Table 4.15*, the average concentration of all nutrient elements in the reclaimed wastewater, except for boron and copper, was well below the acceptable minimum levels for normal hydroponics application. Also, the pH range 7.8 to 9.2 was of some concern. The sodium

Element	Range (mg/l)
Nitrogen (Nitrate form)	1-10
Nitrogen (Ammonium form)	0.1-4
Phosphorus	0.18-0.48
Potassium	12-15
Calcium	13-15
Magnesium	4-8
Sulphur	25-35
Iron	< 0.02-0.06
Boron	0.1-0.2
Zinc	0.017
Copper	< 0.01-0.05
Manganese	0.01-0.02
Molybdenum	-
Sodium	80-90
Chloride	65-75
Total hardness (as $CaCO_3$)	70
pH	7.8-9.2
Electrical conductivity (EC)	0.5-0.6
Dissolved oxygen	7.0-13
Suspended solids	13-20
Biochemical oxygen demand	3.0-6.0

Table 4.15 Characteristics of reclaimed wastewater

GROUP A
Pot Number in Group
Weight g

Pot 1		Pot 2		Pot 3		Pot 4	
Truss 1.	495	Truss 1.	180	Truss 1.	265	Truss 1.	280
	280		150		240		170
	270		185		190		340
	240		200		245		175
	230		210		240		180
Truss 2.	270	Truss 2.	255		150		160
	340		240	Truss 2.	420	Truss 2.	290
	230		180		220		160
	220		130		210		165
	345	Truss 3.	470		230		140
Truss 3.	240		255	Truss 3.	320		230
	280		290		325		260
	220		160		305		90
	190		190				110
	240		165				305
Truss 4.	350	Truss 4.	195			Truss 3.	260
	310		320				280
							240
							280
							385
							245
							230
						Truss 4.	150
							165
							340
Total	4255	Total	7080	Total	3360	Total	5630

Aggregate yield Group A - 20.325 kg.

Table 4.16 *Yield from Group A - the Control Group - in perlite medium and irrigated with a commercially prepared hydroponics nutrient mixture.*

and chloride levels were of no concern for growing most varieties of tomatoes.

The reason for the very low nitrogen and phosphorus levels in particular, was that the licensing conditions imposed by the Environment Protection Authority (EPA) of NSW, required that the total nitrogen not exceed 10 mg/l and total phosphorus not exceed 0.5 mg/l on a 90 percentile basis, for effluent discharged from the final detention pond into the creek. Other restrictions in regard to biochemical oxygen demand, non filterable residue, grease and oil, faecal coliforms, ammonia nitrogen and pH were also imposed.

A pilot trial involving two each of Grosse Lisse, Mighty Red and Celebrity plants, indicated that major problems existed in using the reclaimed wastewater without modification.

After about six weeks, growth rate slowed considerably and evidence of iron chlorosis and magnesium necrosis began to appear. About a third of flowers dropped and of the

	GROUP B Pot Number in Group Weight g		
Pot 1	**Pot 2**	**Pot 3**	**Pot 4**
Truss 1. 370	Truss 1. 220	Truss 1. 220	Truss 1. 230
340	170	240	250
365	175	90	140
350	100	105	295
280	140	Truss 2. 210	Truss 2. 365
250	160	185	170
180	Truss 2. 260	165	255
Truss 2. 140	205	190	105
340	240	Truss 3. 170	140
260	180	290	Truss 3. 275
190	Truss 3. 330	195	180
240	190	120	205
	230	130	265
	160		140
	Truss 4. 140		240
	360		360
	255		
Total 3305	Total 3515	Total 2310	Total 3615
	Aggregate yield Group B - 12.745 kg.		

Table 4.17 *Yield from Group B in perlite medium and irrigated with modified wastewater and foliar sprays.*

fruit which reached mature stage, several had blossom-end rot. Most of the mature leaves were pale, blotchy with purple discolouration, mottled or crinkled and considerable numbers of leaves below the first trusses fell from the plant stems. There was yellowing of many young leaves, with only the main veins being dark green in colour. Roots were poorly developed and dark brown in colour. Only one in four tomatoes which reached the fully ripe stage were considered to be of marketable class.

As a result of this experience, the three Group trial was set up with the wastewater modified to increase nitrogen to about 150 mg/l, calcium to about 100 mg/l phosphorus to 10 mg/l and potassium to about 150 mg/l. The pH was reduced to the range 6.0 to 6.5 using sulphuric acid dosing. Foliar sprays of magnesium sulphate at 2% and chelated iron at 0.02% were also introduced.

Yields from the three Groups, including the individual tomato weights and trusses from which they were picked, are shown in *Tables 4.16, 4.17* and *4.18*.

As was expected, Control Group A produced by far the highest marketable yield up to the fourth truss of each vine. The yield of Group B with perlite medium was 62% of the yield of the Control Group, while Group C was 64%.

Conclusions reached following the limited trials, were that the unmodified reclaimed wastewater was not suitable for commercial cultivation of tomatoes, and even after acid dosing for pH correction and enhancement of some selected elements and use of foliar sprays, yields were considerably lower than what could be expected from employing household mains water, enhanced with a commercially prepared hydroponics nutrient mixture.

GROUP C Pot Number in Group Weight g			
Pot 1	**Pot 2**	**Pot 3**	**Pot 4**
Truss 1. 230	Truss 1. 265	Truss 1. 250	Truss 1. 260
255	155	110	310
550	Truss 2. 480	120	250
305	185	90	320
120	150	Truss 2. 220	290
Truss 2. 230	95	105	Truss 2. 175
180	270	140	255
110	240	80	200
Truss 3. 240	275	65	Truss 3. 210
220	250	Truss 3. 260	130
240	Truss 3. 250	160	205
175	160	105	330
255	190	75	170
220	250		290
190	155		210
Truss 4. 140	260		Truss 4. 140
			145
Total 3665	Total 3630	Total 1860	Total 3890
Aggregate yield Group C - 13.045 kg.			

Table 4.18 *Yield from Group C in granulated rockwool medium and irrigated with modified wastewater and foliar sprays.*

Chapter 5. MEDIA AND CONTAINERS

Chapter 5. MEDIA AND CONTAINERS

Growing media

The growing medium for the cultivation of tomatoes in containers must possess many of the characteristics of soil. It must provide a degree of support for the root system, allow the root system to grow in search of water and nutrients, and must be a means of allowing a supply of oxygen, water and nutrients for the growth and development of the plant.

Many types of materials are available for employment as a medium in containers. The selection of a particular medium is influenced by a number of factors including cost, availability, weight, degree of porosity, resistance to decomposition, inertness, water holding capacity, uniformity and consistency, sterility, longevity, reusability and disposability. Also, the medium should not contain any toxic materials, calcium carbonate, or other substance which may leach out and have a deleterious effect on the nutrient solution, including the pH.

Heat absorption is another important property. A dark coloured medium will quickly heat up when exposed to the sun, resulting in a temperature rise in the root zone. Mixing expanded clay with a dark gravel medium, will reduce the heat rise problem but will add to the cost. Perlite, vermiculite and expanded clay are thermally insulating and will be slower to heat up and cool down compared with most gravels.

Good moisture retention properties are important in container culture. Preferred materials will ensure that water is retained on the surface of the particles, in the air or pore space between particles, and within the particles for porous materials.

Particles should not be too fine, as they may not drain sufficiently and so starve the roots of oxygen. On the other hand, particles should not be too coarse. Coarse impervious gravels are ideal for large beds, which may be irrigated at frequent intervals, but this practice is often not convenient for pot culture, particularly if a manual feed methods is used to apply the nutrient solution.

When comparing different media used in hydroponics, it is usual to refer to the 'total pore space', which is the percentage of its volume that is not filled with solids. A total pore space of 20%, means that in every litre of material, there is 200 ml of pore space and 800 ml of solid material. Total pore space is important, but pore shape and size are also vital factors. Plant roots may find it more difficult to push through a medium with mainly small or long narrow pores, than through one with large pores formed by approximately round materials.

The porosity of the medium is a major factor in the cultivation of tomatoes in containers. Some typical media have levels ranging from about 10% to 40%. With a 10% level medium, the water level will be high shortly after application and less frequent watering will be required than for a medium with higher air filled porosity.

Media with air filled porosity of about 30% are desirable where good aeration is a consideration. It is also a reasonable compromise with water retention capability. With this media, tomato seeds will result in about 85% germination and in an average growing environment, seedlings will reach a height of about 27 cm after five weeks. If 40% material is used, frequent watering is essential and for a fully grown plant, this may require feeds of at least twice a day during warm weather. Media used in container culture, and principal properties include:

• Sand

Sand is one of the cheapest materials available. However, care should be taken to ensure that it is not contaminated with soil and that it is suitable for hydroponics. It should be neither too fine nor too coarse. Particle size distribution should be considered when selecting sand. Use of incorrect size can result in disaster, as many growers have found out to their cost. In order to retain a reasonably good balance between aeration and nutrient and water retention, particle sizes should be in the range 0.1 to 1.00 mm diameter, with an average of 0.25 to 0.50 mm.

Sand which has come from a salt water environment, should be thoroughly washed with fresh water until all traces of salt have been removed. Shell grit mixed with sand will cause trouble, if not appropriately treated. Shell grit is mainly calcareous material and if released into the nutrient solution will cause the pH to rise. The increased alkalinity is likely to tie up iron from the nutrient mixture, resulting in iron deficiency in the plants.

With container culture using sand as the medium, experience has shown that the trickle method of nutrient application is the best arrangement. The nutrient solution should be fed at each irrigation cycle, owing to the relatively low nutrient retention of sand. There is no advantage in applying water only, during some of the cycles. Frequency of application depends on the growth stage of the plant, and the temperature, but will range from two to three times during daylight hours and once at night, during the summer season. With small plants, no more than 500 ml would be sufficient, but when the plant is very large, near the cropping stage, up to four litres per day may be required for some varieties.

• Gravel

Gravel is not widely used in container culture, although some growers have obtained good crops with continuous drip feed systems. Crushed granite or quartz, the most popular types of gravel, are virtually non-porous and will dry out quickly on a hot day. Particles should be no less than 2 mm in diameter and no greater than 8 mm, for pots of diameter 30 cm. A mix of 30/70 using 2 mm and 8 mm gravel, gave good results for a 50-pot trial growing Ultra Boy variety.

A problem with crushed stone, is that it has sharp edges which may cut into the stem and roots, if there is movement of the plant due to wind. For this reason, some growers prefer river gravel, which is reasonably smooth.

As with sand, particles should not be of calcareous material, so that problems will not be encountered with pH shift. Gravel has a number of advantages, and the water holding problem can be minimised by using a mix of about 40% perlite and 60% gravel by volume. One installation using 10 pots with this mix, had good success with Rouge de Marmande tomatoes as a winter crop.

• Scoria

This is a surface type of volcanic rock, and has good water retention properties. Unless available from local sources, scoria can be expensive due to high transport costs.

Although it can be used without other materials in pots, it is in many cases used only to a depth of about 50 mm on the bottom, because of its high cost. When used with perlite and vermiculite in this way, the scoria prevents the other medium from being washed out through the drainage holes during flushing operations.

Scoria has a number of desirable characteristics as a medium in container culture. These include:

• Compared with gravel and sand, it is lighter in weight. Density is about 600 to 1000 kg per cubic metre.

• Because it was originally produced under intense heat, it is inert.

• Generally sterile.

• Obtainable in various sizes.

• Long life.

• Very porous, containing many air cells and pockets.

• Water retention is about 250 to 350 kg per cubic metre.

• Good insulating qualities, which minimises heat transfer from the walls of black plastic pots in the sun.

• Good capilliary properties.

Scoria is generally available in sizes of 5 mm plus fines, 9 mm plus fines, 10 mm, 14 mm and 20 mm. The most popular size for pot culture is 10 mm. It allows good air movement through the medium and is ideal for situations where the pot stands in a reservoir of nutrients. Where the pots are fed by an intermittent trickle system, the incorporation of some fines helps to improve the water retention properties.

It is a mistake to use scoria dust. It will compact, almost rocklike, and prevent water flowing through it. Some growers have had so much trouble with the dust, that they sieve it out.

Many tomato growers have expressed disappointment with the use of scoria. They found that after a full 12 month cycle, adsorption of the nutrient salts on the rock was a problem. The salts were extremely difficult to remove by normal water flushing methods. They also found that tiny roots grew into the pores, making sterilization between crops difficult. To overcome the root problem, the scoria was stockpiled in a holding bay for a year or so, to allow the root matter to decompose. It could then be removed by flushing with a strong jet of water.

Problems with pH have been noted with this medium. The pH of scoria from some sources is very alkaline, giving a pH in the range 8.5 to 10.0. For normal use, this is well above the acceptable level for tomatoes. Fortunately, the value falls after the application of the nutrient mixture, but this may take a couple of months if the plants are fed by a trickle process. The scoria may eventually reach a level of about 5.8 and then hold at that value.

Although it could be expected that the high initial pH value would cause problems because of deficiencies in the availability of some elements, field experience has not shown this to be so. However, some growers have observed a higher than usual number of fruit with blossom-end rot, during the first crop.

• Vermiculite

Vermiculite is a micaceous material, which is expanded when heated to a high temperature. It is basically a complex hydrated magnesium aluminium iron silicate, and is mined as plates or lamellae, which are very thin. Mica is probably best known for its use as an electrical insulator in toaster and iron elements.

When heated to a very high temperature, moisture trapped between the plates is turned into steam, causing the plates to expand to about twelve times their preheated thickness. This process, known as exfoliation, results in the formation of crumb-like structures which are very porous, giving vermiculite a high water retention capacity.

Vermiculite is widely used for many industrial purposes, but all grades are not suitable for hydroponics. Some grades have a high pH - frequently in excess of 9 - and can have a deleterious impact on the nutrient pH value, unless suitable acid is added. There have also been reports that vermiculite sometimes contains appreciable quantities of magnesium, which quickly reacts with potassium and ammonium in the nutrient solution.

As a hydroponic medium, vermiculite is lightweight when dry and is extensively used in pot culture. However, it does not have a long life and is therefore not popular with some growers. After the tomato plant has completed its growth cycle and the roots are removed, the vermiculite may be broken up, so losing much of its porous properties. The very small pieces of mica are themselves impervious and the medium can become a 'stew' when water is applied, making it unsuitable for pot culture. Sometimes sand is mixed with vermiculite, but this action only hastens the breakdown process. On a use-once-only basis, vermiculite is a good medium and finds wide application in the cultivation of tomato seedlings. It will hold water for long periods on hot days and provides excellent aeration for the roots.

Vermiculite is available from hydroponic stockists in 5, 10, 40 and 100 litre bags.

• Expanded clay

Expanded clay is popular with small installations, particularly in decorative pots for indoor plants, although patio installations growing miniature tomatoes like Sweet 100 are quite common. The material is structurally stable, lightweight and non-decomposable. It is widely known as Leca (Light expanded clay aggregate) which is also a trade name.

The clay when mined has the property of expanding at a particular temperature, and great numbers of air bubbles form in the otherwise heavy clay. It is this highly porous characteristic, which allows the passage of water and air in the plant root zone. The baking temperature which brings about reaction of the clay's carbonates to form the honeycomb structure, is about 1200°C.

The pellets weigh about 700 kg per cubic metre. If put in water, they will float to the surface and hence when used in pots are not suitable for any situation where the container is flooded. Horticultural grade expanded clay pellets are expensive and some growers have experimented with construction grade pellets, made for aggregate in concrete work. However, these pellets have a fine coating of calcium oxide, which should be removed before using the pellets in a hydroponic installation. An easy method of removing the coating is to soak the pellets in a weak solution of phosphoric or sulphuric acid overnight and then thoroughly rinse several times. Expanded clay is available in 5, 10, 40 and 100 litre bags

• **Perlite**

Perlite is a volcanic rock material and in composition is a potassium sodium aluminium silicate. It expands to some thirteen times its own volume, when heated to about 900°C. During the heating process, the mineral particles pop up like popcorn and form a snow white kernel material, so light that it weighs only 64 to 128 kg per cubic metre.

Each kernel of perlite is comprised of tiny air cells or bubbles, with the surface being covered with tiny cavities, which provide an extremely large surface area. These surface cavities trap moisture and make it available to the plant roots. Because of the physical shape of the perlite particles, large air gaps are formed between adjacent particles, good aeration for the root system. The principal characteristics of perlite may be summarised as follows:

• Sterile
  Perlite as purchased from the manufacturer is sterile and free of disease.

• Neutral
  It has essentially a neutral pH with any variation being within the range 6.5 to 7.5.

• Long life
  It is a hard inorganic material, that can be readily shaken from the plant roots and reused.

• Lightweight
  Perlite is extremely lightweight when dry, making it easy to handle and economic to freight.

• Insulation
  The cellular structure of perlite granules creates an ideal thermal insulator, so protecting the plant roots from extreme variations in temperature.

• Aeration
  Perlite does not compact and so maintains an ideal balance of air and moisture for the roots in the growing medium. (About 98% of all the oxygen a plant uses is absorbed through its root system).

• Drainage
  The medium cannot be over watered. The surface of the particles is such, that water does not fill up completely every pore. Excess water drains off. Air space is about 45%.

• Absorbent
  Perlite absorbs up to five times its own weight in water and makes moisture and nutrients readily available to the plant over a relatively long period of time. Its water holding capacity is 250 to 300 litres per cubic metre of material.

• Reusable
  Perlite can be reused many times. There is some difference in crop yield for reused perlite, compared with new material, but care should be taken to thoroughly sterilize old material, preferably using steam. The use of fungicides results in a significant drop in yield, in reusing the medium for the cultivation of tomatoes. However, the obvious cost benefit of reusing the perlite must be carefully considered and balanced against the increased risk of disease problems, particularly in a commercial enterprise.

One minor problem experienced with perlite is that, being white, growth of algae is encouraged on the light exposed surface. This can be easily corrected by placing a cover on the pot top, to exclude the light. The cover also assists in reducing evaporation during a hot day.

On the plus side, the whiteness can be put to advantage when tomatoes are grown in a glasshouse during cloudy weather. The white perlite will reflect light back up to the leaves, so increasing photosynthetic activity and growth. The same applies to seedlings grown under artificial light.

• Synthetics

Some growers have used polystyrene beads or foam as a medium in containers, but when used alone, they have not been a success with tomatoes. Whereas perlite gives a water retention of about 23% of the total pore space, water only occupies about 5% of the total pore space with polystyrene beads, and only 4% in the case of polystyrene foam. This means that plants grown in a polystyrene medium, must be watered much more frequently, compared with a perlite medium. Polystyrene does not hold enough water to increase its density appreciably and experience has shown that when the nutrient solution is applied, the polystyrene is likely to float out of the container, if the rate of application is higher than the capacity of the drainage holes to dispose of the liquid.

Some success has been achieved by mixing peat with polystyrene, but there are many other media that are more successful for growing tomatoes. Mixtures of foam chips and sand have also been tried with varying results. This has, in some installations, produced good yields with College Challenger varieties, probably because the sand traps the moisture and the polystyrene chips ensure good aeration.

One grower who had access to a large supply of shredded polyurethane, had some good results with a trial of 25 pots growing Burnley Gem variety. Polyurethane does not have good capilliary properties and needs frequent application of the nutrient solution. The material gives good aeration at the root zone, but algae forms rapidly if light is not excluded. Another synthetic is polyester fleece sandwiched between two layers of plastic foil.

• Coconut husk

Coconut husk or coir, the fibre produced by a coconut, has had wide application for many years in the manufacture of rope, matting, brooms and in potting mixes for growing orchids, but in recent times it has found application in hydroponics installations, particularly as a medium in container cultivation.

In appearance it looks somewhat like peat, but does not have the disadvantages of peat regarding acidity, impurities and, in the case of South Australian peat, high salinity.

Experience indicates that the use of coconut husk as supplied commercially, does not require liming or other treatment to raise the pH. Coconut husk medium will readily stabilise at pH 6.3, with suitable nutrient solution, and has a life span before decomposition, greater than peat. Air space is about 30%.

A considerable amount of investigation work, in the use of coconut husk medium in soilless cultivation of tomatoes, was undertaken in several Asian countries and results were so encouraging that it is now widely used in hydroponic installations in the region.

The most common medium used in Asia is a product sold as Cocomix, a combination of shredded coconut husk and sand in various mix ratios, to suit specific needs of the grower. Tomatoes grown in containers of various volumes, including 4, 6, 8 and 10 litres, produced plants with leaf, stem and dry root weights equal to plants grown in other media and with average total fruit yields of 7.8 kg per plant. Some plants produced fruit from up to 12 trusses, but the percentage of marketable fruit is not known.

Some trials in Adelaide to compare yields from a number of media using a selection of tomato varieties, examined coconut husk, scoria, gravel, sawdust, peat and granulated rockwool. The total yields from five varieties grown in coconut husk gave good results. Only plants in scoria and granulated rockwool produced better yields and these by only small margins of 3.9% in the case of scoria, and 1.2% in the case of granulated rockwool. Compared with peat and sawdust, coconut husk was better by 11% and 30% respectively. The varieties trialled were Gardeners Delight, College Challenger, Grosse Lisse, Potentate and Floradel.

Several coconut husk products are available in Australia, one of which (Supreme

Horticultural Coir, distributed by Hydro-Coir Products) consists of compressed one litre blocks imported from Sri Lanka. One block in 5 litres of water will produce 6-7 litres of coir plant growing medium.

One NSW tomato grower with a large commercial enterprise, employed a mixture of coconut husk and sand on a 50/50 basis with considerable success. He purchased the coconut husk material from a Sydney distributor, who marketed it as cocopeat. It was supplied in compressed block form. The mixture was placed in lay-flat bags, also known as grow bag pillows, manufactured from heavy duty UV stabilised panda film material, which is black on the inside and white on the outside. Plant growth with the medium and the bags was very consistent and resulted in high yields from the plants. The grower, who had previously employed vertical bags for growing tomatoes, found that the flat bags were easier to maintain. They are available in packs of 150 bags.

• Zeolite

A material that has been receiving considerable attention overseas for application as a hydroponic growing medium, is zeolite. Trial installations have been set-up in USA, Turkey, Jersey Islands, and Cuba, among other places, during the past 7 years.

Zeolite is a natural mineral, which is part of a group of hydrated alumino silicates and carries a negative charge, balanced by freely moving cations with positive charges. This provides an ideal trap for positive ions, like nitrogen-rich ammonium and potash, which are then released when demanded by plants. Zeolites have an open framework with a network of pores, giving a large surface area for trapping and exchanging valuable nutrients. It is marginally alkaline.

There are many variations of zeolite available, all with different properties. Zeolite applications include water purification, mine wastewater clean-up, sewage treatment, replacement of phosphate detergents, air pollution control, soil quality improvement, slow release fertilisers, heavy metal traps, pesticide carriers and others. One of the best known applications is as cat litter. It has the ability to readily adsorb onto its granules, ammonium as well as large quantities of water. It is available in Australia from Zeolite Australia, Ltd.

In 1988, an installation was established in Cuba to monitor the performance of Tropic variety tomatoes grown in containers, using natural zeolite and a new zeolite substrate known as NEREA. The Tropic variety is well known in Australia and was very popular as a table tomato many years ago, but unfortunately seed is difficult to obtain today. The Cuban trials showed that hydroponic growth of tomatoes was better than usually observed with plants grown in traditional substrates, yields were high and less water, energy and fertilisers were required.

In Jersey Island trials, which have been ongoing for a number years, crops grown include carnations, peppers and tomatoes. One of the major investigations includes the long term reuse of zeolite as a medium. Results to date are encouraging, but much more work has yet to be carried out. Growing containers included 9 litre polythene bags for the peppers and tomatoes.

Conclusions to date for natural Australian zeolite are that it:

• Retains fertiliser longer than many other substrates.

• Improves cation exchange capacity of mixes.

• Reduces leaching characteristics of applied nutrients.

• Reduces fertiliser costs.

• Offers excellent capilliary action and moisture retention.

• Enables improved plant growing characteristics. The material is available in a range of particle sizes

• Rockwool

Rockwool was first employed as a substrate for hydroponics during 1969 in Denmark. It is composed of fibres 0.005 mm in diameter, which are woven into slabs and stabilised through the addition of phenolic resins and a wetting agent, to produce a horticultural product. Rockwool manufactured for insulation purposes is not suitable for hydroponics.

The rockwool fibres consist mainly of oxides of silica and calcium, together with smaller quantities of iron, aluminium and magnesium.

Rockwool is marketed under a number of different names, with Grodan and Growool being well known brands in Australia. The material is available in slab and small blocks of varying dimensions, fibre orientation and density of fibre. In addition, a number of grades of loose rockwool, referred to as flock or granulated rockwool, are available and are used for cultivation of tomatoes in pots and containers.

The most widely employed application of rockwool for cultivation of tomatoes, is in the form of slabs of size 750 mm x 300 mm x 75 mm high, which are available in wrapped or raw form. Holes are cut in the top of the plastic for planting purposes and slits are cut in the lower part of the side to provide for nutrient solution drainage. The most common method of applying the nutrient solution is by a drip feed system, with one dripper per plant.

One of the outstanding features of rockwool is its integrated propagation and growing system.

The main characteristics of rockwool include:

- Lightweight with density of only 70 kg per cubic metre when dry.

- Exceptional water holding capability, with 97% void space.

- Good air retention property. In practice a slab usually contains two parts water to one part air.

- Because of the high temperature required for its manufacture, rockwool is sterile when new.

- Material is inert and has no effect on the composition of the nutrient solution being used.

- As the material does not absorb or exchange nutrient ions, all traces of salts can be removed from the slab by soaking and flushing with fresh water.

- Sterilization of the slab is possible using low pressure steam or chemicals.

- Slabs can be easily cut into any shape to cater for a wide range of container shapes and sizes.

- In addition to slabs, the material is available in the form of propagating blocks, wrapped cubes with or without holes, and flock or granulated material in various grades.

- Rockwool has no pH buffer capacity and after a short period of use will stabilise at the pH of the solution in the feed system.

- The insulation properties of rockwool have a temperature stabilising influence on the plant root system.

There are also some disadvantages with rockwool including:

- The material is not biodegradable and some overseas environmental protection authorities are concerned about means of effectively disposing of spent rockwool.

- It is almost impossible to remove all traces of root material of a large tomato plant. A problem exists with microbial reaction on decaying root material and the resultant effect on components of the nutrient solution, particularly nitrogen in the root zone area of a growing plant.

For cultivation of plants in pots, rockwool has been cut into blocks of sizes to suit the pot, as shown in *Figure 5.1*. The seed is grown in a 38 mm square propagation block and when roots appear on the sides, the block is placed in a 75 mm square growing block, which has a hole in which the propagation block is inserted. When roots break the walls of the growing block, it is then placed in the permanent growing pot. The bottom 4-5 cm of the pot sometimes contains 3-5 mm gravel, to assist with drainage. Two pieces of appropriate diameters are then cut from a standard 75 mm slab and placed in the pot. The top layer has a cut-out of sufficient size to accommodate the growing block. Alternatively, fine flock or granulated rockwool may be used in lieu of the slab material. It is available in 120 litre bags.

Good crop yields have been obtained with rockwool and drip feed system, with the slab arrangement showing a 3% yield improvement over the flock material, provided water is not allowed to accumulate at the bottom of the slab.

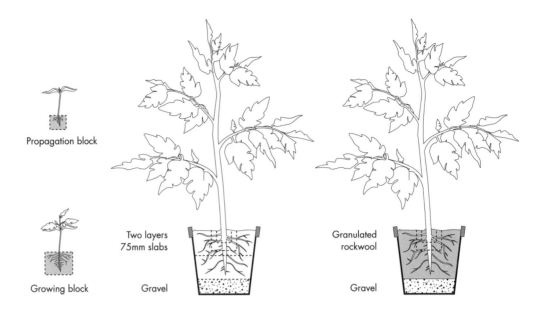

Figure 5.1 *Use of rockwool in pots.*

Labels: Propagation block / Growing block / Two layers 75mm slabs / Gravel / Granulated rockwool / Gravel

• Peat moss

Peat moss has been popular with tomato growers since the 1950's. In pot culture, it is seldom employed by itself but is mixed with perlite, vermiculite, expanded clay, small gravel or sand.

Although sand and peat combinations produce crops with good yields, it is not popular with many flat dwellers, because of weight problem when the medium is fully saturated. One of the advantages of using pots is that they can be shifted to get the best benefits of the sun, but a large pot of sandy peat is not easily shifted.

Peat is usually supplied through horticultural outlets in a form compressed about 2:1. Bag sizes vary to about 170 litre and are supplied from sources in Russia, Germany, Sweden, Ireland, Canada and New Zealand. Peat from Australian sources has seldom proved satisfactory for hydroponics. Some sources have a high level of contaminated soil, while others are highly saline.

The composition of peat deposits varies widely from one source to another. Factors which influence acceptability include the vegetation from which it originated, mineral content (particularly sodium), state of decomposition and the degree of acidity.

The most popular type used for hydroponics is peat moss. It is derived from sphagnum and has a high moisture holding capacity, generally 10 times its dry weight. The pH is in the range 3.8 to 4.5 for most products. Peat has high buffer capacity, equal to about vermiculite. This means that it has high resistance to change in pH from added acid or alkali, although dolomite has been used successfully to raise the pH to an acceptable level for tomatoes. Dry peat usually presents a wetting problem, and some growers have found that besides using wetting solutions, boiling or very hot water will fix the problem. If not properly wetted, there is likelihood of local pockets in the root environment developing. This may upset controlled growth. A dry pocket may result in the death of a seedling.

Although hydroponicists who use peat mixtures have developed their own preferred ratios, a mixture of 1:1 of peat and vermiculite or perlite by volume, has been found to produce good yields with most varieties of tomatoes. Vermiculite will give a pot life of about 2 years before breaking down, but perlite in the mixture can be expected to give a useful life of 4-5 years. However, there is a tendency for commercial growers not to reuse media because of yield reduction.

A number of growers using vertical containers, where depth was greater than the diameter, experienced problems growing tomatoes with peat on its own, peat/sand mixture or peat/sawdust mixture. The problem was greatest with nutrient feed systems which were of the continuous flow type, or intermittent irrigation systems where 'on' periods were long and 'off' periods were short.

The plant root system appeared to be effected by lack of sufficient oxygen. It is well known that failure of respiration because of insufficient oxygen, results in loss of energy and cessation of the functions of life.

Dissolved oxygen in a nutrient solution would typically be at least 8 ppm at 25°C, but measurement of solution passing through the medium of one installation with a peat/sand mixture, revealed a dissolved oxygen level of 0.5-1 ppm over a 24 hour period. It was assumed by the Chemist that the low level of dissolved oxygen was associated with a gaseous product of anaerobic microbial respiration.

Inhibition of respiration results in lower root pressure flow, which may reduce transport of calcium to the fruit. The result would probably be an increase in fruit with blossom end rot if the plant survived long enough.

Some growers who have employed peat moss as part a mixture (typically 60% peat moss and 40% perlite), have experienced disease problems which they considered originated in the peat. They then adopted a sterilization program before mixing the peat with the perlite and putting it in the growing containers. Unfortunately, the steam sterilization process caused the sphagnum to collapse, and consequently destroyed the essential air spaces and water retention properties.

Spagnum peat moss (left) a product of the former USSR and (right) a 100 litre bag of P500 Australian perlite. Both are widely employed as medium either on their own or mixed with other types of media for cultivation of tomatoes in pots, vertical bags, lay-flat bags or polystyrene containers of various shapes and dimensions

• Peat-lite

This is a mixture of peat moss, perlite and vermiculite in the ratio 40/30/30. It is available from some hydroponics stockists already prepared and includes dolomite or lime and a wetting agent, to take account of the high acidity and wetting problems associated with peat moss.

Although not widely used by tomato growers in Australia, it is very popular in the USA where growers use the medium in plastic bags, about 30 cm diameter and 30 cm high.

• Wood by-products

Wood shavings and sawdust are probably the cheapest media materials, if the grower lives near a sawmill. Many tomato growers overseas have had great success with sawdust. However, care should be taken in selecting the material, because some sawdust contains substances which are toxic to tomatoes. In Australia, trials using sawdust from mills which cut turpentine, cedar, eucalyptus trees and a few other species have been disappointing.

One of the difficulties is obtaining a consistent supply of sawdust, of composition known to be suitable for hydroponics. Most small sawmill owners place all sawdust in a common heap, and material from a wide ranges of tree varieties would be included in the heap, some of it not suitable for hydroponic application.

Fresh sawdust usually has an extreme interaction with the nutrient solution, due to organic decomposition.

Sawdust on its own as a medium has been found to exhibit the same low oxygen problems as peat. In fact, problems can be experienced with low oxygen levels, in any medium which is organic, because mixtures of organic matter and nutrients result in increased microbial activity (respiration) occurring during the degradation of the organic matter.

Although wood products have reasonably good water holding properties, some growers have questioned their nutrient holding capabilities. Nitrogen management is especially important with some sawdusts, in order to avoid a deficiency. Sawdusts which have high carbon:nitrogen ratios, require extra nitrogen in the nutrient mixture, to avoid the competitive demand for nitrogen between micro-organisms and the plants. If additional nitrogen is not added, where for example pine sawdust is employed, the deficiency that may develop may give the impression of toxicity. Pine has a high Carbon:Nitrogen ratio and decomposes rapidly.

A major problem experienced with containers such as lay-flat bags, which have a wide dimension, is that the nutrient solution does not readily spread laterally throughout the medium. Fine sawdust has better ability to laterally transfer moisture, but the mixture usually becomes very dense after a period, causing a problem with gas transfer into and out of the plant root zone and impeding drainage of excess water. Usually only slow rate drip feed systems are suitable for use with a fine sawdust medium.

Variety	No. of plants	Peat	Peat Sawdust	Perlite Sand	Perlite	Perlite Scoria
			25%/75%	50%/50%		70%/30%
Apollo	5	5.4	-	5.9	6.6	6.5
Better Boy	4	6.1	-	-	6.5	6.2
Mighty Red	6	5.9	-	6.8	7.0	-
Ultra Boy	4	6.0	-	6.9	7.8	-
Grosse Lisse	6	5.9	5.5	-	7.5	7.0
Magnifico	5	-	-	6.5	6.9	6.8
College Challenger	4	-	5.6	-	-	-

Table 5.1 *Typical average yield in kg per plant of ripe and green mature fruit up to 4th truss, using various media. Harvested during October/November period.*

To overcome some of the water distribution difficulties with sawdust, some growers mix other media with the sawdust. A mixture of peat and sawdust has resulted in reasonably good yields with Grosse Lisse and College Challenger. The best results were achieved with a 25% peat/75% *pinus radiata* sawdust, with the nutrient solution supplemented by additional potassium to the extent of about 10% increase on the general purpose solution. The higher potassium level resulted in larger stem diameter, firmer fruit, better shelf life and no fruit with blossom-end rot, compared with plants grown without the additional potassium.

Table 5.1 shows the results of yield trials employing various media in 30 cm diameter pots with nutrient mixture strength CF26-28. *Table 5.2* indicates typical pH values for the most widely used media, for growing tomatoes in containers. Some media produce readings outside these ranges, depending on the source or manufacturing processes.

Buffering

Plant cells are protected against drastic changes in pH by the action of buffers in the cell. These buffers are generally organic acids or salts of weak acids, such as phosphoric acid, and others which originate in substances taken up by the plant from its growing environment. The cation components of buffer systems, other than hydrogen ions, are usually metals. In fact, minerals play important roles in cells. In addition to taking part in buffer actions, they regulate osmosis, affect cell permeability and serve as structural components of cells.

The capacity of a buffer system to resist changes in pH, is greatest when

Medium	pH
Calcium carbonate sand	8.0 - 8.3
Expanded clay - Leca	6.2 - 6.4
Expanded clay - Argex	5.9 - 6.3
Gravel-calcareous	7.2 - 7.6
(treated with phosphate)	6.4 - 6.8
Peat moss	3.8 - 4.5
(treated with 3 g/l lime)	5.5 - 5.8
Perlite	6.5 - 7.5
Pine bark	6.0 - 6.5
Phenolic resin	6.0 - 7.5
Rockwool (after stabilization)	5.8 - 6.3
Scoria	8.5 - 10.0
Urethane resin	6.0 - 9.0
Vermiculite	7.0 - 7.5
Coconut husk	6.0 - 6.3

Table 5.2 *Typical pH values of various media*

the concentrations of proton donor and proton acceptor are equal. As the ratio changes in either direction, the buffer becomes less effective.

An important factor in any growing medium, and the water employed in growing tomatoes in containers, is the amount of buffering action in it. The ability of the growing medium to resist changes in pH, is called the buffer capacity. When the water used in the nutrient solution has a relatively high bicarbonate content, and consequently a high buffering capacity, more acid would be required to bring the feed solution to the desired pH level, compared with rain water.

Buffering action is a characteristic enabling the medium to exchange nutrient ions, to create a balance in the medium. The action is basically the ability of the medium to absorb the ion charge which is excessively abundant, and release one which is low in supply.

When the plant roots absorb nutrients from the solution surrounding them, the immediate zone is depleted of nutrients, even though there may be ample concentration in the surrounding area. The ready movement of replacement nutrients into the depleted zone can be a major obstacle in ensuring continuous provision of optimum nutrition to the plants. The more efficient the nutrient replacement activity , the lower the absolute concentration of the solution required to meet the needs of the plant for development and production.

A system's resistance to the formation of this zone of nutrient depletion, is determined by a number of factors including:

• The volume of nutrient solution which moves through the root zone per unit of time. Feed systems including drip, flow, spray and jet systems are superior to static types in this regard and this accounts for the improved total yields and weight of individual tomatoes. Systems with the faster nutrient flow rates, such as flow, spray and jet, also result in higher production compared with the slower flowing drip system.

• Good management practice in ensuring the nutrient solution and water level are maintained within optimum levels.

• Appropriate volume capacity of the solution in the feed system. The larger the volume per plant, the slower the fall in individual element concentration.

It is generally accepted that the higher the buffering ability of the medium, the higher the optimum pH for maximum nutrient availability. Some tests have indicated that the optimum solution for vermiculite and mixtures with peat is 6.2 to 6.6, while for perlite, scoria and sand with low buffering action, the optimum is around 5.4 to 5.8.

Housekeeping

Good housekeeping is essential if the medium is to be effective in acting as a totally inert substance. If care is taken in selecting a good medium, then it is unlikely that any problems will be encountered from toxicity or disease introduced by the medium itself. Problems usually come from substances introduced by the grower, often during seedling transplanting operations.

The nutrient solution applied to the medium is not fully absorbed by the plant. Over a period of time, there will be some deposition of salts in the medium, mainly as a result of evaporation. Evidence of this will be clearly seen around the edges of the drain holes at the bottom of the pot, or at the high water mark where pots stand in a reservoir. If salts are allowed to accumulate in the medium, they may cause an imbalance in the nutrient solution. Salt levels may rise to toxic levels causing the plants to be stressed with a resultant drop in yield.

When the plants are at the seedling stage and in small pots, the salts can be removed simply by immersing each pot in fresh water, letting them stand for a while to dissolve the salts, and then removing them to drain. For large pots in which plants are fully grown or tied to supports, this dipping process is not practicable. One of the best arrangements is to fit a rose to a hose and spray at mains pressure. The amount of water used for the flush should be about that held by an empty pot of the same size. The water should be drained away and not returned to the nutrient tank, unless the tank is to be emptied. The flushing process will also be beneficial to the root system, in driving out trapped carbon dioxide and replenishing the oxygen supply in the root zone.

Tomato growers have their own theories on the frequency of flushing. Practices vary from two weekly to six weekly intervals, to never. Observations of the behaviour of plants seem to indicate that those which have been flushed at the shorter intervals during their fruit bearing life, appear to be much healthier than those flushed at longer intervals.

Another housekeeping factor concerns the introduction of soil and diseased vegetable matter. Soil on transplant seedlings should be washed from the roots by dunking them in water, taking care not to damage the fine roots. The water used should be clear and fit for human consumption. If the water is pumped from a dam or well, a lookout should be kept for any sign of mud or decayed vegetation when the water level is low.

Sterilization

One of the major advantages of soilless culture is that, to start with, the pot and medium do not contain soil borne diseases or pests. New containers are considered to be clean, provided they have not been in contact with soil. To prevent this advantage being lost, the grower has to be on guard so that problems are not introduced as a result of poor hygiene, improperly treated seeds and the introduction of soil on the roots of seedlings.

Fungal spores, insect eggs, etc, may be in soil attached to the gardener's boots, on the hands, on clothes or even under finger nails. Hands should be thoroughly washed before working on the hydroponic unit. Some growers provide a dish of disinfectant, specifically marked for the purpose. Suitable disinfectants include Dettol or 2% sodium hypochlorite.

If containers are being reused, they should be cleaned by removal of medium, thoroughly washed with water and detergent, followed by sterilization with sodium hypochlorite, Dettol or other recommended chemical.

Several chemicals are available for sterilization of the medium, but the most readily available and easy to use are hypochlorites. Calcium hypochlorite is used in swimming pools and is usually available in powder form. Sodium hypochlorite is a bleach and the sterilizer is available in liquid form. A recommended concentration is 10,000 ppm and directions for making up a solution of this concentration is usually provided on the container. For maximum effectiveness, chlorine solutions should have the pH adjusted to a reading between 8 and 10. Hydrochloric acid can be used for this purpose.

A typical pot sterilization procedure is as follows:

- Cut the plant stem about 100 mm above the top of the medium.

- Upend the pot in a plastic tub.

- Grab the stem and vigorously shake the root system.

- The medium should fall away easily from the roots

- Return the medium to the pot.

- Thoroughly wash the medium using a rose with full pressure.

- Leave the pot to drain for about two hours.

- Mix up sterilization solution to 10,000 ppm in a plastic watering can with a rose fitted.

- Thoroughly saturate the medium until there is a good flow from the bottom.

- Leave to stand overnight.

- Thoroughly wash the medium using a rose at high pressure so that there is a good flow of water from the bottom of the pot for about one minute.

- Leave the pot to drain, then store for future use.

Any grower who wishes to grow a healthy crop of tomato plants should not smoke while working on the installation. Tobacco leaf is a ready carrier of virus diseases, which can be very destructive to tomatoes. Thorough washing of the hands is essential if the grower wishes to maintain the habit of smoking and production of a disease free crop.

Tools, particularly secateurs, should be kept clean and sterilized after cutting diseased plants. Many growers scrub their hands with carbolic soap and hot water after handling diseased plants, following a clean-up operation. All diseased plants, including the complete root system, should be removed from the site.

Types of containers

Many different types of containers are available in which to successfully grow tomatoes. The most popular types include plastic, glass, clay, concrete or fibre pots, plastic bags, gullies, lightweight polystyrene containers and polyethelene-lined wooden barrels. These are available in a wide range of shapes, sizes and colours. Bag systems are available as Layflat Bags, or Up-right Bags.

One of the outstanding advantages of growing tomatoes in containers, is that it can be done without owning even a square metre of land. They will grow just as successfully on a patio, on the roof of a building, or even in a window box if the environmental conditions are suitable.

All varieties of tomatoes grow well in containers but some are more suited to restricted situations than others. A window box may not be a good place to grow a tall plant like Burnley Bounty, but it would be an ideal place to grow miniature fruit types with a small bush.

Besides taking up less space, tomatoes grown in containers are mobile. They can be shifted into locations which make the best use of the sun or which shield them from cold winds or frost.

Pots are usually round with one or more holes in the bottom for drainage, whilst other containers may be round, square, triangular or rectangular in shape. Plastic bags holding up to 10 litres of medium are also popular for some applications.

The preferred growing arrangement is to have one tomato plant per pot or bag, but for a large polystyrene container one metre in length, up to three plants may be grown.

Plastic pots are non porous, whereas clay and polystyrene types are porous. The porous types have a number of disadvantages, which include:

- They may dry out quickly on a hot day.

- If they weep, algae will grow on the outside making the container unsightly.

- New clay pots frequently absorb nitrates.

- Micro organisms penetrate the walls and may be difficult to remove during the sterilization process.

- Most are heavy and not easy to move.

- They are expensive, especially some of the terracotta types.

Terracotta pots have been used since ancient times. They held flowering plants, because blossoms were credited with absorbing fumes from lamps and with neutralising the intoxicating properties of wine.

Today, plastic pots are by far the most popular for growing tomatoes.

Advantages include:

- Relatively cheap.

- Lightweight and easy to handle.

- Long life.

- No pollution or absorption of nutrient elements.

- Algae easily contained.

- Plants can be removed without disturbing the roots of other plants in the system.

- Individual pots can be easily sterilized.

- There is no competition between plants for nutrients.

- Wide range of sizes available.

Plastic pots are available in a range of colours and designs. One popular design is the 'terra pot', a plastic imitation of terracotta for use on balconies and patios.

Two methods of supporting small tomatoes such as pixies, growing in a pot. A wire frame with grid openings large enough to allow fruit to be picked and removed from the side can be tied to the rim of the pot or a tripod made from three garden stakes tied to the rim of the pot are both suitable.

These pots retain the traditional shape and curvature of the time-honoured Roman clay pot, including the authentic clay colour, textured surface finish and even kiln ring marks inside the lip.

The size of the pot is important in growing tomatoes. The tall plant variety needs adequate volume in which to develop an effective root system. The pot should be relatively deep, so that the roots of the seedling can be buried deeply enough during transplant and also to reduce drying out of the medium. A 30 cm diameter pot is preferable to a 20 cm size for the tall varieties. As a general rule, the plant will produce a greater yield with the larger pot and will also crop over a longer period.

Depending on the method of feeding, the plant in a small pot will deplete the nutrient solution, particularly nitrogen, more quickly than one growing in a large pot. However, the earlier absorption permits earlier accumulation of carbohydrates and flower-forming hormones, which in turn are associated with flower bud formation, flowering and fruiting. This may be used to advantage to speed up an early crop.

Except for a few special hydroponic installations, such as siphon draining technique, pots should have adequate drainage holes. With clay or ceramic pots it is usual to have a single hole in the bottom, whereas for plastic types a number of holes are provided around the junction of the wall and base plate. Where fine medium such as perlite or vermiculite is being used, steps should be taken to prevent the medium being washed out through the

An installation comprising four pots per 900mm by 300mm by 150mm polystyrene container fitted with cut-out top boards to accommodate the pots being prepared for growing Tiny Tim tomatoes. Medium is perlite on a 30mm base of scoria with nutrient solution being fed by drip arrangement. Pots stood in a 50mm reservoir of nutrient solution.

Polystyrene containers 900mm by 300mm by 150mm with masonite cut outs to accommodate two 30cm and one 20cm diameter plastic pots. Each pot provided with individual nutrient feed line. "A" frame supports plastic rope to which plant stems are tied. Containers are designed to provide for either free drain or reservoir operation.

holes during application of the nutrient solution, or during flushing operations. To assist in this regard, a piece of plastic shadecloth, crushed stone or scoria are all suitable.

Besides their application for housing rockwool slabs, lay-flat plastic bags (also known as pillows or grow bags) are widely employed for growing tomatoes in a range of media including perlite, peat, sawdust, coconut husk, vermiculite and others.

Some growers have successfully used vertically mounted black plastic bags, usually 8-10 litre capacity, for growing tomatoes, but the lay-flat version is much more widely employed. Capacities of bags range from 25 to 60 litres or more, with the 25 litre bag being used for up to four plants and the 60 litre bag for up to six plants. Bag lengths vary from 750 mm to 1000 mm or more, with 300 mm being a typical width. However, some cherry tomato growers have experimented with bags about 2 metres long and 250 mm wide to accommodate eight or more plants. The growers claimed that the single row of plants facilitated harvesting by allowing easy access to both sides of the growing row. One grower used a medium of 15% peat/25% bark/60% perlite, with solution being applied by drip feed, midway between the plant stems.

The majority of lay-flat bags are made from double sided polythene plastic, white on the outside to minimise temperature buildup inside the bag and to improve light intensity around the growing plants, and black on the inside to prevent the development of algae.

Nutrient feed arrangements are usually drip-feed irrigation, with about 10% surplus drained to waste, but up to 30% should be put to waste if the initial water has a high sodium chloride level. Growers have certain preferences for nutrient feed arrangements. Some employ one lateral dripper per plant, while others prefer one lateral dripper per bag. Waste may go to ground, or to a storage tank below ground level for re-use on other crops or recirculation. The usual method of using lay-flat bags is to maintain a reservoir of nutrient solution in the bag. This may be done by employing a Bag Reservoir system, or a Gulley Reservoir system.

For Ausperl Grow Bags, which have dimensions 750 mm x 300 mm x 100 mm and contain approximately 25 litres of medium (usually perlite) per bag, the recommendations for

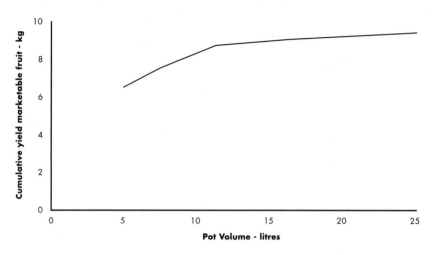

Figure 5.2 *Yield versus pot volume.*

using the bags with the Bag Reservoir system is to slit the bag horizontally 20 mm up from the base so that a reservoir of 20 mm of nutrient solution is formed in the basal layers of the perlite. The reservoir level would be the same for other media, including vermiculite, peat, coconut husk and combinations of these with perlite.

The 20 mm reservoir applies to plants which have been well established in the growing bag. In the case of seedlings which have been grown in 75 mm rockwool cubes and placed onto the grow bag, the bag slit is first made at 75 mm above the bag bottom. This is because the dry surface of the perlite may draw the water out of the rockwool block, causing the block to dry out and possibly bringing about death of the seedling. When the seedling plants have become well established in 2-3 weeks, the second slit can then be made at the 20 mm level. Some growers propagate the seedlings in perlite-filled plastic containers, so that the two levels of slits are not required.

In this way, every bag throughout the installation has even watering, floor grading is not critical, it does not depend on complex irrigating systems and flushing of the bag is easily carried out.

For a Gully Reservoir system, whole rows of growing bags are wrapped in an outer polythene gully and reservoirs 30-40 mm deep are created. To ensure movement of water between the Gully Reservoir and the bags, the bags are slit vertically along their bottom edges The Gully Reservoir system provides a larger buffer reservoir of nutrient solution than the Bag Reservoir system, and may be of advantage for fully grown plants during high temperature conditions, when plants have a high water uptake.

The Ausperl Grow Bags have a nominal capacity of 25 litres of perlite. Plant density usually ranges from 2 to 4 plants per bag. For two plants, this would mean a growing volume of 12.5 litres per plant and for four plants, the volume would be a little over 6 litres per plant. Trials with some varieties, show a reduction in yield per plant as the growing volume is reduced.

With some installations, the irrigation frequency is regulated by an electronic processing device, which automatically adjusts the solution application frequency after taking into account the total solar energy in the growing area, the air temperature and the relative humidity.

Trials with Mighty Red variety and using a medium mixture of 80% perlite/20% scoria in lay-flat bags, gave almost similar yields to plants grown in plastic pots, when calculated on the basis of litres of medium per plant. As shown in *Figure 5.2*, the yield of marketable fruit from a 12 litre pot was approximately 9 kg and for a 5 litre pot about 6.7 kg. One reason for the lower yield with the smaller pot was the high percentage of unmarketable fruit, due mainly to blossom end rot and some sun scald. With the lay-flat bags, yields averaged 9.1 kg per plant, for three plants in a bag with approximately 36 litres of medium, and 7.5 kg per plant for three plants in a bag with 16 litres of medium.

From the graph, it would appear that a medium volume of above about 12 litres per plant, for either pots or lay-flat bags, could not be economically justified.

In recent years, the Active Drainage (AD) system has been developed for use with lay-flat bags, using rockwool slabs as medium. It offers positive root zone moisture control. With this system, instead of excess nutrient solution being drained by gravity via slits near the base of the wrapper, excess nutrient solution is siphoned out of the bag. Drainage can be controlled to any pre-set moisture level, giving ability to control the slab moisture content with stage of plant growth, or environmental conditions such as cloudy weather or high temperature.

Growool wrapped slabs of size 750mm by 300mm by 75mm set up for drip feed arrangement prior to placement of growing plants in cubes. The rockwool cubes are placed in the slits on top of the slabs. Typically two plants are grown per slab. Slits in the sides of the containers allow surplus nutrient to drain out except for a small portion of about 10mm depth.

An installation employing Ausperl Grow Bags filled with perlite and placed on a plastic sheet over a coarse gravel bed. Four plants were planted per bag providing a growing medium volume of about six litres per plant. The seedlings were established in perlite in small plastic containers before being transferred to the grow bags. The secondary nutrient distribution feeder with drip laterals were supported by a steel cable fixed level with the top of the plastic containers.

Variety	Daily production rate-g/plant Standard pot	Daily production rate-g/plant Air cell pot
Apollo	66.9	67.3
Burnley Bounty	75.1	77.2
Grosse Lisse	68.5	70.3
Magnifico	80.2	83.5
Mighty Red	77.2	76.1

Table 5.3 *Average daily production rate for standard and air cell pots.*

Above: Standard 30cm diameter plastic pot with wall cut outs to make 42% air cell container. Plastic fly screen or other suitable material can be used to contain medium within the pot. A 42% air cell container with perlite will dry out too quickly under most growing environments and 5 to 30% air space has been found to be more satisfactory using the same feed systems as employed with full wall pots.

The system makes it simpler to return excess solution to the main storage tank, compared with the slit bag arrangement. The return solution is also cleaner and does not require filtering.

Bench installation is simplified with the AD arrangement, as gradient problems are simplified, particularly if the growing area is very flat. As the bags are mounted well above floor level, a suitable return pipe gradient can be achieved irrespective of the level of the growing bags.

Measurements indicate that water content and nutrient levels are more evenly distributed within the slab and between slabs, compared with the conventional slit bag system.

An important advantage which has been of assistance to some growers, where there has been interruption to nutrient feed, or a row has to be taken out of service for urgent maintenance, is that the siphon system can be made inoperative in any particular control section, allowing the bag to hold a quantity of nutrient solution to keep plants supplied while the installation is out of service. With the conventional slit bag system, the plants could be left without solution for as long as the system is out of service.

A problem with small plastic bags is that they easily fall over, especially when the plants are large and unsupported and a lightweight medium like perlite is used. Some growers support the bags inside a Besser concrete block, or by temporary timber planks.

A major disadvantage with plastic pots and bags is associated with aeration, especially for those containers where the depth is greater than the diameter. As the plant grows, the root system of a large plant becomes very dense and the air spaces between the particles of perlite or other medium is reduced considerably. This makes it difficult for oxygen in the air to find its way down through the medium to roots near the bottom of the container. Air cannot enter via walls because they are impervious. In addition to the need for oxygen to be accessible to the roots, those gases given off, such as carbon dioxide, ethylene etc, must be able to escape from the root environment.

Where flushing is undertaken at frequent intervals, oxygenated water passes down past the entire root system and gases are flushed out. However, if the system operates on a drip feed or similar principal, some provision must be made to improve the environment by providing static aeration techniques. One system called the 'air cell pot', has vertical slots regularly spaced along the pot walls. Cut-outs of at least 10% of the surface area of the pot is typical. The medium is prevented from falling out of the pot by a strip of shadecloth which is placed over the inside wall, before pouring in the medium. Another method is to use air pipes. These are 25 mm plastic water pipes of the same height as the pot and drilled with many holes over the length of the pipe. One or two are inserted in the pot and this allows free movement of air up and down the pipe.

In addition to improved aeration, air cell pots prevent the circling of roots around the wall and so encourage the formation of a branched root system. This makes better use of the volumetric contents of the pot. When the tip of a root grows to the cut-out section of the wall, it dries out and dies when it becomes exposed to the atmosphere.

Table 5.3 shows the average daily production rate of marketable fruit from trials with plants of five varieties, using 30 cm diameter standard pots and 30 cm diameter air cell pots with 10% wall cutouts. The study was conducted over a period of about 90 days, using a growing medium of 50/50 perlite and scoria, and fed by a jet system with a nutrient solution of conductivity CF24-26.

The pot size has an important influence on the marketable fruit yield.

Tables 5.4, 5.5 and *5.6* show the weight of individual marketable fruit for each truss up to and including the fourth truss, harvested during a trial of nine Grosse Lisse plants in three Groups. Each group comprised three plants in 30 cm diameter plastic pots, with medium

Growth comparisons of 20cm and 30cm air cell pots with 30cm full wall pot growing the same variety in perlite medium and fed from the same supply tank. At the time the photograph was taken the plant in the 30cm full wall pot was 90cm high. The plant in the 20cm air cell pat was 128cm high while the plant in the 30cm air cell pot was 150cm high.

of perlite, scoria and peat in the ratio 70/20/10 prepared to compare three different passive aeration arrangements of the medium. All plants were irrigated with a nutrient supply from a common source and given a 10 minute cycle three times daily, using a spray system with nutrient return.

Pots for Group A were standard pots with air acting only on the top surface of the medium. Group B were standard pots, with a single 25 mm diameter perforated plastic air pipe mounted vertically and located about 2 cm from the plant stem. It extended from the base of the pot to about 3 cm above the surface of the medium. As well as the top surface being exposed to the atmosphere, a section of the medium right down to the base was also exposed. Group C were standard pots with vertical strip cut-outs in the wall, providing 10% exposure to the atmosphere. Plastic mesh prevented the medium from falling out of the pot. In this arrangement, part of the medium at the side walls was exposed to the air, as well as the top of the pot.

Results indicated that increased exposure of the medium to the air produced increase in fruit yield, compared with a standard pot with only the top surface of the medium being exposed. The perforated air pipe Group gave an increase in yield of marketable fruit of just over 1 kg and the air cell Group gave an increase in yield of 2.7 kg.

Group A produced 49 fruit with an average weight of 241 gm, Group B produced 56 fruit with an average weight of 229 gm and Group C produced 60 fruit with an average weight of 242 gm.

In addition to allowing air to enter low down in the medium, the pipe and air cell systems also allow gases produced by the roots, such as carbon dioxide and ethylene, to escape from the pot more readily, so enhancing the growing environment.

Figure 5.2 shows results of trials using Mighty Red variety grown in pots of various volumes, using medium mixture of 80/20 perlite/scoria with a flow feed system. The pots were spaced uniformly at 0.5 metres apart.

It is evident that a pot with a volume of about 12 litres of medium, with a standard 30 cm diameter, is sufficient for good development and production of a crop yield of A Grade or No 1 Grade marketable tomatoes. It produces a much higher yield than pots of lower capacity and there was insignificant improvement for pots above 12 litre capacity. For the very small improvement in yield for pots above 12 litres, there are some disadvantages. These include higher cost of the pots, higher cost of the medium, less plants per unit area and greater vegetative growth. The greater vegetative growth can result in problems with shading of adjacent plants. Pots below 12 litres produced a high proportion of blossom-end rot fruit.

Growing plants in pots creates an environment which differs considerably from that with soil growing techniques. In some cases, the restricted environment can result in lower yield and considerable research is currently being undertaken in pot design to overcome the shortcomings.

Research currently being undertaken by the Queensland Department of Primary Industries includes the development of a method of deflecting the plant roots, so that they do not circle around the pot walls. The technique involves the use of a suitable material such as flexible plastic or fibreglass sheet with a certain design configuration. The device discourages the roots from accumulating at the edges of the pot and directs them to the interior of the pot, to take better advantage of nutrients and water in the medium.

A popular container which simplifies feed arrangements is the gully. Instead of providing individual feed lines to each plant, as for pots and bags, nutrient solution is applied at one end of the gully and flows down past each plant in turn, eventually being returned to the storage tank. It is based on the NFT principle, but operates with an intermittent irrigation cycle and employs a flowing stream of solution rather than a film.

In a typical installation to cater for 12 indeterminate tomato plants, a standard 6 metre long, 150 mm x 75 mm plastic gully is used, with cut-outs made to accommodate the medium, which comprises four Growool WC 75 cubes strapped together with tape to form a square block. Half of the plastic wrapping of each cube is cut away to allow the passing solution to migrate into the four cubes of the block. As the square block format takes up the complete space between the 75 mm vertical walls, two sections of perforated 20 mm plastic pipes, slightly longer than the growing block, are inserted between the block and the

Table 5.4 Yield (grams) from Group A employing standard pots.

	Pot 1	Pot 2	Pot 3
Truss 1.	325	165	235
	145	335	255
	220	295	405
	305	305	355
	220	405	125
	335	220	235
Truss 2.	265	165	185
	195	220	140
	405	335	105
	95	260	385
Truss 3.	225	65	265
	365	195	260
	295	330	275
	305	225	305
Truss 4.	140	85	225
	225	190	75
			115
Total	4.065 kg	3.795 kg	3.945 kg

Aggregate yield 11.805 kg

Table 5.5 Yield (grams) from Group B employing standard pot with perforated air pipe to provide passive aeration.

	Pot 1	Pot 2	Pot 3
Truss 1.	235	270	305
	302	166	265
	485	252	405
	295	335	225
	166	440	265
	195	235	105
Truss 2.	240	85	85
	195	220	195
	115	305	305
	265	195	225
Truss 3.	255	250	265
	115	185	165
	305	195	295
	225	265	85
Truss 4.	285	165	235
	95	270	155
	225	225	285
	302	154	90
	110		
Total	4.410 kg	4.212 kg	4.220 kg

Aggregate yield 12.842 kg

Table 5.6 Yield (grams) from Group C employing 10% air cell pot to provide passive aeration.

	Pot 1	Pot 2	Pot 3
Truss 1.	295	330	115
	335	355	320
	165	265	155
	410	195	275
	225	280	220
	110	225	335
Truss 2.	220	105	115
	225	235	265
	290	260	220
	405	305	295
Truss 3.	360	225	260
	110	405	360
	85	330	385
	245	265	215
	220	270	95
Truss 4.	175	285	105
	255	305	235
	190	115	150
	265	95	110
	110	220	
	305		
	220		
Total	5.220 kg	5.070 kg	4.230 kg

Aggregate yield 14.520 kg

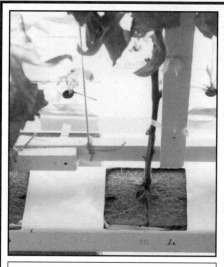

A multiple growing container comprising 150mm plastic gully with cutouts to accommodate four Growool WC75 cubes tied together for each plant. The split plastic cover has been removed to show the block and plant root system in photograph (Top). Nutrient was supplied by flow feed arrangement at 15 minute intervals three times daily. Photograph (Right) shows part of a crop of cherry tomatoes in the gully. Trials with Gross Lisse, Mighty Red and Sweet 100 varieties indicated yields comparable with plants grown in 30cm pots with perlite grown at the same time and irrigated from the same nutrient storage tank.

gully walls. A cut-out in the block will facilitate placement of the pipes. The purpose of the perforated pipes is to enable the solution to pass fairly rapidly down the gully, without having a back up of water. The pipes being perforated, will allow the solution passing through them to also pass into the feed block. With solution impacting on the block from the front and two sides, the block is soon saturated.

The square sections removed from the gully in making the cut-outs for the Growool block, have 20 mm holes drilled in the centre and are then cut up to provide two sections which will fit around the plant stem. This covers the Growool block, to prevent algae growth and to minimise loss of water due to evaporation.

Because the Growool blocks are saturated with solution during each irrigation cycle, they retain sufficient solution to meet the plants needs during summer, full-production periods. A flow rate of 1.5 litres per minute for 15 minutes, at cycles of 7 am, 1 pm and 5 pm are adequate for most varieties of tomatoes.

Good yields are produced with the system, and there are usually very few fruit which are unmarketable. There is not a great deal of difference in total yield, number of fruit and fruit size for any of the plants located anywhere in the gully.

With a trial of eight Grosse Lisse and four Mighty Red harvested during the February/March period, the results are shown in Tables 5.7 and 5.8 for two plants from each variety. The figures relate to Grosse Lisse in compartments 1 and 8 and Mighty Red in compartments 9 and 12, and are taken from data obtained to the fifth truss point, up to the time when the trial was terminated. Details of ripe fruit suitable for the table, form the basis of the Tables. Sizes and weights of green fruit still on the vines when the trial was terminated, have not been shown.

The Grosse Lisse plant in compartment 1 produced a yield of ripe fruit of 4.907 kg, with 26 fruit of average weight 188 g, and diameters varying from 62 mm to 95 mm. The same variety in compartment 8 produced a yield weight of 4.949 kg, with 23 fruit of average weight 215 g, and diameters varying from 68 mm to 102 mm. Productivity of plants in intermediate compartments were broadly similar.

Table 5.7 — Grosse Lisse, compartments 1 and 8

Plant compartment 1			Plant compartment 8		
Truss no.	Fruit dia.-mm	Fruit wt-g	Truss no.	Fruit dia.-mm	Fruit wt-g
1	80	200	1	85	240
	90	250		75	180
	70	170		80	202
	95	300		75	180
	82	210		70	170
	62	135		68	162
	78	193	2	90	285
	70	170		80	200
2	85	250		75	183
	75	183		74	178
	70	170		75	184
	68	165		85	250
	72	175	3	80	202
	72	176		95	295
	79	195		77	190
3	68	165		85	250
	70	170	4	75	185
	78	195		80	200
4	65	120		85	250
	67	155	5	102	340
	82	210		86	255
	82	210		77	190
5	74	178		74	178
	70	172			
	76	185			
	81	205			

Total yield 4.907 kg
Average weight 26 fruit - 188 g.

Total yield 4.949 kg
Average weight 23 fruit - 215 g.

Table 5.7 *Fruit produced by Grosse Lisse in compartments 1 and 8 of a 12 compartment gully system.*

Table 5.8 — Mighty Red, compartments 9 and 12

Plant compartment 9			Plant compartment 12		
Truss no.	Fruit dia.-mm	Fruit wt-g	Truss no.	Fruit dia.-mm	Fruit wt-g
1	70	168	1	70	171
	70	170		72	175
	72	175		70	170
	78	194		65	158
	80	200		65	160
	66	160		60	125
	50	90	2	75	180
2	82	210		65	120
	83	215		80	200
	75	180		63	140
	68	156		90	285
	60	125	3	68	160
	67	155		75	180
	62	135		80	201
	61	130		70	169
3	72	176		95	303
	70	168	4	74	178
	60	128		95	296
	62	136		90	285
4	95	302		75	182
	100	325	5	85	250
	95	303		80	201
5	96	300		82	210
	88	260			
	95	302			

Total yield 4.863 kg
Average weight 25 fruit - 194 g.

Total yield 4.5 kg
Average weight 23 fruit - 195 g.

Table 5.8 *Fruit produced by Mighty Red in compartments 9 and 12 of a 12 compartment gulley system.*

The Mighty Red variety were planted in the last four compartments of the gully and results were as expected from this variety. Plant in compartment 9 produced a yield of 4.863 kg, with 25 fruit being of average weight 194 g. Fruit diameters ranged from 50 mm to 100 mm and maximum weight was 325 g. The plant in compartment 12 produced a yield of ripe fruit of 4.5 kg, with 23 fruit averaging 195 g. Diameters ranged from 63 mm to 95 mm with the largest fruit weighing 296 g.

A feature of the gully system design is that it provides a well-aerated nutrient solution at the point where the solution enters the gully. The feed solution falls from a vertical pipe with an adjustable tap fitted, and as the solution impacts on the base of the gully, it creates a mass of bubbles. The tap allows control of the solution feed rate into the gully.

A characteristic of this arrangement is that the root systems are only immersed in water for 15 minutes at 7 am, 1pm and 5pm. On shut-down of the pump, the solution drains out of the gully and water trapped in the Growool blocks is gradually taken up by the plants, although the root zone is never completely dry with proper system design. The exposure of the roots to the air is of great benefit to the plant. Gases can readily diffuse into and out of the root mass. The diffusion rate of gases in air is many thousand times more rapid than in water.

One well known Australian company which produces a range of hydroponics equipment for the growing of tomatoes and other crops is Auto-Pot Pty Ltd, with research and development facilities in Melbourne. Headed by Jim Fah, inventions have been covered by patents in Australia, USA, UK, Japan, Taiwan and Malaysia.

The company's products, which have been exported to many countries including USA, Japan, Saudi Arabia, UK, Israel and South East Asia, have been awarded a number of exhibition prizes including Inventors Association of Victoria First Prize 1992, and Best Victorian Invention at the Royal Melbourne Show 1992.

The heart of the Auto-Pot Systems is the 'SMART-Valve' invented by Jim Fah. The valve controls the entry of the nutrient solution into a container or reservoir. It is a very small unpowered plastic valve, that allows the nutrient solution to enter the container to a depth of about 35 mm. At that level, the valve shuts off the supply from the storage tank until all the solution in the reservoir has been fully taken up by the plant. The operation provides the plant root system with a watering cycle followed by a drying out period, to allow the roots to absorb oxygen from the air via the medium in the growing pot.

Because the valve is so small and relatively cheap, each container is provided with its own valve. This enables the plants in each container to dictate their watering cycles. Changes in the environment such as temperature, wind etc allow the valve to respond immediately to the needs of the plant.

The system differs from other static feed systems which rely on the conventional ball-cock type float valve, in that it allows total reduction of the nutrient solution to zero level, before the reservoir is refilled. Once the water has been taken up from the reservoir to the extent that the film of water under the valve has gone, the valve reopens, allowing another supply of solution to refill the reservoir to the 35 mm level.

Features of the Auto-Pot Systems employing the SMART-Valve include:

- Efficient use of the nutrient solution. Except for a small evaporation loss from the surface of the pot medium, all water supplied to the reservoir is available to the plant.

- There is no solution run off to waste, or recycling of the solution by any mechanical or pressure means.

- Over or underwatering of plants cannot occur. Solution enters the reservoir to a predetermined level - typically 35 mm - and is replaced immediately all the solution has been taken up by the plant.

- No battery or mains electric power or compressed air is required to operate the system. The solution is either gravity fed in the case of the tank-fed system, or by water pressure in the tap-fed system.

- The systems are completely automatic with no financial outlay being required for provision of electric power cabling, pumps, piping, dosing systems, computers etc.

- Cheap and simple installation, with all connections being by 4 mm soft plastic tubing that is joined or junctioned by inexpensive press-in type joiners. The thin tubing can be easily attached to walls, rafters etc, when connecting storage tank output to the containers.

- The SMART-Valve enables self-scheduling of the nutrient supply and automatically caters for plant needs throughout the entire growing and production periods.

- Except for maintaining nutrient solution supply in the storage tank, no human intervention is required for operation of the system.

There are two main types of operating systems covered by the Auto-Pot design. They are:

- **Gravity feed system**

This unit comprises the growing pots, container, the SMART-Valve and nutrient supply tank. In general, the gravity feed design is suitable for any number of containers from one up to about 200. However, where more than a dozen or so containers are required, some growers prefer a pressure-fed system. Change over from gravity feed to pressure feed is simple.

A popular Auto Pot Systems Automatic Hydro Pak kit assembled and growing tomatoes in perlite medium in two 250mm diameter plastic pots. A SMART-Valve which controls supply of nutrient level from a 35 litre tank is located in a cavity between the cavities for the pots. One grower claimed he grew tomato plants about 10m high in a well lit factory using the system.

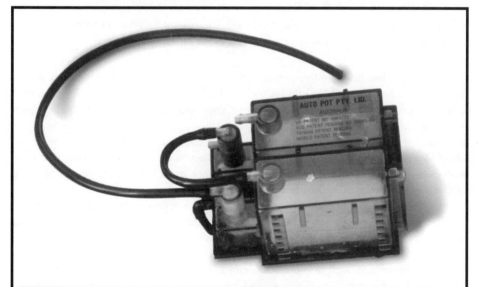

The SMART-Valve, part of the Auto-Pot Systems used to control supply of nutrient solution into a container or reservoir. The valve allows the solution to enter the container to a depth of about 35mm and then shuts off the supply until all solution in the reservoir has been taken up by the plant. When the container is empty, the valve opens to allow the container to be refilled to the 35mm level.

• Pressure feed system

This design, which requires mains pressure water for operation, can be operated with up to 200 containers, catering for some 800 individual plants in 250 mm diameter plastic pots filled with perlite or other suitable medium. The water can be supplied either from the council water distribution system, or a country home supply that has pressure at the tap provided by either motor or header tank.

The unit comprises growing containers, each of which has a built-in SMART-Valve, a network of delivery tubing, a fertigator and a tap adaptor incorporating a pressure-reducing valve to limit water pressure to a predetermined level.

The fertigation unit comprises three bottles. The first is filled with Part A nutrient solution, the second filled with Part B nutrient solution and the third is a flow indicator which serves as a sedimentor and mixer, and provides a visual check of the rate of flow. An injector in the cap of the bottles with the nutrient solutions, adds a minute dose of fertiliser to the water as it passes to the SMART-Valve. Feeding is automatic, every time nutrient solution passes to the reservoir.

Included in the range of Auto-Pot equipment are a number of kits.

- Kit No 1 comprises a 12 litre, high-density polystyrene container (700 mm x 200 mm x 200 mm deep) with lid, perlite medium, nutrients supplied as Part A and Part B, a 10 litre capacity see-through storage tank, in-line filter, SMART-Valve, tubing for connection of the nutrient storage tank supply to the container, and instruction book. This kit has been successfully employed for cultivation of many varieties of tomatoes. One installation grew three Zebra variety per container, in a medium comprising 75% perlite and 25% vermiculite. Two cherry tomatoes per container were grown in another installation, using the same medium mixture of perlite and vermiculite. Yield details are not available, but photographs of the plants indicate that the yields and fruit sizes would have been at least equal to the best of other growing systems.

- Kit No 2 comprises the same components as Kit No 1, except the container size is 700 mm x 300 mm x 100 mm deep. This system with the shallower container is ideal for smaller tomato varieties such as Pixie and Tiny Tim.

- Hydropak kit. This consists of a tray which accommodates two 250 mm grow pots and houses the SMART-Valve between the cavities for the pots, bag of perlite medium, nutrients, filter, tubing and instruction book. It is ideal for growing two tomato plants, with reports indicating excellent yields.

- Capilliary mat kit. This kit uses the SMART-Valve to control the flow of nutrient solution to the mat, but the way the solution is delivered to the plants, is different.

The kit comprises flat polystyrene foam container, 10 litre nutrient storage tank, A and B nutrients, in line filter, SMART-Valve, rockwool cubes and plastic tubing. An absorbent mat is laid on the flat bottom surface of the container, with parts of the mat dropping down to be level with the base of the SMART-Valve.

When nutrient solution floods the bottom of the container, following operation of the SMART-Valve, the capilliary mat draws nutrients to its surface. A pot with perlite, or a rockwool cube, simply sits on the capilliary mat. Mats are available in a range of sizes from 600 mm x 1200 mm, to 1200 mm x 2400 mm.

The technique is highly successful, with one trial with a Grosse Lisse tomato producing a plant 2 metres high and with a high yield of marketable fruit when grown in a 100 mm rockwool cube placed on the mat.

Other kits include a container to accommodate six 150 mm diameter pots, four 250 mm diameter pots, oblong wall planters 1000 mm x 320 mm x 220 mm deep to accommodate three 250 mm pots, round twin wall planters designed to take pots from 300 mm to 400 mm diameter and others.

When containers are located outside and subject to flooding from rain, an automatic SMART-Siphon is available. This unit is automatically activated by excess water and reduces the water table to 10% of the normal automatic maximum.

Vertical columns

Vertical columns, usually in the form of integral or stacked containers of various designs, have been employed with some degree of success in growing tomatoes. The technique involves filling a vertical container with medium, feeding nutrient at the top and inserting plants in the vertical side, either through a slit if the material is thin plastic sheet material, or into protuberances such as elbows, if the container is of solid material. The systems are very popular with strawberry growers and relatively expensive terracotta types, with integrated protuberances, can be purchased for placement on a balcony or patio.

In addition to commercially produced products, a wide range of home made systems have been employed in tomato cultivation. Columns can be made up of stacked metal drums, large diameter plastic pipe, plastic sacks, stacked plastic crates or stacked hollow masonry building blocks.

One grower had considerable success with stacked plastic crates. Four crates, approximately 30 cm cube size, were tied together with bent steel straps and placed on a spaced pair of 50 mm x 75 mm timber rails about 60 cm above the ground. A 25 mm hole was drilled in the bottom of each crate to allow nutrient solution to pass from one crate to the next below. The bottom crate was provided with a fitting linked into a rigid 75 mm plastic pipe, located a few centimetres beneath the crate. This allowed waste nutrient solution to be returned to the nutrient storage tank. Experience with an earlier installation, indicated that letting the surplus solution go to ground, created an unacceptable working environment for staff and was also a wasteful practice.

An overhead pipe system enabled nutrient to be supplied to the top crate by a flow-feed system. Medium in the crates was a mixture of perlite, vermiculite and coconut husk in the ratio 50/20/30.

Irrigation was on the basis of three feeds daily at 7 am, noon and 5 pm during summer, with 1.5 litres per minute being fed for 20 minute periods. In cooler months, feed cycles were restricted to 9 am and 3 pm.

Initially, the grower employed continuous nutrient at the rate of 0.5 litre per minute, but found that intermittent feeding three times daily produced fruit which matured and ripened faster. Total yield was about the same.

The pH was maintained in the range 6.1 to 6.5 and the solution in the supply tank dumped every six weeks. At that time, all columns were given a one hour continuous flow feed of plain water, to minimise salt build up.

Each crate accommodated one plant, using a plan of one plant per vertical side of the column, which gave four plants per column equally spaced around the column.

Seedlings were inserted into the medium at one of the crate handle cut-outs. The cut-outs measured 12 cm x 4 cm, giving plenty of space for plant stem growth.

The grower specialised in cherry type tomatoes, including Yellow Cherry Cocktail, Yellow Currant, Gardeners Delight, Sweet 100, Orange Sunrise, Bite Size, Goldilocks and several unnamed varieties. Tomatoes were produced throughout the year and the grower was hard pressed to meet the demand, as he had a reputation for high quality produce. He supplied restaurants, fast food outlets, hotels and airline food divisions.

Customers had specific requirements. Some required small, medium and large sizes only, while others wanted a mixture of small, medium and large sizes. The specifications dictated that small fruit were to be in the range 15 to 24 mm diameter, medium in the range 25 to 30 mm, and large in the range 31 to 35 mm. Fruit below 15 mm were rejected and fruit above 35 mm diameter were sent to a local growers fruit and vegetable market.

The greenhouse was fitted with manually operated roof screens, which were brought into use during the hot summer periods. No heating was provided during winter. As the plants were basically growing in a circular pattern, the grower initially encountered a small problem with yields from plants growing on the southern side, due to insufficient light. He improved the situation considerably by installing a 'pyramid cord' pattern and placing aluminium foil along the southern wall of the greenhouse. He estimated that yields from plants on the southern side increased from 75% to about 90% of that of plants on the northern side of the column.

Replanting of columns took place on a rotation basis, organised so that 1/3 crop was at peak production, 1/3 was six weeks off starting production and 1/3 was being replanted. The different varieties which had different production characteristics ensured there was always a continuous supply of ripe fruit. Harvesting was carried out on Tuesday and Sunday each week.

Because coconut husk is an organic substance and breaks down in time, and vermiculate also has a tendency to break down, new medium was used at each replanting stage. Earlier experience had shown that yields after reusing medium, were well down on those for new medium. There was also a high percentage of unmarketable fruit. The grower considered decaying roots which could not be removed, used up nitrogen from the nutrient solution and not all salts could be removed by the flushing operation.

The grower's long experience in growing cherry tomatoes indicated that best yields were produced with low levels of nutrient conductivity, usually CF20 or less. Increasing the conductivity to CF25 - 30 will, as a general rule, reduce the number of fruit per truss, the average fruit weight and total yield, by up to 20%. However, percentage of soluble solids is raised and sugar Brix level is increased. The extent of the increases vary with the variety, and the season at time of harvesting.

Increased conductivity of the nutrient feed solution will result in a superior tomato in terms of sugar Brix level, higher pH, a better acidity/sourness ratio, firmer fruit, longer shelf life and overall better acceptability by the consumer.

Typical yields using the vertical column arrangement of stacked crates were in the range 12 - 14 kg per square metre, for nutrient concentrations of CF25 - 30, and 15 - 17 kg per square metre for nutrient solution CF18 - 20 for summer cropping. Sweet Bite was at the lower range point and Gardeners Delight at the higher end.

Hollow masonry building blocks of moulded concrete construction have been used by tomato growers for both greenhouse and outdoor hydroponics installations. Blocks similar to stretcher block design are available in a range of sizes with two or three hollow compartments.

One two-compartment product used for wall construction, approximately 250 mm wide, 450 mm long and 220 mm deep, was employed by a farmer with an outdoor system. Two blocks were stacked to provide vertical growing containers for the tomato plants. Each row

Three polystyrene containers widely employed in growing tomatoes. They are usually fitted with small plastic taps to enable the nutrient solution to be drained out or set at a fixed level as reservoir, typically 50mm. It is usual practice to paint the inside of the containers to minimize water seepage loss. Sizes are (L to R), 900mm by 300mm by 150mm; 550mm sides by 250mm; and 975mm by 375mm by 225mm.

of double blocks was placed in a plastic covered scooped out channel in the soil, about 100 mm deep, allowing excess solution to flow down to a catchment dam on the property. The dam provided water for pasture irrigation purposes. End blocks were used with the bottom course to ensure stability of the structure.

The vines were supported by a trellis comprising top and bottom galvanised wires, spaced about 1.5 m apart and held in position by wooden strain posts at the end of each row and drilled intermediate hardwood droppers. The two wires were used to support long-life, waterproof, strong cord placed into a V pattern, by winding the roll of cord up and down over the wires along the full length of the trellis. The bottom of the V was located at each plant position. The two wires of the V enabled the grower to grow each plant with two stems.

The grower switched to hydroponic cultivation following a nematode disease problem with soil-grown tomatoes. Because the installation operated on an intermittent feed basis, with surplus solution flowing away from the containers to the dam, he experienced no problem during periods of heavy rainfall.

The installation initially comprised six rows of blocks, each 40 metres in length. But following success with the early crops, he extended the installation to nearly double capacity over a five year period.

Nutrient feed arrangement comprised a drip-fed system, providing nutrients at the rate of 600 ml per minute for 10 minutes at three hourly intervals, 6 am to 6 pm, with one feed at midnight. The nutrient storage tanks comprised two large concrete tanks coated with bitumen on the inside, and placed on mounds so the bottoms were about 1.5 metre above ground level. Water was provided by a bore on the property giving high quality water.

The pH was adjusted as necessary to be within the range 5.9 to 6.2 and conductivity set in the range CF24 to CF28. Plants were at different stages of growth to ensure fruit supply over a long period. To cater for newly planted seedlings, the grower fed them with solution of CF15 for four weeks after plant out. He used four 200 litre plastic drums on a four wheel cart, to shift the feed tanks to the seedling areas.

Before switching to hydroponics, the grower undertook a series of trials to investigate the characteristics of various media which could be purchased from local produce stores. He decided to employ the system of stacked masonry hollow blocks, after reading about an installation used by a farmer in the USA who had used the system with much success.

Using a prototype of his proposed wall of masonry blocks, he planted five varieties of tomatoes in six different media. Four seedlings of each variety were planted in the vertical columns of the block compartments, raised 1 cm above ground.

Records made of the yield results, up to and including the fourth truss of each plant, are shown in *Table 5.9*. The total yields included marketable and unmarketable fruit. The highest yield was provided by Floradel grown in granulated rockwool and Potentate grown in gravel. Both varieties produced an average yield of 6.1 kg, but Potentate included three unmarketable tomatoes with blossom-end rot. College Challenger yield was just slightly lower at 6.05 kg when grown in scoria.

		Coconut husk	Scoria	Gravel	Sawdust	Peat	Granulated rockwool
1	Gardeners Delight	2.9 kg	3.2 kg	2.05 kg	1.9 kg	3.1 kg	3.15 kg
2	College Challenger	5.85	6.05	4.51	2.9	4.5	4.95
3	Grosse Lisse	5.6	5.55	4.95	4.1	5.05	5.75
4	Potentate	4.9	5.2	6.1	3.8	4.4	5.15
5	Floradel	5.55	5.8	5.95	4.65	4.85	6.1
	Total yield	24.8 kg	25.8 kg	23.5 kg	17.35 kg	21.9 kg	25.1 kg

Table 5.9 *Average yields produced by selected varieties growing in hollow vertical masonry blocks filled with different media. Harvested to fourth truss plants 2-5.*

In comparing the various media, yield weights in descending order were produced by scoria, granulated rockwool, coconut husk, gravel, peat and sawdust.

The *Pinus radiata* sawdust trial was a disappointment. Fruit size was small, plants lacked vigour and showed signs of iron deficiency. Two of the plants died before completion of the trial. The sawdust remained excessively wet, even two hours after cessation of nutrient feed cycle. Floradel seemed to handle the wet sawdust best but even so, yield was much lower than that produced by plants in other media. Peat also did not enable plants to provide good yields. Grosse Lisse produced the best yield with peat, at 5.05 kg average over four plants.

To check on the likelihood of leaching of lime from the concrete blocks into the nutrient solution, the grower painted every second block with bitumen placed on the inside walls. During the trials, he could find no measureable difference in plant behaviour between plants in painted and unpainted containers.

In the permanent installation, the grower adopted the practice of restricting plant growth to six trusses, in order to produce two good crops per year with a third of lower yield. However, selected plants were allowed to grow beyond six trusses, to observe yield patterns. Records kept of one Grosse Lisse plant indicated a yield of 10.1 kg from 14 trusses, after growing through summer and autumn seasons. Normal production averaged 8.3 kg for plants grown through summer and early autumn, and 5.1 kg for plants grown during spring and early summer.

There are a number of advantages in growing tomatoes in containers with systems employing nutrient return principles. They include:

- Most system designs are relatively easy to install and economical to provide.
- With individual containers, there is no mass entanglement of roots with other plants, as is the case with NFT systems.
- Many media are recyclable and easily sterilized.
- Containers with integral vine support systems can be shifted to take advantage of changed environmental conditions.
- Plastic pots and similar containers have long life, are easily cleaned and readily storable.
- The growing area is easily kept clean.
- Most media provide a root support system.
- Plants can be readily removed from the installation without upsetting adjacent plants.
- Nutrient feed systems can be operated on a pulsed arrangement, so minimising electric power charges for pump motors.
- Irrigation cycles can be computerised, taking account of environmental growing conditions to feed the correct amount of solution and at the time required by the plant, as determined by sensors.

Chapter 6. GROWTH FACTORS

Chapter 6. GROWTH FACTORS

Growth and development

Many factors affect plant growth. Whether it is grown outside in the field, or in a controlled environment such as a glasshouse or polyhouse, the plant will be subjected to conditions of radiation, water and air. Artificial light may be an additional condition for some controlled situations. In commercial production of tomatoes, other factors, such as the use of growth regulators, may be important. The growth of the crop can be retarded, if necessary, by the application of appropriate chemicals, and harvest maturity is now widely regulated by the application of ethephon.

In external cultivation, water application may be spasmodic if by rainfall, or regular if by sprinkler, but for a glasshouse, application would be under regular control and may even include dissolved fertiliser such as for a hydroponics system.

Air has a considerable influence on growth of the plant. In an external environment, temperature is not controllable and neither are direction and velocity of the air. Air conditions may be such that considerable damage may be done to the plant. However, pollination is assisted by air movement and insects. In the enclosed situation, temperature may be controlled with air conditioning or heating equipment, there will be no damage due to wind gusts, but there could be a problem with pollination and also in some specific situations, a low level of carbon dioxide.

The parts of the plant above and below the medium are subjected to different conditions. Factors which affect the part above the medium, include temperature of the leaf and stem, the assimilation rate, the leaf transpiration rate and water potential in the form of osmotic pressure, and the plant sap flow rate. The part below the surface of the medium is basically the root system, which is influenced by the environment and the actual root conditions. The environment includes the pH of the water, the oxygen level, the water holding properties of the medium and the concentration of the nutrient solution. The root conditions which influence the plant growth include temperature, respiration, osmotic pressure, and the absorption rate of water, oxygen and minerals in the nutrient solution.

A tomato plant has two important phases related to its capacity to grow and to produce fruit. They are called vegetative and reproductive phases. The vegetative phase is involved with the development of the stems, leaves and root system, while the reproductive phase is concerned with the formation and development of the buds, flowers and fruit.

In the vegetative phase, new cells are made, cells are enlarged and tissue is formed. The production of new cells requires carbohydrates to manufacture the protoplasm - the material basis of all living matter - and the walls. The enlargement of new cells requires the presence of sugars, water and hormones which give the walls capacity to stretch. When the cells increase in size, the walls become thicker, resulting from additional cellulose produced by the sugars. The new tissues result in thickening of the walls of the cells of the stem epidermis, and the development of the conducting tubes for passage of water and dissolved nutrient elements in the stem and root system. All these factors require carbohydrates for the development of stems, leaves and roots so that in the vegetative phase, the plant will use most of the carbohydrates it is manufacturing.

Sometimes plants will exhibit abnormal vegetative and blossom development. This is a genetic disorder known as 'bullishness'. Frequently about two plants per thousand are affected and they should be removed to eliminate light competition.

In the reproductive phase, several important processes are involved. These include a slow down in the making of new cells, maturation of the tissues, thickening of the fibres, production of hormones and the development of buds, flowers and fruit. As with the vegetative process, these require carbohydrates, mainly sugars and starches, so that the plant is storing a large part of the carbohydrates it is making.

The growth and development may be likened to a pendulum swing. At one point the vegetative phase may be dominant, when the plant is in a vigorous growth stage, in another the reproductive phase may be dominant when the plant is cropping, and in the third there may be a point where neither phase dominates.

The dominance of the vegetative phase occurs usually when the plant is in the early stage of growth, there is a rapid rate of photosynthesis, the temperature is optimum for a rapid rate of cell division, there is an abundant supply of water and nutrients, and large amounts of carbohydrates combine with nitrogen compounds to form the protoplasm.

Plants should not be allowed to produce excessively strong vegetative vigour during the pre-fruiting period. Not only will the plants be difficult to train, but more importantly unsatisfactory setting and development of the first few fruit trusses will result in reduction in early yield and quality of the fruit.

Some growers frequently curb vegetative growth and improve setting of the first truss, by raising the strength of the nutrient solution. This restricts water uptake by the plant, but in a number of cases has resulted in a higher than average loss of marketable fruit by blossom-end rot. Some varieties, particularly late varieties, react quickly to very high nutrient concentrations by wilting. Other growers prefer a strength of CF30-32 and maintain this level for two or three weeks after plant-out of the seedlings. This tends to restrain root growth and through this, the vegetative development. Probably the best and safest way to balance vegetative growth with container grown tomatoes is to restrict the nitrogen supply.

When the reproductive phase is dominant, carbohydrate accumulation overshadows carbohydrate utilisation. The effect is that the plant would be stunted, the stem would be woody, the leaves would be moderately small and the length of the stem between two successive nodes would be short. Flowers and fruit would be evident, conducting tissues would be well developed and cell walls would be hard. Because the plant is stunted, the crop yield would be low. This condition of the plant may result from a number of conditions, including insufficient light, unsuitable temperature environment, insufficient water, inadequate or an unbalanced nutrient supply.

In a balanced state, where neither the vegetative nor reproductive phase dominates, the plant would be moderately vegetative and would carry a good yield of tomatoes. Flowering and fruiting would proceed simultaneously with the growth and development of leaves, stem and root system. This condition, characterised by moderate vigour of leaves, stem and roots, is the ideal situation sought by tomato growers and is achieved where there is plenty of light to ensure a high rate of photosynthesis, temperature is optimum and there is an adequate supply of water, nutrients and oxygen to the root system. These factors are known as the limiting factors in plant production.

The development or rate of growth of any of the processes is governed by the rate of the slowest factor. A few examples are as follows:

- The rate of development of the stem and leaves of a plant is dependent on the amount of nitrogen absorbed and assimilated with the sugars. If the supply of nitrogen in the nutrient solution is low, the production of new protoplasm is low and consequently the rate of development of the stems and leaves will be low. It would serve no purpose in adding extra phosphorus, iron, sulphur or any other element. It has to be nitrate.

- The yield of tomatoes will fall if the plant has been subjected to a period of water shortage. This will frequently happen with a container during hot weather, if the plant is fully grown and does not receive regular and frequent supply of water. Although light, temperature and other conditions may be suitable, the plant will only respond to an increase in water supply.

- Plants grown under a large tree or other place where there is a deficiency of light, will not produce a good yield even though all other factors are satisfactory. The plant will only respond to an increase in light level on the leaves.

Nitrogen plays such a major role in determining the growth characteristics, fruit yield and fruit quality, that some growers employ a stepped nitrogen schedule, starting at the seedling stage and continuing through to about development of the fourth or fifth cluster of flowers, at which stage the solution makeup remains unchanged until termination of the crop. Growers who adopt this practice also vary the potassium level at the same time to ensure the N/K ratio remains relatively constant.

A trial employing a nutrient solution with nitrogen 180 ppm and potassium 280 ppm, involved six Celebrity tomatoes grown in perlite/scoria/peat mixture in the ratio

50/30/20. The trial used 30 cm pots and a flow feed irrigating system with pulsed feed cycles of 10 minutes on, and two hours off, between 6 am and 6 pm.

Details of the step schedule are shown in *Table 6.1*. Total nitrogen concentration was initially set at 80 ppm and potassium at 120 ppm, when the seedling were planted in the pots. All other element levels in the solution were unaltered.

At the emergence of flowers on the second truss of all three plants, the nitrogen level was raised to 110 ppm and potassium to 160 ppm. Levels were increased to 140 ppm for nitrogen and 210 for potassium on appearance of the third cluster, and on the appearance of flowers on the fourth trusses, all element concentrations were the same as those in the nutrient solution feeding three plants in the control group. At this point, all six plants were being fed from a common nutrient supply source with concentration CF25-28 and pH 6.0-6.3.

In terms of growth characteristics, the three plants in the control group were much more vigorous, being about 20-30 cm taller after 5 weeks. However, there were fewer flowers on the first trusses. Because of the fast growth characteristic, the first trusses of the control group were much higher on the plant stems. The first truss of Pot 1 was at 75 cm, Pot 2 was at 60 cm and Pot 3 was at 80 cm, compared with 30 cm for Pot 4 plant, 36 cm for Pot 5 plant and 32 cm for Pot 6 plant.

Individual fruit weights and total yield details are outlined in *Tables 6.2* and *6.3* for fruit harvested during September/October.

The control group with full strength nutrient solution throughout the entire growing period, from seedling to trial termination, produced only 60 marketable tomatoes, compared to for plants fed with the stepped N and K increases. However, the combined yield and average weights of fruit for each of the three plants was greater.

It is of interest that fruit on first trusses of the control group plants numbered 13, compared with 17 for the other group. There was very little difference in sugar Brix level and pH of selected fruit from the two groups. The pH averaged 4.35 and sugar Brix level 5.8%.

The trial showed that for Celebrity variety, the stepped irrigation arrangement produced an average yield of 4.385 kg per plant, compared with 4.621 kg for the control group without any modification of the nutrient solution during the growing season.

However, some other varieties, particularly if grown in other seasons and in a different environment, may produce a reverse result to that obtained with Celebrity.

Element	Step 1 Seedling 1st cluster	Step 2 1st-2nd cluster	Step 3 2nd-3rd cluster	Step 4 3rd-4th cluster
N	80 ppm	110 ppm	140 ppm	180 ppm
K	120	160	210	280
P	60	60	60	60
Ca	120	120	120	120
Mg	36	36	36	36
S	120	120	120	120
Fe	2.4	2.4	2.4	2.4
B	0.36	0.36	0.36	0.36
Zn	0.04	0.04	0.04	0.04
Cu	0.02	0.02	0.02	0.02
Mn	0.36	0.36	0.36	0.36
Mo	0.01	0.01	0.01	0.01

Table 6.1 Nutrient schedule for various stages of growth.

Pot 1		Pot 2		Pot 3	
Truss no.	Fruit wt-g	Truss no.	Fruit wt-g	Truss no.	Fruit wt-g
1	202	1	265	1	185
	250		230		255
	195		195		270
	265		220		262
	193		205		202
	185	2	135		110
2	240		185	2	222
	235		262		156
	115		245		185
	190		80		242
	275	3	175	3	258
	202		225		270
3	155		263		220
	225		242		155
	195		195		95
	210	4	250	4	210
	120		215		156
	255		155		258
4	185		165		266
	220		225		90
	205				150
	135		85		110
	160				
Total yield 4.612 kg Average weight 23 fruit - 200 g		Total yield 4.217 kg Average weight 21 fruit - 200 g		Total yield 4.327 kg Average weight 22 fruit - 196 g	

Table 6.2 Yields from plants irrigated with nutrients solution with stepped increases in N and K.

Pot 1		Pot 2		Pot 3	
Truss no.	Fruit wt-g	Truss no.	Fruit wt-g	Truss no.	Fruit wt-g
1	266	1	220	1	258
	202		282		265
	274		205		277
	225		190		205
2	185		234	2	260
	265	2	187		244
	270		254		154
	190		266		274
	244		232		256
	212		195	3	250
3	244		133		166
	265	3	223		265
	278		185		276
	252		165		120
	214		225	4	210
4	144		242		255
	255	4	263		276
	265		272		269
	277		258		211
	230		268		
	115				
Total yield 4.872 kg Average weight 21 fruit - 232 g		Total yield 4.499 kg Average weight 20 fruit - 224 g		Total yield 4.491 kg Average weight 19 fruit - 236 g	

Table 6.3 Yields from plants irrigated with full strength nutrients solution from seedling stage.

Photosynthesis and light

We all need food if we are to survive and grow. We cannot make food, only plants can do that. All our food supply can be traced back to plant life. Even the meat we eat has its origin in plants, since animals feed on plants in order to grow.

Chlorophyll, a green pigment which gives a plant its green colour, absorbs light and working with carbon dioxide and water produces sugars. The process by which these sugars are produced is called photosynthesis. Some of the sugars are used as a source of energy and excess is stored in various parts of the plant.

The process is a series of complicated reactions requiring both dark and light periods. The process which takes place during a period of available light is a photochemical reaction, whilst that which takes place during a period of darkness is called the dark reaction and is basically an enzyme reaction. The plant requires a dark or rest period for the final conversion of carbon dioxide and water into sugars and the release of oxygen. Oxygen is also essential for our welfare, so that we are doubly dependent on plants. They provide us with food to eat and oxygen to breathe.

The extent or rate of photosynthesis performed by a plant depends on a number of factors. These include:

- The quality and intensity of the light.
- The temperature.
- The amount of oxygen and carbon dioxide.
- Water.
- Enzymes.
- Essential mineral elements.

Except for plants grown in heavy shade conditions, there is often sufficient sunlight incident on the leaves to saturate their photosynthetic capacity. Light is a form of electromagnetic radiation and can be separated into a spectrum resembling a rainbow. The colours range from violet through blue, green, yellow, orange to red, with the maximum intensity of emitted light lying in the orange part of the spectrum.

Researchers have found that the most effective light for photosynthesis is red and blue. These colours are strongly absorbed by chlorophyll. Investigations have shown that tomato plants grown in red or blue light produce a greater dry weight over the same period than plants grown in white light exposure. Some growers advocate that pots and containers should be painted red or blue to take advantage of this colour preference by chlorophyll. The wavelength or colour spectrum of light is generally altered by the colour of the reflective surface. A blue surface will reflect blue and a red surface will reflect red.

No overall good will result, however, if lights which are excessively strong in blue or red emissions are installed. If there is too much blue light and not enough red, the plant will be short and dark in colour. If on the other hand there is too much red and not enough blue light, the stem will be soft and thin with long spaces between the internodes. However, there is some evidence that short periods of strong red light will stimulate a flowering response.

Tomatoes grown in a greenhouse where shadecloth is used, will exhibit significant variations in yield with changes in light level below the optimum level. For the situation where shadecloth allows only 50% of the light, field trials indicate that the fruit yield will be about 20% lower compared with a no shadecloth environment. If the shadecloth admits only 25% of the light, the yield may drop to about 50%.

Care is needed in selecting shadecloth for the cultivation of tomatoes. Woven mesh can be relied upon to give the guaranteed amount of light transmission during most of the day, because the material strands are thin and flat. However, there are some problems. Because the strands are relatively thick, full transmission is only possible with the sun directly overhead. At other times during morning and afternoon, with the sun at an angle, the light gap between the strands is reduced, resulting in less light passing through the material. Shadecloth is available in colours of green and brown, plus white and black. Black has the longest life span as it does not deteriorate as rapidly as other colours. White shadecloth is used extensively in the cultivation of tomato seedlings. The direct sunlight is reduced substantially, but light which does pass through is dispersed, providing a high light level within the shade house. This is beneficial to seedling growth.

With deficient light intensity, the amount of energy available for the union of carbon dioxide and water is low. This results in a comparatively low rate of production of sugars. Thus growth, development and consequently yields, are lower. In winter periods when light levels are low, some growers cover the glasshouse floor with white plastic sheeting or polystyrene granules. These light reflecting materials increase the amount of light reaching the plants. Growers have reported crop yield gains of 25% compared with glasshouses with untreated floors.

Too much light on the leaves may also result in reduction of crop yield. There are at least two reasons for this. Firstly, the excess light increases the temperature of the leaves and the rate of absorption of water cannot keep up with the rate of transpiration. The diffusion of carbon dioxide in the leaves slows down, because the stomata close following loss of turgor by the guard cells. The overall result is that there is a low supply of sugars for growth and development. Secondly, the leaves of many varieties of tomato plants will turn yellowish-green, or even scorch with excess light. This reduces the amount of photosynthesis and is known as solarization.

Temperature and carbon dioxide also have an important influence on the rate of photosynthesis and hence on the rate of food production. Plants are able to use more light with warmer temperatures. However, there is an optimum temperature which varies with the species of plant.

Carbon dioxide exists in the atmosphere at a level of about 300 ppm and this is usually sufficient to meet plant needs. However, if plants are grown in a greenhouse with inadequate ventilation, the available carbon dioxide may be used up quickly by a thick growth of advanced plants. If the level falls below about 200 ppm, growth and fruit crop will be reduced. If the glasshouse cannot be ventilated due to cold weather etc, then the carbon dioxide should be made up by providing a carbon dioxide generator. Kerosene and other heaters also can produce carbon dioxide when the fuels are completely burned.

Respiration

Plants do a considerable amount of work and therefore require a supply of energy. Some of the work functions include lifting water and minerals from the root area to the leaves and other parts, lifting leaves, stem and fruit against gravity, growing roots, stems and leaves and forming new tissues in the growth and reproducing process.

The plant obtains its supply of energy from food substances - sugars. Through a series of complicated processes, the potential energy which is locked in the sugar is released. Oxygen is an essential element and in the process, waste products are formed and need disposal. This is all part of respiration. Basically, sugar is changed into pyrruvic acid, releasing energy. The pyrruvic acid is then processed in a citric acid cycle, releasing more energy and producing by-products of carbon dioxide and hydrogen.

Respiration takes place in two ways. One is external respiration, so called because it takes place outside the cells of the plant. Oxygen is taken from the surrounding atmosphere and passed through the leaf stomata. Carbon dioxide and water are passed out. Internal respiration consists of all the chemical processes which take place when the food substances are broken down and energy and waste products are released. It takes place inside the cells. In essence, respiration is the controlled release of energy.

Respiration goes on all the time. When the plant is making food during daylight hours by the process of photosynthesis, it needs energy to make that food, as well as for the normal functions of growing and reproducing. When it is dark and photosynthesis is at a standstill, respiration continues.

Photosynthesis and respiration are to a certain extent opposite processes as summarised by the following:

Photosynthesis	Respiration
Active only during daylight hours.	Active during daylight and dark periods.
Energy is stored.	Energy is released.
Carbon dioxide taken in and oxygen given out.	Oxygen taken in and carbon dioxide given out.
Occurs only in green parts of the plant	Occurs in all parts of the plant.
Plant substance is built up.	Plant substance is broken down.

The leaf

The primary function of the leaf is to manufacture the initial food substance. The surface of the leaf is covered by a layer of cells which form the epidermis or skin. This layer is very important in minimising water loss. It is covered with a waxy material which retards the evaporation of water.

The leaf contains sausage-shaped guard cells which contain chlorophyll for food manufacture. The walls of these cells vary in thickness, with the inner walls being next to openings called 'stomata' through which carbon dioxide, oxygen and water vapour diffuse.

As is the case with most other plant leaves, light directly influences the shape of the guard cells of a tomato plant and also the opening of the stomata. Under environmental conditions where there is adequate light and the plant has sufficient water, the guard cells are fully stretched and the stomata are usually open. When there is no light, the guard cells are limp and the stomata are closed.

An adequate supply of water in the medium is essential for the welfare of the plant. If the water supply is inadequate for the plant's need, the guard cells lose their turgidity and this results in a decrease in size of the stomata. This causes a twofold effect. The amount of water being lost by the plant through transpiration is reduced and the rate of diffusion of carbon dioxide from the atmosphere into the plant is decreased. The reduced intake of carbon dioxide decreases the rate of photosynthesis, which in turn results in a decrease in the rate of sugar manufacture. The growth slows and the crop yield falls.

The leaves of the tomato plant are alternate, compound, well developed, relatively large with broad leaflets in some varieties, and narrower leaflets with others. They possess glandular hairs which when handled roughly, liberate the odour and yellow-green stain characteristic of the tomato plant.

The veins of the leaf are in close contact with the manufacturing cells and conduct the food, hormones and vitamins from the cells, as well as conducting water and nutrients to the cells. A large tomato plant requires a considerable amount of water. In soil, a typical tall variety will require some 150 litres as a result of transpiration losses during its growing season. The transpiration rate of hydroponically grown plants is 10 to 30% higher than for soil grown plants, so we are looking at about 180 litres of water consumption. This transpiration function is important in the movement of inorganic salts and organic compounds through the plant and also for uptake of carbon dioxide and the liberation of oxygen. Factors which affect the rate of transpiration include temperature, relative humidity, air movement, light intensity and the concentration of the nutrient solution.

When tomatoes are grown in a glasshouse during summer, very high temperatures may be reached if ventilation is poor or cooling is not provided. This situation frequently results in curling of the leaf and is a warning to the grower to watch out for future blossom-end rot of the fruit. Leaf curl could also result from disease, but this is less likely in hydroponics because the fungi causing disease live in the soil.

In addition to being vital to the life of the plant, the leaf is important to the commercial hydroponicist, as leaf analysis is the best way to determine plant nutrient status and thus to obtain information on what changes, if any, may be required in the nutrient mixture. Analysis is performed on the petioles for the macronutrients and on the blades for the micronutrients.

The leaf plays an important role in the final colour of the tomato. Fruit protected by leaves are considerably cooler than those exposed to the sun on a hot day, and the colour development is correspondingly better.

The number of leaves that form on the plant before appearance of the first cluster of flowers varies with the cultivar, but the growing environmental conditions have an effect on all cultivars. Grosse Lisse, Burnley Bounty, Mighty Red and many others produce six to seven leaves before the first flower cluster forms and from that point, new clusters will form at intervals of three leaves.

The stem

The stem has several important functions. Besides serving as the connecting body between the roots and the leaves, it provides for growth in length, holds the leaves in the light, stores manufactured foods, particularly carbohydrates, and supports the flowers and the fruit.

The main features or components of the stem are the epidermis, the cortex, vascular bundles and pith. An important function of the epidermis is to keep absorbed water within the plant. It has a layer of waxlike material which greatly reduces the rate of transpiration of the stem.

Massive root system of Super Beefsteak plant being one of two grown in Ausperl Growbag of dimensions 750mm by 300mm by 100mm and drip fed at a rate of 300ml per minute for 10 minutes duration each hour between 6am and 6pm. Outside these hours feed cycles were at 3 hourly intervals. Of two fruit picked from the first truss of this plant one weighed 610g while the other weighed 590g.

The cortex contains, among other things, dead tissues which are thick-walled elongated fibres, which give strength and rigidity to the stem. By this means, it is able to hold the leaves in the light and to support the heavy crop of fruit.

The vascular bundle contains the transportation trunks, the primary phloem and the primary xylem. Because of their structure, they provide rigidity and strength to the stem. The function of the phloem is the transportation of manufactured compounds such as foods, vitamins and hormones, while the role of the xylem is the transportation of water and the dissolved nutrients from the roots up through the stem to the leaves.

The pith is made up of large, thin-walled cells and is located in the central part of the stem. It stores food, particularly starch the most important reserve carbohydrate.

A considerable force is required to pull water through the stem to the leaves of the plant.

Factors which allow this to be done include:

- Water molecules adhere to one another and when a molecule evaporates, it pulls on the one below and this in turn pulls on the one below that, and so on.
- Water adheres to most surfaces and by adhering to the walls of the xylem vessels, counters the effect of gravity.
- Water is evaporated from the foliage as a result of energy provided by the sun.
- The diameter of the xylem cells is very small, so reducing the force required to pull water through the vessels.

The root system

When tomatoes are grown in containers, the hydroponicist gets to know a lot about the behaviour of the root system of different varieties. The roots are hidden in the medium and the first sign that something has gone wrong will show up in the leaves. Sometimes a root problem may be slow in developing, but at other times collapse of the plant may take place within a few hours, particularly in hot weather. The root system has a number of functions:

- Absorbing water, oxygen and nutrients dissolved in the water.
- Providing for growth and extension.
- Providing an anchorage for the stem. This requires that primary and secondary roots grow larger, as more plant support is needed.
- Storing food which has been made in the leaves and which is not needed elsewhere in the plant.
- Giving off CO_2 (root respiration) and different organic waste products.

One of the many functions of the root system is to take up water from the medium. The necessary pull or suction comes mainly from the transpiration of water from leaves. As the water is lost by the leaves, the deficiency is signalled to the root system which is able to draw water in from the medium. The demands are easily met when there is plenty of water surrounding the roots, but as the nearby water is taken up, greater suction is necessary to draw in water from distant places.

If there is some water in the immediate vicinity of the root area, but insufficient to prevent a wilt stage during the heat of the day, the plant will generally recover by next morning. However, if there is not sufficient water to allow recovery during the night period, the plant will wilt permanently. It will shed leaves in an effort to survive, but will eventually die. Wilting will be a problem in container culture with a large plant, unless water is supplied regularly and in sufficient quantity to meet the plant needs. If supply is erratic, the plant will be stressed.

The suction exerted by the roots in drawing up water is measured in units called kilopascals (kPa). Suction can be considered as a negative pressure. A suction of less than 0.5 kPa is enough to take in the first water from a well saturated medium. If barely damp, the suction level will rise to perhaps 60-70 kPa. Fortunately, high pressures are not experienced in a well cared for hydroponics installation. For a 20 cm pot, the average suction would be of the order of 1 kPa for a well watered container. Sufficient water should be applied to ensure that roots do not dry beyond about 5 kPa for porous media.

The root system of a tomato seedling consists of a tap root and a subordinate system of lateral branches. If the seed is planted directly in the container, then the seedling will grow into a plant without any disruption to the tap root, except that the container will cause it to grow around the walls after it encounters the bottom. If however the seedling is grown in a punnet or similar type container, the tap root will most likely be destroyed during the transplant operation. The laterals will thicken up and become well developed, and adventitious roots will shoot out from the part of the stem below the surface of the medium. If grown in soil, these lateral and adventitious roots may reach out a metre or more, but in a pot they form a dense root growth which when removed from the pot, gives the appearance of a large sponge.

The root is made up of living tissues and like all living tissues is always respiring i.e. it is continuously taking in oxygen and giving off carbon dioxide. During the growing process a large tomato bush has a high rate of respiration and consequently needs plenty of oxygen. Failure of respiration due to lack of sufficient oxygen results in loss of energy and cessation of the functions of life.

The oxygen is available in the atmosphere and in water trapped in the medium. In soil culture, if the ground is kept friable, oxygen from the atmosphere is readily available because of the large surface area. The roots can therefore spread out just below the surface and also deep down in the soil. With some of the large plants, roots will extend out a metre or more from the stem. One of the major advantages of the small root system of plants grown hydroponically in containers, is that the saved metabolic energy can be diverted into the production of the fruit, with a potentially higher yield.

In pot culture, the surface area exposed to the atmosphere is very small. To compound the problem, the side and bottom of the pot are usually impervious, so that a plant is at a disadvantage compared with a soil grown plant in so far as access to the atmosphere is concerned. This is the main reason why pot roots are concentrated near the surface, rather than lower down, and also why a 30 cm pot has a larger growth and higher yield compared with a 20 cm pot, when both are operated under similar drain-through conditions. However, air cell pots or perforated air tubes in the pots will minimise this problem.

In addition to the thick roots which are easily seen when the plant is removed from the growing medium, there are myriads of root hairs. These are very fine and can usually only be seen by using a hand lens or a microscope. It is these root hairs which take in the water and the nutrients. The root hairs are tubular extensions of single root cells and develop from the embryonic zone or root tip. As the roots grow longer and the embryonic zones are extended, the root hairs die. In hot weather, if insufficient water is supplied to the container, the root hairs will be unable to take enough water to meet the plants immediate needs and wilting will probably occur. Large plants may use about 3.75 litres per day on a hot dry day.

Any environmental condition which is unfavourable to the root system, whether it be deficient oxygen, physical obstruction, temperature extremes etc, will affect the plant's performance. The roots will draw extra energy from the main body of the plant in an effort to overcome the adversity and this will show up as reduced fruit size and reduced growth. Overall stunting of a whole plant is frequently a sign of all nutrient disorders, but root stunting is characteristic of calcium deficiency, acidity, aluminium toxicity or copper toxicity. The shortened roots become thickened, the laterals become stubby and peg like, with the whole root system being discoloured brown or grey.

Reservoirs are extensively used in pot culture, particularly when the plants are at an advanced stage, so that there are not excessively large cycles in moisture content in the medium. Removal of the root system from the pot will clearly show the behaviour of the roots in areas of different moisture content. The roots reveal in their structure that the practice of alternating the water level between high and low is not one to which they are naturally adapted. It is essential, therefore, that this be taken into account in determining the amount of water held by the reservoir container. It will need to have a greater volume if the frequency of the nutrient supply cycle is low, compared with a more frequent supply cycle.

With a reservoir, an examination of the root structure will show that above the water level there is a mass of very fine root hairs which are adapted to absorb air-moisture, while below are the smooth thicker roots with their innumerable smooth lateral roots which grow into the nutrient solution at the bottom of the pot and even out through the drainage holes into the reservoir.

In summary, the criteria which constitute a good environment for the root system include:

- A supply of suitable nutrients and water.

- Protection of roots against high temperatures.

- Media that will allow some physical support for the plant.

- Removal of carbon dioxide from the root area.

- Freedom from toxic agents, root pathogens and pests.

- A microbial population to decompose dead roots, tissues and root secretions.

- A supply of oxygen to allow aerobic respiration, providing the energy for the root functions.

JET   **DRIP**   **FLOW**

Roots of three Mighty Red plants grown in 30cm diameter plastic pots and irrigated (L to R) by jet, drip and flow feed systems. Irrigation was carried out three times daily at periods of 10 minutes duration. There was not a great deal of difference between plants fed by jet and flow feed systems but they were both larger by weight measurements than the plant fed by the drip feed system

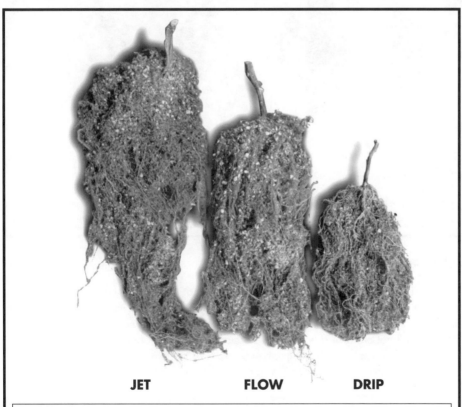

JET   **FLOW**   **DRIP**

Comparison of root systems of Ox Heart grown in separate polystyrene triangular containers 550mm sides and 250mm deep employing medium of perlite over a base of 30mm scoria. Nutrient feed was applied (L to R) as jet, flow and drip feed systems from a common supply tank and irrigated for 10 minute intervals three times daily.

20cm pot   **30cm pot**

Burnley Bounty root systems (L to R) from 20 and 30cm diameter plastic pots after 12 weeks, employing perlite over a base of 30mm gravel and fed from a common nutrient supply of concentration CF25 using a static feed system.

20cm pot   **30cm pot**

Root mats of Grosse Lisse at different growing periods in 20 and 30cm diameter plastic pots and fed with nutrient solution from a common source. Growing medium for all containers was perlite over a 30mm scoria base. For both the 2 month and the 4/3 month growing periods, the root mats in the 30cm pots were larger than those in the 20cm pots. (L to R) 2 mth & 4 mth (20 cm pot) and 2 mth & 3 mth (30 cm pot).

Aeration

It is considered by many experienced growers that aeration of the medium is just as important as the make-up of the nutrient solution. Without an adequate supply of oxygen around the root system, the minerals in the nutrient solution will not be fully taken up and the plant will not produce a good crop. Fortunately in a hydroponic installation, the roots do not have to compete with soil micro-organisms for the available oxygen.

Aeration of the plant root system has a major influence on both the vegetative and reproductive phases of plant growth. The air relations impact on the respiratory requirements of the roots, as needed for the continual growth of new root tissue and root hairs. The roots need oxygen to make new cells, to repair cells and to take up nutrients and water. If the oxygen supply is exhausted or is cut off, changes take place in the roots very quickly. The uptake of nutrients and water stops, alcohol and ethylene are produced in the roots,

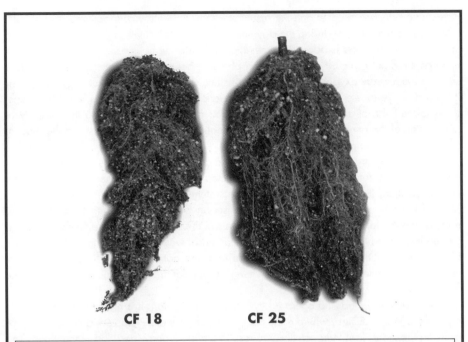

CF 18 **CF 25**

Growth of root mats of Sweet Bite cherry tomatoes grown in 22 litre lay-flat bags filled with 75% perlite/25% peat medium mixture and drip fed with nutrient solution CF18(L) and CF25(R). Each bag contained three plants. On total weight, the roots of the plants in bag fed by CF25 solution was approximately 15% greater than those in bag fed with CF18 solution.

Burnley Bounty **Ox Heart** **Mighty Red**

Comparison of root systems (L to R) of Burnley Bounty, Ox Heart and Mighty Red grown in 30cm diameter pots and fed with nutrient solution from a common source at concentration CF25. Medium for all pots was perlite over a 30mm base of gravel. Ox Heart produced the largest root mass followed by Burnley Bounty with Mighty Red being the smallest.

hormone production is upset and the results are seen through wilted tops and dying roots. It has been estimated that during the day time when growth activity is greatest, the demand for oxygen by the roots is about 10 times higher than at night time.

Since the plant gives off oxygen during photosynthesis, it might be assumed that there should be adequate oxygen to meet the plant's needs. There is, but not at all points where it is used. Oxygen is a gas and while freely available around the leaves, it seldom penetrates to the full root area. The aeration problems are basically related to the difficulty of penetration of the atmosphere to the roots, gaseous diffusion by the roots and the amount of oxygen in the water.

Plant growth characteristics are influenced to a considerable extent by the degree of aeration in the root zone. When trials are conducted with different methods of applying the nutrient solution, it soon becomes clear which systems or techniques provide the best aeration of the root zone. Without an adequate supply of air down amongst the roots, new roots cannot be formed and as a result minerals in the solution are not absorbed. Also, if the medium in the lower levels of the pot is starved of well aerated solution, the roots will be thick up near the surface and thin down near the bottom. This is frequently encountered with very fine sand, particularly where the pot depth is very much greater than the diameter.

With a well designed and operated hydroponic installation, it is not excess water that is a problem. Water culture, where roots are continually in water, is a very successful way of growing tomatoes. Problems are likely to result from inadequate aeration of the water. The roots must have direct access to oxygen in solution. This can be achieved by thoroughly aerating the water in a number of ways. Without aeration, very little oxygen would penetrate the water to reach the roots. The rate of diffusion through the water is only about 1/10,000 of the rate through air.

In addition to supplying oxygen to the roots, aeration plays another important role. Insufficient aeration results in the plant becoming chlorotic through lack of iron, as this element appears to be absorbed mainly through new roots whose growth is critically dependent on good aeration requirements. Aeration also appears to influence the amount of potassium absorbed. However, it is not clear whether this problem is directly due to poor oxygen supply, or whether it is related to the absorption of iron which acts as a carrier of potassium.

Aerated feed systems

In container culture of tomatoes, the watering can with a rose is one of the most effective means of ensuring a highly aerated solution is supplied to the root system. With a very porous medium, stale air, salts and gases will be flushed out with well aerated water. Unfortunately, the watering can technique is not acceptable where many plants are grown, so some other method needs to be adopted.

Generally, gravity feed using drip, flow, spray or jet feed systems have proved to be very successful and can be employed in semi-automatic or fully automatic modes. Trials have indicated that the flow, spray and jet feed arrangements give superior results compared with drip feed, with jet feed being the most productive.

A typical drip feed installation employs a small bore feeder tube, about 1 to 1fi mm diameter, to provide a slow rate of nutrient supply on a regular basis for a fixed time. The amount delivered depends on the pressure of the liquid in the supply line and the period of application. The main drawback with the arrangement is that the pot is moistened in only a relatively narrow vertical core area. Salts can often be seen on the outer perimeter of the core and the only contribution of oxygen via the solution is that which is already dissolved in the water and any that the droplet may absorb from the atmosphere.

In the flow feed system, the feed tube is much larger, being about 3 mm diameter, so that the solution is supplied in a stream rather than in droplets. In a typical system, the vertical tube from the main supply line is fitted with a three-way plastic fitting, so that the solution flows in opposite directions across the surface of the medium. The advantage of this is that the water stream covers a wide area of the medium surface and in flowing through the medium, gives greater water penetration.

The spray feed system produces slightly better results in crop yield and vegetative weight than the flow feed arrangement and considerably more than the drip feed method. There are two variations of the spray feed system, both of which give good results. One is to attach a plastic spray nozzle to the rim of the pot just above the medium, to give a spray arc of about 90 degrees to cover most of the medium surface. The other is to use a jet stream from a plastic fitting about 2 mm diameter, pushed into the main feeder and located about 180-200 mm above the surface of the medium. The stream is directed to a point near the pot centre, but 3 to 4 cm away from the plant stem.

The spray system, by virtue of its fine spray action through the air, absorbs oxygen and carries it down to the roots. The jet stream, provided the feed tank has a head of at least one metre, causes the water to strike the medium particles at high velocity, creating a mass of bubbles on the surface at the point of impact, and for several centimetres down into the root zone. By nature of its impact and dispersion, the solution covers a large area of a 30 cm pot.

In terms of vegetative growth, the jet stream feed gave the best results in a winter glasshouse trial of Burnley Bounty as shown *Figure 6.1*. For green weight of leaves, stems and roots in plants grown in 30 cm diameter pots, there was not much difference between the aerated systems, but there was a significant difference compared with an unaerated system. The unaerated set-up was basically an enclosed supply drum, with ball-valve feed to a reservoir in which the pots stood. The water in the reservoir was not exposed to the atmosphere.

In dry root weights, the differences were not as great as for total vegetative figures. With Burnley Bounty and Grosse Lisse varieties weights were much the same, but with the jet feed system, Burnley Bounty produced on average a much larger root system. Details of the root weights are shown in *Figure 6.2*.

In the overall crop yield results, there was not much variation in aggregate weight between the flow, spray and jet systems, using Burnley Bounty as samples. The drip feed yield was much lower than the other aerated systems, but well ahead of the static or unaerated system. The static feed yield average weight was little more than half the jet feed arrangement, as shown in *Figure 6.3*.

The trials clearly show the beneficial effect which vigorous aeration of the nutrient solution has on overall performance. The jet, spray, flow and drip feed systems used solution from a common tank, so that the oxygen levels in the liquid at the branch points were identical. Additional oxygen fed to the plants was determined by the particular system and the aeration it introduced. The drip feed would have added a small amount, the flow feed a little more, with spray and jet feeds being subjected to greater aeration.

The static feed system is widely used by hydroponicists, but a major disadvantage is that it is not very effective in providing a good supply of oxygen to the whole plant root system. The bottom of the container is saturated with the nutrient solution and as a result of capilliary action, moisture is also available at higher levels.

With a 30 cm diameter pot using perlite, moisture content near the top is 20 to 23% as shown in *Figure 6.4*. The new growth and root hairs are well down in the pot for a large plant, where they absorb water and the nutrients. However, oxygen is absorbed throughout the entire root system, including the mature roots near the top where root hairs are no longer active. Hence, the root system will absorb a greater amount of oxygen from those nutrient feed systems which use well aerated solutions, and which are fed at the top of the pot to allow the solution to pass through the entire root growing zone.

Meeting the oxygen demand

Researchers have found that a mature, indeterminate tomato plant root system, requires 320 ml of oxygen per hour for growth and development.

Under normal conditions, oxygen enters water by diffusion. The amount absorbed by the water depends upon a number of factors including temperature, barometric pressure, the partial oxygen pressure and the extent of the water surface area exposed to the atmosphere. The exposed surface area of water can be increased in several ways,

Root mats produced by four Grosse Lisse plants grown in four 75mm cube rockwool blocks tied together and irrigated by flow fed system in a 150mm plastic gully at 15 minute intervals three times daily. Grooves on sides of blocks accommodated plastic pipe sections as feed bypass to prevent solution backup in the gulley.

Pots fitted with perforated plastic pipe to improve aeration at the lower levels in the medium. The pipe drilled with 3mm holes extends to the bottom of the pot and allows the air to penetrate to all levels of the root zone. It also allows gases generated in the root zone to escape to the atmosphere. A trial with Grosse Lisse variety, gave yield increase of over 8% for plants enhanced with passive aeration using the pipes compared with plants grown without the pipes.

including:

- Feeding compressed air into the water using a fish pond pump or similar device.
- Agitating the water using moving blades or paddles.
- Spraying the return water into the storage tank using a rose.
- Causing return water to fall from sufficient height to create a splash condition.
- Using a small air-bleed in the suction side of a submersible pump, to feed a venturi located in the tank solution.

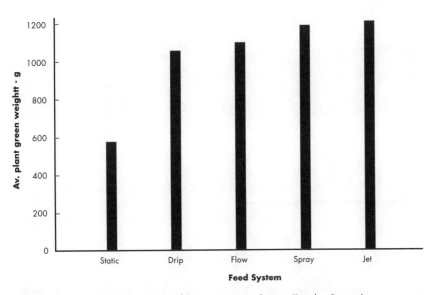

Figure 6.1 *Average plant weight of leaves, stem and roots (Burnley Bounty).*

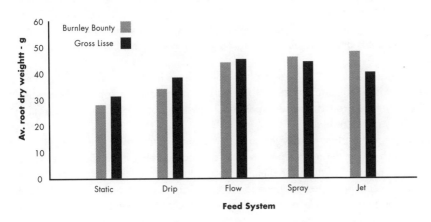

Figure 6.2 *Average root dry weight with different feed systems (Burnley Bounty & Grosse Lisse).*

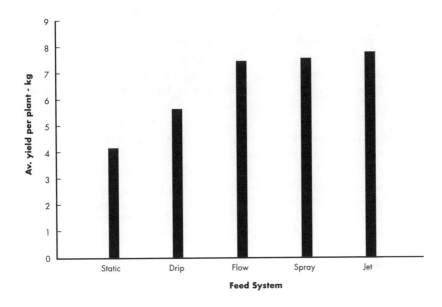

Figure 6.3 *Average crop yield per plant with different feed systems (Burnley Bounty).*

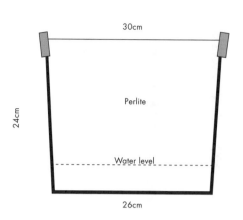

Height cm	Moisture % v/v
20	20
16	23
12	25
8	28
4	32
0	Saturation
-4	

30cm

24cm

Perlite

Water level

26cm

Figure 6.4 *Moisture profile for 30cm pot with perlite in reservoir.*

Other methods which have been used with varying degrees of success include the timed injection of oxygen bubbles and the use of chemicals which release oxygen at a slow rate.

Temperature is a very important factor in the amount of available oxygen. At a temperature of 0°C, the amount of dissolved oxygen in fresh water is typically 14 ppm, but if the temperature of the water rises to 30°C, the oxygen level would fall to about half i.e. 7 ppm. For an average temperature of 19°C, the amount of oxygen in water is about 9 ppm at 100% saturation. It is difficult to obtain 100% saturation conditions, but 95% is a practical possibility.

Over the range 10° to 30°C, a large plant will increase its demand for oxygen some 3 to 4 times, so it is essential to ensure that the nutrient temperature is kept low by storing it in tanks buried in the ground. Feeder pipes should, where possible, be sheltered from the sun, particularly if they're black.

The demand by the plant for oxygen falls significantly during the night time. Also, the demand is much lower during a typical winter day compared with a summer day, and pumps used to increase aeration for summer crops can be cut back to less frequent operation during winter. Some growers have found that night aeration or continuous air saturation is not good for high crop yield and they restrict forced aeration of the nutrient solution to the day time period. However, researchers in Japan have found that root pressure flow is low at night if the oxygen is deficient. The low root pressure flow reduces calcium transport to the fruit. The reduced calcium is an important factor in the occurrence of blossom-end rot of the fruit.

Reference has already been made to the dense root mat which builds up near the surface of the pot. This introduces a problem in that the greater the density of the root mat, the more difficult it is for gases which are produced around the root system, such as carbon dioxide and ethylene, to escape. This is a particular problem with plastic and similar materials which do allow air movement through the walls.

Air cell pots will help to reduce this problem by providing an improved root environment. Not only does it show up in improved crop yield, but the roots are more evenly distributed throughout the pot. Without slots, as used in normal pots, roots are usually very dense close to the wall surface. In addition to allowing gases to escape, the slots allow oxygen to enter from the atmosphere, so improving the aeration throughout the growing medium. Optimum yield with air cell pots is obtained when the slot area is approximately 10-20% of the total wall area. Above this, the medium dries out rapidly during hot summer months and irrigation cycles have to be increased so that a wilt condition does not develop.

Heat and temperature

Pots sizes are usually relatively small and respond quickly to changes in temperature. A number of factors influence the amount of heat absorbed or reflected by the pot. These include colour, insulation properties and the degree of light penetration. The most influential of these factors is colour. A light coloured pot will reflect heat, while a dark coloured one may absorb a considerable amount.

The majority of pots used by tomato growers are made from black plastic material which can become very hot if exposed to the sun on a hot day. This could result in damage to the root system. In a well developed plant, the roots will be concentrated on the inside surface of the pot and could be in contact with a hot surface. Heat from the walls is transferred to the medium. *Figure 6.5* shows temperature variations of perlite in a 30 cm diameter black pot during a typical summer day in Adelaide.

To minimise heat build-up problems, some growers use white plastic bags in lieu of black ones, or they paint black pots with white plastic paint. The cost of a white plastic pot is very much greater than for a black model and in addition, it does not have the same life when exposed to long periods of sunlight. The white outer surface of a painted black pot reduces the temperature significantly during summer, but observations of the cultivation of tomatoes in a glasshouse during winter did not show any significant difference in crop yields between black surface and white surface containers.

A plant takes advantage of the daytime and night time periods during a given 24 hour period, to perform two important functions in its growth and development. During the daytime it makes initial foods and related substances and during the night period it makes new cells and elongates them. The optimum daytime temperature for this to happen is in the range 23°C to 27°C and for night time, the range is 15°C to 18°C. These temperatures, combined with adequate light, good nutrition, suitable water and carbon dioxide, are conducive to the manufacture and accumulation of adequate supplies of carbohydrates necessary for maximum set and production of good quality marketable fruit.

Control of the night-time temperature is particularly important and is the main reason why many growers find that investment in a glasshouse or polyhouse is a profitable move. Proper temperature control has a marked effect on the yield. It is common practice to maintain the night-time temperature within the upper half of the optimum range when the plants are in the vigorous stage, and within the lower half of the optimum range when plants are fruiting.

The high cost of heating a glasshouse during the cold winter nights, has led some growers to experiment with a combination of lowered night air temperatures and nutrient solution heating, during the plant-out and early establishment stage. However, trials have not been encouraging. Solution temperatures and night-time atmospheric temperatures influence crop yields independently. Warming of the root zone between 20°C and 30°C does not compensate fully for the delayed fruiting of plants grown under conditions where the night-time air temperatures are low.

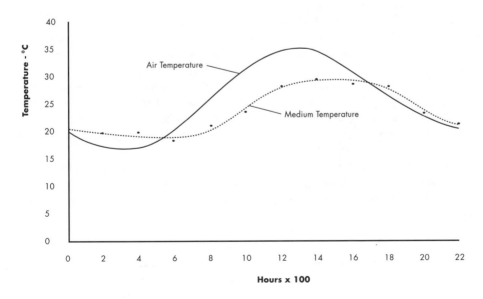

Figure 6.5 Pot medium temperature variations.

Wide fluctuations in temperature are detrimental to tomatoes. During a warm day, plants manufacture a high amount of carbohydrate which is available to be used up at night as food, to provide energy for growth, if the temperature is suitable. However, when the night-time temperature is low, the plant's rate of growth will also be low and the plant cannot make use of all the surplus food produced during the day. This results in the plant becoming stunted, fruit being small in size, frequent cracking of skins and the development of curled leaves which are slow to unfold.

Temperature also influences the sweetness of a tomato. High temperatures do not result in sweet fruit. Sugar is converted to starch, starch is converted to sugar and sugar is converted to carbon dioxide and water. All these reactions are decreased with drop in temperature, but the decrease is not uniform. Conversion of starch to sugar is higher than the others, so that sugar is accumulated and remains at a high level. With high temperatures, the conversion of sugar to carbon dioxide and water is greater than the other reactions, resulting in a low level of sugar.

During the summer growing period, the problem is one of getting rid of heat, or controlling the growing environment, so that the plant is not put under excessive stress. Factors which will minimise heat related problems include provisioning of shadecloth, white washing glass or providing a blower system to create a gentle movement of air over the leaves, keeping the nutrient solution and the storage tank out of direct sunlight, providing a fog or mist system where glass or polythene is used, increasing the number of watering cycles during the hottest periods and leaving healthy leaves on plants to shelter fruit and stems.

Seeds and seedlings

Although healthy seeds may give the appearance of being dead, they are in a dormant stage. The seeds are complete embryos waiting to become active plants. They are protected from environmental damage, diseases and predators by a hard protective coating and a low rate of metabolism. Some seeds can be eaten by birds and animals and pass through the digestive system without any harm to their reproductive process.

The germination process is started by water. The water softens the protective coating and is absorbed by the endosperm inside. The endosperm expands, bursts the coating and allows the embryo to grow. The water also activates enzymes in the embryo. If the temperature is right, the enzymes accelerate the rate of metabolic activity in the embryo and plant life begins.

Commercially produced tomato seeds are relatively cheap and the grower can have a high level of confidence that the seeds will produce tomatoes that are true to type, have a high germination potential, produce vigorous seedlings that are free of seed-carried diseases, and are free of weed seeds.

Many home growers, flushed with the success of a particular plant, often have visions of keeping seeds from the treasured tomato in the hope of repeating the performance with their own seeds the following season. Unfortunately they are frequently disappointed with the results.

There are a number of factors to be taken into account if home saved seeds are to produce satisfactory results. Even though the tomato is a so-called self pollinated plant, some cross pollination is likely to occur with other varieties that may be grown close by. Bees moving from garden to garden may also cause cross pollination. This does not promote uniformity in plant performance.

Seeds from exceptionally good single plants of some varieties, may be saved separately with good chances of retaining the characteristics of that single plant. In self pollinated crops, seeds produced in each fruit will theoretically contain identical genetic information, so that seeds saved from different tomatoes from the same plant will produce identical offspring, even if the tomatoes on the selected plant look different. It is not advisable for the home gardener to keep the seeds of hybrid varieties, expecting to obtain a repeat performance of a good yield. The seeds will segregate and most probably would produce less desirable types. Hybrid seeds are specially bred to produce a desired result from the first generation of the seed. Frequently, second or third generation seeds will not reproduce plants true to type.

Seed packets containing hybrid seeds are usually designated 'F1 Hybrid'. This stands for "first filial" and is the product of crossing two genetically different parent plants, both of which have been highly inbred in order to concentrate some desired characteristics. The first generation F1 of a good cross is usually vigorous and frequently superior to its parents, but succeeding generations tend to revert to the highly inbred parents. Some hybrid seeds are sterile.

If the decision is made to save seed from a particular variety the fruit should be chosen from healthy bushes which exhibit vigorous leaf growth and bear a good crop of uniform well shaped fruit. The fruit should be left on the plant until the fully ripe stage, but picked before it becomes over ripe and starts to decay. If the seed is to be saved from only a few tomatoes, the centre is scraped out with a small spoon, washed in a sieve under running water and then put out to dry in a warm place. When thoroughly dry, the seeds can be stored in a small paper envelope. Seeds should not be saved from diseased plants or those

Cherry tomatoes growing in Ausperl Grow Bags raised above the floor level on steel tubular frames and planted with density of two plants per 25 litre perlite filled bag. The design of the frame allowed the bottom section of the plant to be lowered on to the frame in order to maintain the top part of the stem to a reasonable height for harvesting purposes.

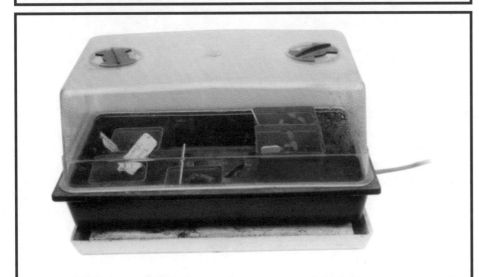

Miniplant propagator providing a controlled environment in which to raise tomato seedlings. The unit consists of a clear lighweight cover with two adjustable vents, growing pots and a specially designed tray unit with drainage holes. A heating pad allows the system to be heated as required.

with abnormal growth characteristics.

Another method preferred by many growers is to squeeze the seed from several selected tomatoes into a cup or plastic container, add some water and let the mixture ferment at room temperature for several days, stirring a couple of times a day. After a few days, the good seeds will fall to the bottom of the container and the bad seeds and pulp will float to the top and can be washed away. The seeds are then dried thoroughly, labelled and stored. The fermentation process is said to kill some seed borne diseases.

For the grower who wishes to go about the process of seed extraction in a more professional manner, the techniques have been well documented in many Department of Agriculture publications. They involve the use of a number of chemicals and heat treatment of the seed in order to control bacterial canker, some fungus diseases and tobacco mosaic virus. There are currently 27 seedborne diseases known to be well established in tomatoes in Australia.

Disease organisms can be carried externally on the seed coat or internally in the seed. Fungicidal dusts can be used to give a high level of control on the external contaminants, but they are useless in dealing with internally borne pathogens. These require heat or soak treatment.

Proper storage of seed is important if good results are to be achieved. While seeds are in a storage condition, respiration continues - even though at a slow rate. The environment has a major influence on the storage life of the seed. If the humidity is high, moisture is absorbed and this in combination with the stored food, forms soluble food. The result is an increase in the respiration rate and a decrease in the storage life. As a rough guide, the life of a seed may be doubled by either reducing the seed moisture by 10%, or reducing storage temperature by 5%.

Commercially available seeds are usually sold in sealed metalized packets to ensure a long storage life. The packets are typically made of aluminium foil laminated to polythene or mylar. An airtight tin or dark glass jar is a satisfactory alternative for the home gardener. However, when sealing seed in a tin or jar, it is best done when the weather is cold and very dry. If sealed on a hot day with high humidity, the humidity of the entrapped air will rise when the temperature falls, causing potential harm to the seeds. Some gardeners place the seeds in a small paper envelope and enclose it in an air tight container with a quantity of silica gel. Silica gel has the ability to absorb any entrapped moisture. Optimum seed moisture is about 5%.

Tomato seeds are generally reliable for about five years, if properly stored. If stored in a refrigerator at 0° to 5°C, the life is greatly increased.

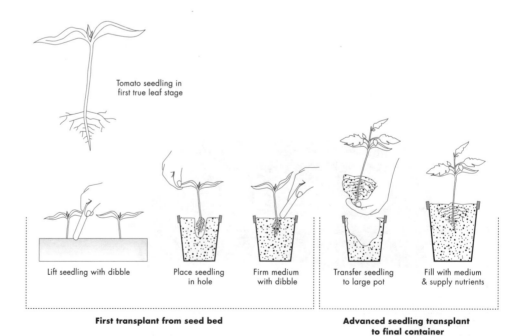

Tomato seedling in first true leaf stage

Lift seedling with dibble

Place seedling in hole

Firm medium with dibble

Transfer seedling to large pot

Fill with medium & supply nutrients

First transplant from seed bed

Advanced seedling transplant to final container

Figure 6.6 Seedling transplant procedure.

Seeds can be placed directly in the container in which the plants will spend their productive lives, but this practice is wasteful of space in the early stages. The usual procedure is to raise seedlings in seed trays or other containers and transplant the seedlings into their pots when they have reached a suitable size. Tomato seeds are lightweight and average about 300 seeds to the gram.

A wide range of containers are available in which to germinate seeds and raise the seedlings, but those preferred by many small scale growers include flexible PVC trays, jiffy or peat pots, oasis foam blocks, small plastic pots and rockwool cubes. The most popular container, where several dozen or more plants are required, is the multi-cell system. This uses lightweight trays with eight or ten cells of an inverted pyramid shape. The arrangement allows easy removal of the plants and a hole in the base of each cell allows root pruning and encouragement of lateral root development.

The advantage of cell or single pot cultivation is that transplant shock is almost eliminated. When properly handled, individually grown seedlings can be transplanted without injury and almost 100% survival can be obtained.

Temperature control is important in seed germination. The optimum germination temperature is 24°C. Temperatures outside the range 10°C to 30°C will result in considerable failure. Seeds are covered with a mass of fine hairs and under favourable conditions will germinate in five to ten days, depending on temperature. At 25°C the average time for seeds to emerge is six days, but at 10°C which is the bottom of the germination range, it takes about 43 days for seedlings to appear. Only water should be applied until the seeds germinate. High concentration of nutrients can inhibit germination.

A point of interest to commercial growers is that from a harvest timing aspect, there is very little difference between early and late sowings. Although an early sowing may take 20 to 25 days for plants to emerge and a later sowing only seven days, the difference in time which elapses from emergence to harvest is usually only a few days.

On transplant, best results are obtained with seedlings using a half strength nutrient solution. Even quarter strength is preferred with some varieties. Magnifico, Roma and

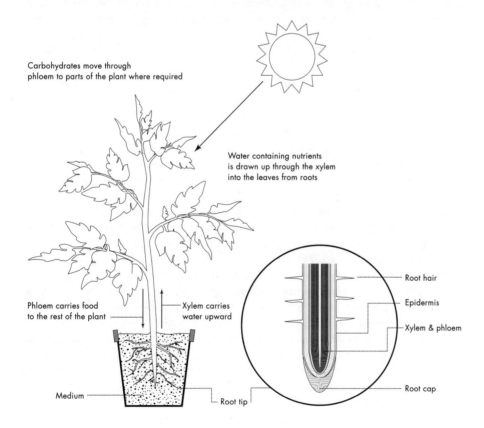

Carbohydrates move through phloem to parts of the plant where required

Water containing nutrients is drawn up through the xylem into the leaves from roots

Phloem carries food to the rest of the plant

Xylem carries water upward

Medium

Root tip

Root hair

Epidermis

Xylem & phloem

Root cap

Figure 6.7 Seedling transportation system.

Longkeeper are some varieties which prefer low strength mixture during the first ten days after breaking surface. If the strength is too high for these and some others, there will be leaf tip burn. Grosse Lisse and Jubilee have a tendency to run to lanky growth unless the nitrogen level is kept low for the first two weeks. The level should be no greater than 60 ppm.

Whatever method is used to grow seedlings, great care needs to be exercised during the transplant phase. Tomato plants, if well conditioned, can take a fair amount of rough treatment but retardation of growth and development will occur to some degree. The smaller the extent of disturbance to the root system, the less the effect. That is why jiffy pots and rockwool cubes are so popular where small numbers of seedlings are involved. when the seedling is growing, most of the water loss takes place through the leaves, but if the root hair system is extensively damaged in the transplant operation, the water being drawn up to the leaves from the root system will be interrupted or severely restricted. The result is that the leaf guard cells lose turgor, the stomata partially or completely close, the rate of diffusion of carbon dioxide into the leaves is reduced and the production of primary food is reduced. The growth and development will be reduced until the root system begins to function in the uptake of liquid, to the same degree as before the transplant operation. If the weather is hot, the seedling may wilt - the extent depending on the severity and duration of the water deficit within the plant. The larger the seedling and the greater the damage to the root system, the longer it will take to recover.

Figure 6.6 illustrates typical transplant procedure. At first leaf stage, the plant is transplanted into a small pot and when at an advanced stage of about 15-20 cm height, is transferred to its permanent growing container. *Figure 6.7* shows the food and nutrient transportation systems of a seedling when fully established.

Pruning and supporting

Growers have various view points with regard to the pruning of shoots and leaves of tomato plants. One aim is to increase the size of the fruit, but this is often done at the expense of the total weight of the crop. Another aim of pruning is to reduce the size of the vigorous varieties, making it easier to tie them to stakes and to make spraying more effective. Some varieties will grow to enormous size if well fed and left unpruned. One vine in England is reported to have grown to a height of over 6 metres and to have produced a crop of some 18 kg.

The requirement for supporting the plant by stake, trellis, frame or other means will be influenced by the growth pattern of the particular variety. All tomato varieties belong to two growth classifications. They are determinate or indeterminate, although some growers also refer to a third classification called semideterminate. Within the determinate and indeterminate classifications are to be found dwarf and miniature varieties.

Determinate varieties have fairly short stems ending in a flower cluster. With a healthy plant, there are fewer than three leaves between the flower clusters. They are bushy plants and do not require staking, although a strong wire frame raised about 15 cm above the surface of the medium will prevent fruit rotting and will also minimise the spread of disease, particularly fungi types. These varieties make growth quickly and then stop growing while the fruit set and ripen. Experience has shown that if these bushes are pruned, the crop yield will be considerably reduced. For pot cultivation, they tend to take up a lot of floor or ground area and therefore are not as popular as indeterminates with many growers. Another factor is that the plant's entire production of tomatoes comes to an end over a very short period - sometimes within a few days. Many householders prefer the crop to be spread over a long period but 'bottlers' may have other views.

Indeterminate varieties have stems which continually increase in length and can be heavily pruned. Their form is such that there is a flower cluster followed by three leaves, and so on as the plant continues in growth. They are ideal for staking, attaching to a frame or for enclosing within a circular wire cage, where it is desired to have maximum vertical growth and minimum horizontal spread.

Tall varieties are usually subjected to a fair amount of stem pruning when grown in pots. Unless the plant is grown against a large support, such as a wire trellis, it is usual practice to prune to a single stem or sometimes to a double stem. Side shoots are frequently pruned out once a week, so that the shoots are removed before they become woody. When the stem has reached its maximum support point, the top may be cut off. Under a favourable environment, these varieties will grow in containers and develop fruit for a period of two years and sometimes longer. This is one of the reasons why they are so popular with growers who have a small glasshouse.

In single stem pruning, all side shoots are cut away from the main stem. The side shoots are the suckers which grow in the axils, the angle between the leaf stalk and its parent stem. In double stem pruning, all suckers except the first sucker just below the first flower cluster are removed. This first sucker is allowed to develop into a second stem. All subsequent suckers are removed from both stems. *Figure 6.8* illustrates sucker removal procedure.

A disadvantage of single stem pruning is that the leaf growth may not be sufficient to shield the fruit from the direct rays of the hot sun, resulting in sunscald and a lower marketable yield. Also, with some varieties fruit cracking is more prevalent, compared with two stem or multiple stem growth. Better Boy and Gardeners Delight are varieties which have this problem.

If the main growing point is cut off, the supply of available nitrogen to other parts of the plant will be increased. This results in promotion of cell making and the utilization of carbohydrates The vegetative phase will therefore be enhanced and the reproductive phase retarded. The stimulation of the vegetative phase at the expense of producing more fruit, might not be what the grower would prefer. However, if the plant has been in production for a long time and the stem is showing signs of old age, cutting off the growing point will in many cases help to promote vigour and rejuvenation. Some trials with Moon Shot variety indicated that with a vigorous pruning program at the end of the crop, a second year crop produced fruit much larger than the first year crop, but with a total weight only two

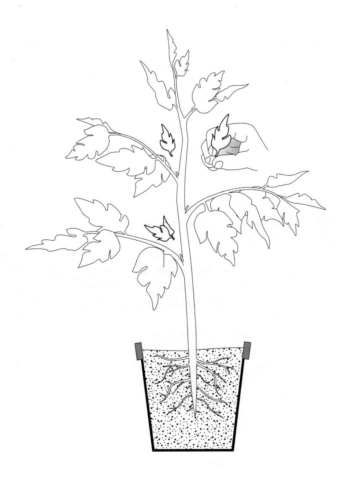

Figure 6.8 Pinch out suckers to allow only one or two main stems with indeterminate tomato plants.

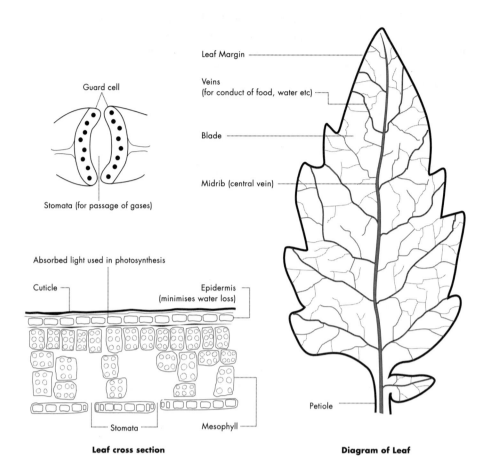

Guard cell

Stomata (for passage of gases)

Leaf Margin

Veins
(for conduct of food, water etc)

Blade

Midrib (central vein)

Absorbed light used in photosynthesis

Cuticle

Epidermis
(minimises water loss)

Stomata

Mesophyll

Petiole

Leaf cross section

Diagram of Leaf

Figure 6.9 *Various parts of a leaf.*

thirds that of the first year crop yield.

Some growers cut off more than just the growing point. They cut off growth so that only a single truss is left on the plant. The first truss usually produces the greatest yield of all trusses and tomatoes ripen before those higher up on the stem. The cut off point varies with growers, but those who practice this technique usually leave at least three healthy leaves above the truss.

A major advantage of such practice is that tomatoes can be grown for a whole year cycle on a quick follow through basis, provided they are protected from frost and cold winds. The most widely practiced stopping procedure with hydroponicists, is to let the plant grow to the stage where it produces five or six trusses and then lop off the growing point. The first truss will frequently produce the greatest number of fruit, with the numbers decreasing for other trusses up the stem. Many growers pick off some fruit so that no one truss carries more than 8 tomatoes. It is not unusual for some plants to have up to 20 flowers on a truss, with 90% fruit formation.

Dwarf tomato plants are in the main self supporting and are very popular for pot cultivation. Many people with only small balconies or restricted growing areas find these varieties ideal. They are determinates and are characterised by a strong central stem, which provides good support for branches and the fruit. However, as the medium used in hydroponics does not generally provide a secure anchorage for the roots, it is good practice to enclose the bush in a wire cage and to tie the cage to the rim of the pot.

The miniature varieties are also determinates, but are mainly grown as ornamentals rather than for supply of fruit. As they typically grow to a height of 20 to 25 cm, they can be successfully grown in a 20 cm diameter pot. Pruning is generally not necessary for these or the dwarf varieties.

Excessive pruning of leaves can be disastrous if taken to the extreme. Leaves are vital to the life of the plant. *Figure 6.9* illustrates various parts of a tomato plant leaf and some of their important functions.

Summarising, the advantages and disadvantages of pruning are:

Advantages

- Plants are easier to dust or spray.
- Plants may be grown closer together.
- Less horizontal space is required if plants are staked.
- Greater air movement around fruit and stem.
- Rate of ripening of fruit is not effected.
- Facilitates harvesting.
- Size of fruit more uniform.

Disadvantages

- Total yield is reduced, for some varieties.
- Removal of leaves and stem leader results in decreased food production.
- Takes time.
- Fruit may be subject to sunscald.
- Plants usually have to be supported, resulting in increased costs for stakes and twine.
- Disease may enter at the cut.

When supporting the stem, care must be taken in the selection of the tie material. Hard plastic string is not suitable, as it will injure the stem and allow disease to enter. It may also damage the phloem. The phloem is close to the outer portion of the stem and carries sugar produced by the leaves, hormones, other growth regulators and products of metabolism to those parts of the plant requiring such materials. If the phloem is damaged by a cord or tie, the new growth of the plant may survive reasonably well, but certain older parts and fruit dependent on the phloem vessels could suffer from a reduction of critical sugars and other life-supporting substances. Soft, thick twine or 15 mm wide cotton tape is suitable, but ties should be sufficiently loose to allow for later increase in diameter of the stem. It is good practice to tie the stem so that the fruits are away from the stem, so that they do not rub against the stake or support. Velcro is another suitable material.

Attention must also be given to support of the fruit. The weight exerted on the stem by a truss of large fruit can be very great. The record books indicate that single tomatoes have reached weights up to 1.45 kg and the weight of a truss of fruit has reached 9.17 kg. Not all gardeners can expect to achieve results like that, but it does highlight the need to pay attention to staking and fruit supporting methods.

Wooden stakes about 25 mm square are probably the most widely used stakes for supporting tomato plants. For soil culture, one stake driven into the soil near the plant is usually sufficient. However, in hydroponic pot culture, securing the stake is not so simple. If the pot is placed on soil it is not a major problem, as the stake can be driven into the soil close to the pot. An alternative is to use three stakes spaced around the pot at 120 degree intervals, tied together at the top, and each stake tied to the rim of the plastic pot by tape or wire. Stakes should be about 1.8 m long for indeterminate varieties.

Another widely employed method to support the plant is the use of wire cylinders. They are easily made and the bottom of the cylinder can be tied to the inside lip of the plastic pot, to keep it firmly in position. No tying of the stem is necessary and it is usually convenient to let two or three stems grow. About one metre is the maximum height for a wire cylinder, otherwise a gust of wind may blow the pot over. If the pot stands against a wall, there is little restriction as far as height is concerned, provided it can be secured to the wall.

The mesh size of a wire cylinder should be large enough to allow the passage of a hand and the removal of the fruit. If the cylinders are not in continuous use, they can be stored in a flat package by simply undoing the joining ties and straightening out the wire.

A major advantage of the wire cylinder is that each pot can be made into a miniature polyhouse during cold weather, by slipping a clear plastic bag over the cylinder. Suitable bags can be purchased from supermarkets, or easily made from thin clear plastic sheeting. The A-frame is a popular support for growing tomatoes in containers. A cord is dropped from the top of the frame and tied either to the tomato stem, or to a bottom rail just above the pot. The advantage of using two rails is that the stem is not subjected to the tensile pull of the cord when the plant is heavily laden with fruit. During movement of the plant with harvesting or wind, the stem may become bruised or cut if the bottom rail is not used.

The height of the A-frame is usually fixed at a level where harvesting of fruit can be carried out without the need for the picker to stand on a ladder etc. Although some growers cut the stem off when it reaches the top of the A-frame, others maintain the plant by removal of the lower leaves, leaning and layering the stem at bi-weekly intervals.

Included in commercially available systems designed specifically to support plants, is the Plant Spool made by Australian company Sydage Pty Ltd. Since one spool is employed per plant, it enables a flexible layout in locating the position of the growing containers. The system provides effective plant support, has simple adjustment, has no obstruction at ground level, is reusable, provides easy twine length adjustment, is supplied pre-wound with 10 m of strong polypropylene twine, and the spool is made of UV stabilized thermo-plastic.

An alternative growing technique is to raise the pot above the floor and allow the bush to hang down. This does away with the need for stakes, but introduces another factor i.e. a means of holding the pot about 1.2 m above the floor. Growers in the USA find this method to be particularly suitable for greenhouse cultivation during the cooler months. It is suitable for both determinate and indeterminate varieties.

The pots are normally hung from beams or wires at suitable heights above the floor and drip fed. A continuous drip or two hour cycle feed, with about 50 ml of solution going to waste, has been found to be satisfactory. In some installations, two or three plants occupied a single 30 cm pot, but the amount of marketable fruit was not as high as ground supported installations, due to the high proportion of blotchy fruit. Also, yields seldom exceeded 5 kg per pot. Some growers who have participated in this system, are of the opinion that the plant foliage hanging downwards from the container is not conducive to the production of high yields of marketable fruit.

Other problems encountered by growers include excessive heating of the medium, because of its close proximity to the glasshouse roof. The heavy weight of the fruit tends to crush the stem on the pot lip and in some cases the weight of the fruit pulled the root system out of the container.

In addition to the vertical method of plant training, there is the layering method. One commercial grower estimated yield was greater by 17% for layering, but sunscald was about 10% higher. Some cherry tomatoes will grow to 12m in length.

Greenhouse cultivation

To produce a quality tomato, it is necessary to have a quality environment. Greenhouses are widely employed to create a favourable environment for growing tomatoes, both with soil and soilless cultivation techniques. Because they are a high capital expenditure and maintenance costs are an ongoing expense, it is natural that the grower will endeavour to grow the maximum number of plants that will provide the greatest financial return.

A properly planned layout is essential to make the best possible use of the available space, but at the same time ensuring the environment for the growing plants is conducive to a high crop yield of marketable fruit.

If plant density is too high, typically above four plants per square metre for fully grown indeterminate varieties, the effect may result in:

• Increase in plant height, size and number of leaves, and leaf disease transfer.

• Decrease in number of trusses, flowers and fruit.

• Decrease in average weight of individual tomatoes.

• Decrease in number of marketable fruit.

• Decrease in yield per plant above a certain density. However, trials with some varieties indicated that when expressed on a per metre basis, there were various increases in yield levels with plant density, up to a certain point.

Tomato yields for soil grown crops in greenhouses vary widely, but are usually in the range 25 to 40 kg per square metre. However, some overseas growers report yields of up to 55 kg per square metre. In container cultivation, not a great deal of data is available, but one grower using 30 cm pots with Burnley Bounty and Grosse Lisse varieties produced yields between 35 kg and 45 kg per square meter. The lower figure was for a winter crop.

The management of a greenhouse crop involves a number of factors, including control of the environment, container layout, plant supporting arrangement, nutrient feed system, treatment of water supply, if from a local source, health of the plants, mechanical pollination assistance, pruning and harvesting of the crop.

The on-site cost of installing a typical multispan tunnel, employing a single skin polythene design covering about 30 m square floor space, is of the order of $50 per square metre, including costs associated with automatically controlled natural ventilation equipment.

A major factor influencing the plant density in a greenhouse, is ventilation. A well designed greenhouse enabling good natural ventilation, will allow high plant density, with a well designed layout plan. Ventilation requirements for the purpose of maintaining fresh air movement and prevention of relative humidity buildup are usually low, involving only a few air changes per hour.

However, the high temperature increase within a glasshouse which was not designed to give adequate natural ventilation during periods of high solar radiation, may make it highly desirable for forced ventilation to be applied. To keep temperature to an acceptable level, this may require about 60 air changes an hour, or even more, in some situations. Fan sizes are frequently 1.2 m in diameter and are costly to install and operate.

The installation of large fans placed at ground level can have a bearing on the number of plants which can be placed near the immediate fan area. Some growers have installed fans at a height such that the air stream is above the top of the plants.

In colder climates, heating of the air, nutrient solution or the base area on which the containers are located, may be required. In many cases, heating will determine the profitability of the enterprise.

A wide range of materials have been used over the years to vary light, humidity and temperature conditions within the greenhouse. New technology in film construction has resulted in the production of coextruded films, improved optical properties, anti-droplet materials and films incorporating light modification features. Some films have properties comparable with glass, in terms of optical properties, and offer extremely long life spans.

A multiplicity of woven or cloth type materials for use inside or outside the greenhouse, are available to suit a wide range of specifications. Each material has particular physical, optical, thermal and life characteristics and advice of an expert in the field is necessary to ensure the best material is chosen, to meet the particular needs of the grower and the crop under cultivation.

In the warmer areas of Australia, the grower's greatest need is usually to provide a better daytime environment, through solar radiation modification, but in the cooler areas the main function of the screen may be to provide better heat retention within the greenhouse. Screen materials are available to assist in meeting both these requirements.

Screens can be either manually or automatically controlled. Proper control of screen operation is important and good management will have an important bearing on ultimate crop yield. Computer control will in most cases provide the optimal plant growth conditions, by monitoring temperature, light levels and relative humidity and, if necessary, initiating steps for appropriate action to be taken.

A number of tomato growers have used green coloured woven shadecloth in their greenhouses in recent years, but it was felt amongst some of the growers that plant growth and crop yield were below those previously produced, when light coloured materials were used. Subsequent investigations led to the conclusion that the light spectrum was changed significantly. Light in some bands of the spectrum was absorbed by the green coloured shadecloth and was not available for growth and development of the plant. One of the growers reported that average yields fell from 6.2 kg to 5.7 kg per plant, for plants cut off at the fifth truss point. Another who grew cherry tomatoes, reported that the number of punnets decreased by about 5%, after changing over from unbleached calico shadecloth. He found that whilst the unbleached calico produced good results, it suffered from algae problems from being wet for long periods, due to water droplets falling on the material and being absorbed by it.

Included among the many materials available today, is a series of products produced by Ludvig Svensson of Sweden and known as LS Screens. The aluminised polyester LS Screens combine a high energy saving value of up to 65% with long life, a flexible structure and a shading effect - very useful during bright summer days. Trials employing LS10, LS11 and LS16 designs with a tomato crop resulted in a mean production increase with four cultivars, of 41% with L516, 35% with LS11 and 7% with LS10. The LS10, a non-aluminised screen, had less effect than the other two aluminised screens.

One of the most popular screens used by tomato growers is ULS15, which provides 50% shade and 57% energy saving. When installed as a rolling type installation, trials indicate a number of important features, including improvement in productivity up to 25%, reduction in plant stress, better fruit colour, extended growing season, fewer unmarketable fruit, lower condensation, higher leaf temperature during night period, and lower leaf temperature during day time.

Chapter 7. THE FRUIT

Chapter 7. THE FRUIT

Flowers and fruit

The flower is that part of the plant which is specially adapted for the production of seed, in order to reproduce itself and so keep up a succession of its kind. As fruit size is directly associated with seed content, proper pollination is necessary to assure the development of a satisfactory complement of seeds.

Although the flower is in many respects different from many other parts of the plant, it is in fact a simple shoot modified for the special purpose of reproduction. The position of the flower shows that it is a special form of shoot, for flowers are formed at the apex of the stem, just as are shoots bearing leaves.

The flowers are borne in clusters on the main axis and on lateral branches. The number of clusters varies, depending on the type and variety. It appears that temperature does not appreciably affect the initiation of flower clusters and flowers. However, flowers initiated under cold night conditions are usually larger.

An individual flower consists of groups of modified and highly specialised leaves, arranged concentrically and designed for the purpose of sexual reproduction. These groups are sepals, petals, stamens and pistils. Each group has a specific function. The sepals (collectively called the calyx) which are green in colour, protect the unopened flower bud. The petals are collectively called the corolla, which is sulphur yellow in colour and forms the most conspicuous part of the flower. The stamen produces the pollen and is referred to as the male organ of the plant, while the pistil is referred to as the female organ. A pistil consists of an ovary, style and stigma. *Figure 7.1* is a flower diagram.

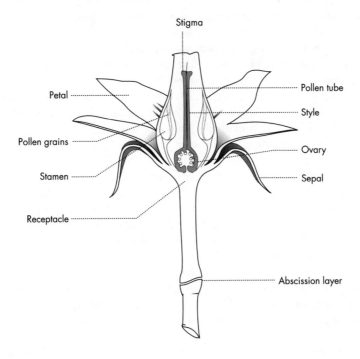

Figure 7.1 Diagram of tomato flower.

The tomato flower is called a 'perfect flower', because both sex organs are in the same flower. Peas, beans, strawberries, carrots and many others grown by hydroponicists are also in this classification. However, cantaloup, watermelon, pumpkin and squash have functional stamens and pistils in separate flowers.

One of the advantages of growing tomatoes in containers is that it is easy to vary the amount of nutrient or water fed to each plant. Some growers take advantage of this to create a stress situation when the plant has reached the growth state where it could bear flowers. Once floral initiation has begun, the process is irreversible and will continue even if environmental conditions which stimulated initiation have changed.

To create the stress condition, the feed supply is cut off, allowing the medium to dry out. Just as the plant shows first signs of temporary wilting, a diluted solution is applied to the pot - usually manually - and then the normal feed resumed. Within a few days the first flush of flowers will appear. Once fruit has formed, this technique should not be repeated as problems will be encountered with blossom-end rot, flower setting and fruit size.

Tomatoes are grown for their fruits, although a commercial grower may grow them for both fruit and seeds. The development of the fruit and seeds depends on the successful union of the sperms and eggs and the subsequent growth of the embryos. The journey of an individual sperm to an individual egg follows a long and tortuous path, in the case of a tomato, and is dependent upon a number of environmental factors, including wind, temperature and humidity.

When grown in the open field, tomatoes are usually wind pollinated, but if grown in an enclosed greenhouse, there may be insufficient movement of air to disturb the pollen. Vibration of the flower clusters is often necessary in a greenhouse. The most effective way is to walk past the plant and hit the supporting rope with a smooth stick, taking care not to bruise the stem. If the environmental conditions are suitable, the fine yellow pollen will be seen falling from the flower. Where only a small number of plants are concerned, hand pollination using a fine soft artist's brush can be undertaken.

Since all flowers in a cluster do not open at the same time, the pollinating process should be repeated as long as there are flowers. In a large greenhouse, a typical practice is to pollinate every second day manually, with a mechanical vibrator. Automatic shaking systems have rarely proved satisfactory.

Many growers use fans or blowers to shift the pollen, but this is not always successful. In fact, if the air flow is too high, the plants may be damaged. Directing the air stream at individual clusters, two or three metres down the row, will give better results than indiscriminately brushing plants with the air stream.

Whatever method is used for pollination, considerable care must be exercised, particularly when using hand held vibrators, as fruit may be scarred or there may be injury to the peduncle of the blossom, resulting in blossom drop.

Pollen will not germinate on a stigma, unless the stigma is in a receptive condition. This is indicated by the petals curling back. Best results are obtained when the relative humidity is about 70%. If humidity is too high, the pollen will remain damp and sticky and will not easily transfer to the stigma. If the humidity is too low, there will be a high probability of desiccation of pollen.

Temperature and light are other important factors in successful germination. The best temperature range is 18°C to 24°C. Outside this range, pollen germination and pollen tube growth are reduced considerably. Below 10°C, fertilisation may fail completely. The pollen tube appears to grow best at about 20°C and even at this temperature, it takes some 60 hours for the pollen tube to reach the ovary. Initiation of the growth of the embryo and endosperm takes place about 80 to 90 hours after pollination.

Prolonged cloudy weather retards germination, resulting in poor fruit set. Pistil length, which affects the ease with which the pollen is transferred from anther to stigma, is inversely related to the amount of light. With some varieties, particularly if grown out of season, the style grows so long that the stigma extends beyond the anthers, making adequate transfer of the pollen difficult.

This problem has been noticed with Kelstar and Ox Heart varieties. Other factors which may cause poor setting include high nitrogen levels and flower damage. Excessive nitrogen will result in heavy foliage growth, excessively thick stems, proliferation of side shoots, increased pistil length and flower shedding. Should the nitrogen level be low in mid-summer, with high light and long days, the pistil will remain down in the flower. Damage to flowers can be caused by insects such as thrip. Damage results in imperfect pollination, poor fruit setting and badly shaped fruit.

Tomatoes were one of the first crops on which growth substances were used to promote fruit set, where pollination does not occur due to either low temperature or low light intensity. Researchers found that indoleacetic acid could bring about fruit set without pollination. Sprays are available under several trade names for this purpose. Directions for use as outlined on the container should be carefully followed. If application strength is too high, the plant growth may be retarded or even stopped altogether. Also, there may be a high number of puffy fruit.

The spray should be confined to the flower cluster. Indiscriminate spraying may result in a considerable reduction in crop yield. The technique adopted by many growers is to cup one gloved hand around the flower cluster and spray with the other, so that the spray does not spread beyond the flowers.

Hormone sprays are very effective and if too many fruit are set, it may be desirable to thin out, so that only about six or seven fruit per cluster are allowed to mature. It is important to get good fruit set on the first truss, as it forces the plant into a reproductive state which favour's greater flower and fruit production as the plant grows.

Pollination serves two purposes; first, the inhibition of flower and fruit abscission and second, to provide the male gamete for fertilisation. These two functions occur separately and even though pollination has occurred and fruit set is obtained, fertilisation may not take place. The reason for this is that the pollen may fail to germinate, or the pollen tube may not grow fast enough to reach the ovary before it is shed.

The successful completion of the sexual process within the flower involves a series of processes or activities. Failure of any of these prevents normal fruit development. They include the following:

- Pollen must be produced.
- The pollen must be capable of developing normally.
- Pollen must alight on, or be transferred to the stigma.
- There must be rapid and complete germination.
- The stigma must be in a receptive condition.
- The pollen tubes must grow through the style.
- The process of fertilisation must take place. The ovary must be retained.
- The ovary must enlarge.

Truss	Flowers	Fruit set
1	6	6
2	8	7
3	8	6
4	10	8
5	20	12
6	19	12
7	18	10

Table 7.1 Numbers of flowers/fruit set, Longkeeper variety

Table 7.1 shows average numbers of flowers and fruit set for a single stem Longkeeper variety, manually pollinated. Ten plants were used in the trial.

Flower or blossom drop is often a problem for both the commercial grower and the home gardener. Care should be taken to ensure that the nutrient mixture contains adequate phosphorus. Experience has shown that in container culture, some varieties of tomatoes require a higher level of phosphorus than others. Levels vary between 30 ppm and 50 ppm. Flower drop can also be encountered in situations where there is not a satisfactory temperature differential between day and night time. There is evidence that flowers which wither and break at the knuckle, resulting in blossom drop, do so when pollination has not taken place because of dryness at the root zone and in the air. Dry set is another flower problem. Growth of the fruit ceases when it reaches the size of a match head. The trouble is due to the air being too hot and dry when pollination is taking place. Figure 7.2 illustrates the problems.

A flower problem which results in unmarketable fruit is caused by damage to the pistil or ovary, or by genetic or environmental factors which cause the flower parts to develop abnormally. The effect on the fruit is known as 'catfacing'. Some varieties are more prone than others. It has been observed with Striped Cavern, Apollo and Magnifico varieties during late summer, but not to any extent which would cause concern. It gets its name from the appearance of the fruit. The fruit is distorted due to creases, indentations and protuberances. In bad cases, there may be signs of scar tissue. Blossom-end rot is one of the major contributors to unmarketable fruit. It occurs as a result of transpiration stress or a calcium deficiency. It is not clear whether the two are interdependent, but when the black spot appears on small fruit, the problem is mainly one of calcium deficiency and on large fruit it is more likely to be the result of a period of insufficient water.

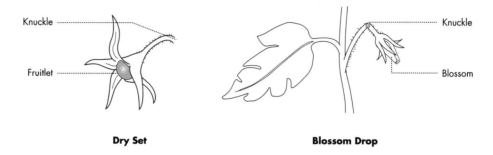

Knuckle

Fruitlet

Dry Set

Knuckle

Blossom

Blossom Drop

Figure 7.2 *Flower problems.*

A foliar spray has been used with some success to reduce blossom-end rot, but once the black spot has appeared it is too late. The root system should be kept moist throughout hot periods of the day. The nutrient solution, which should have the calcium level maintained to the correct level, should be applied twice a day and preferably three times a day during those hot periods when temperatures exceed about 30°C.

In one instance, a commercial grower had a 25% crop loss as a result of BER with Roma variety, following a 24 hour pump failure during his absence. The installation was a drip feed system with irrigation cycles set at 7 am, 10 am, 1 pm, 4 pm and 6 pm, with nutrient feed periods of 20 minutes at each cycle.

Fruit quality

Since the tomato develops from the ovary of a plant after fertilisation has taken place, it is basically a fruit. However, it is classified as a berry, as it is fleshy and houses seeds.

The fruit is an enlarged ovary of two or more compartments or locules, containing seeds imbedded in a gelatin-like placenta. Tomatoes are either bilocular, comprising two compartments, or multilocular containing more than two compartments. Other internal components of the fruit include the mesocarp and the core.

The highest quality tomatoes are obtained when the fruit is allowed to ripen on the vine. Unfortunately, the commercial growers cannot leave the fruit on the vine to reach the red ripe stage. If they did, the fruit would probably be damaged during transport to the market, or be over ripe before it reached the table of the consumer.

Tomatoes colour at a constant rate at a constant temperature and the rate of ripening can be predicted, provided the fruit temperatures are known.

Growers and marketers have available colour photographs which identify various classifications. One ripening guide prepared by the New South Wales Department of Agriculture in 1985, and still used by many people associated with the tomato industry, identifies seven stages of ripening. Stage 1 is 'Green', where the surface of the tomato is completely green with shade variations from light to dark green. The other stages are:

- Stage 2 - 'Breaker', which is taken as the reference point. This stage means that there is a definite break in colour, from green to tannish yellow, pink or red on not more than 10% of the surface.

- Stage 3 - 'Turning', which means that more than 10%, but not more than 30%, of the surface in the aggregate shows a definite change in colour from green to tannish yellow, pink, red or a combination thereof.

- Stage 4 - 'Pink', which means that more than 30%, but not more than 60%, of the surface in the aggregate shows pink or red colour.

- Stage 5 - 'Light Red', which means that more than 60% of the surface in the aggregate shows pinkish red or red, but not more than 90% of the surface is red.

- Stage 6 - 'Red', which means that more than 90% of the surface in the aggregate shows red colour.

- Stage 7 - 'Red Ripe', which means that the entire fruit surface has reached the maximum red colour characteristic of the cultivar. This stage is usually reached six days from the Breaker Stage. at 20°C.

In harvesting tomatoes green, it is inevitable that the grower will include some that are immature, because it is difficult in the field to determine maturity without opening the fruit for inspection.

In general terms, tomatoes harvested immature are of poor quality and when they do finally ripen, they lack flavour and should not be harvested. It is important that the picker be able to accurately identify the mature green stage of the fruit, since the fruit can gain as much as 10% of its final weight in the four days before the first appearance of skin colour.

The distinction between top quality home garden varieties and those grown commercially has tended to fade away, if some of the present seed catalogues are any indication. The same applies to seedlings on the shelves of the local nursery. The result is that if the home gardener is not determined to search for something of above average quality, there is a danger that something from the shelf will be taken that in all probability was bred for fruit which would take a high level of abuse in packing and transport to a far away market. The grower on the other hand, would normally pick the fruit lovingly and carry them only a few metres to the table. The price paid for this, is that the breeding process has resulted in the loss of some of the more desirable characteristics of the tomato, particularly taste, and the tomato would not be enjoyed as much as it should be.

The gardener who has no goal to produce top quality tomatoes for the table will, in purchasing a variety that is readily available, probably end up with a good yield, but with fruit that may be watery, poorly coloured and badly shaped with a tough skin.

The confusing range of fertilisers, many claimed to be specially formulated to produce a bumper crop of tomatoes, is a trap for the unwary. The result is frequently a bush that would match many tropical shrubs in size, but with a disappointing crop of fruit. Fertilisers which are heavily loaded with nitrogen and little potash will produce much bush and little good quality fruit, whereas those loaded with excessive potash and little nitrogen will result in a plant which often produces sweet, excellently coloured and firm fruit, but which are smaller in size compared with those grown in a balanced nutrient mixture.

Adjustment of the conductivity of the nutrient solution can be used to vary the yield and quality of the tomato crop. However, appropriate levels of individual elements must be maintained within certain maximum/minimum boundaries.

Table 7.2 indicates the results of trials with four Mighty Red variety plants fed with nutrient solutions of conductivities CF15, CF25, CF35 and CF45. Yields are for the first four trusses, with 90% of fruit picked at the fully ripe stage and the rest at the pink stage, with harvesting completed during mid September in an unheated glasshouse. All plants were grown in 30 cm plastic pots with perlite medium and using drip feed systems with irrigation cycles three times daily.

Pot 1 fed with nutrients at CF15, produced 18 marketable fruit of total yield 3.078 kg, at average weight 171 g. Pot 2 fed with nutrients at CF25, produced 21 marketable fruit of total yield 5.706 kg, at average weight 271 g. Pot 3 fed with nutrients at CF35 produced 19 marketable fruit at average weight 273 g and Pot 4 fed with nutrients at CF45 produced 18 marketable fruit at average weight 242 g.

Although Pot 2 with nutrient solution at CF25, produced the best performance in terms of total yield, the number of marketable fruit and average fruit weight were only marginally below Pot 3, with solution at CF 35. Fruit from Pot 3 produced the better class of fruit. They coloured more quickly after reaching the fully mature stage, shape characteristics for Mighty Red variety were more uniform, and the sugar Brix level was higher, being 6.5% compared with 6.2% for Pot 2 fruit. Also, unmarketable fruit numbered only two, compared with four from Pot 2 plant.

The total fruit yield for Pot 4 was 826 g lower than for Pot 3 and 1345 g lower than fruit grown in Pot 2. The number of unmarketable fruit was 10, with problems being experienced with blossom-end rot and radial splitting. Three fruit fell off the vine after breaking away at the knuckle, just as they reached the full red stage.

In terms of shelf life, it was evident that increase in conductivity resulted in increase in shelf life. Fruit from Pot 4 gave, on the average, an increase in shelf life of 4 days over fruit harvested from Pot 1.

The trials were completed in mid September, after the plants had grown through a fairly

	Pot 1 CF 15	Pot 2 CF 25	Pot 3 CF 35	Pot 4 CF 45
Truss 1	160 g	240 g	325 g	226 g
	295	265	240	350
	305	385	266	165
	282	366	425	285
	380	105		95
	225	325		
Truss 2	175	306	106	235
	215	285	355	360
	305	240	420	255
	225	250	295	155
		385	150	305
			220	
Truss 3	66	265	105	80
	205	295	225	305
	290	402	420	225
	325	320	335	285
		220	210	290
Truss 4	205	230	380	330
	95	65	220	
	105	220	285	225
	262	255	205	190
		282		
Total	3078 g	5706 g	5187 g	4361 g
	18 fruit 171 g	21 fruit 271 g	19 fruit 273 g	18 fruit 242 g

Table 7.2 *Yields from four Mighty Red variety plants fed with different CF levels of nutrient solution.*

cool season. Tomatoes of Mighty Red grown during the summer period, generally produced much higher yields and higher sugar Brix levels.

The large number of spoilt fruit with blossom-end rot from the Pot 4 plant, was probably due to reduction in calcium and an increase in potassium absorption. It was noticed that once fruit reached the stage of showing the first trace of pink colour, they ripened faster if grown in the higher CF ranges. Of the first two fruit on the first truss of each plant, which were kept under observation, the fruit on Pot 4 plant reached full red stage a full day ahead of fruit on the plant in Pot 1.

In another trial with Ox Heart variety conducted at the same time, poor yields resulted from the plants grown with solutions of CF35 and CF45, because of problems with developing flower trusses. Considerable flower abortion occurred. It was thought at the time, which was late July, that the large root system, a characteristic of Ox Heart, may have been a factor. The two plants were removed from their pots and the large root balls trimmed to remove about one third. of the root system. The plants were placed back in their pots and the perlite medium topped up. Although more flowers set on subsequent trusses, the fruit size of mature ripe fruit was much lower than had been experienced with fruit produced during the summer. Sugar Brix level was 4.5%, a figure much lower than that obtained with summer grown fruit.

A trial of six Yellow Pear varieties grown in coarse peat moss in 20 cm pots, produced some interesting results. Three of the plants were placed in a large container to provide a reservoir for a static feed nutrient feed system, while the other three were fed with a drip feed system at the rate of one litre per minute for 10 minutes, three times daily. The roots of the plants in the static feed system were in a permanently wet environment and produced small fruit, some with radial cracking, and all three plants gave symptoms of magnesium deficiency. Those in the drip feed system gave average yield of 3.2 kg per plant and fruit was of good quality, with sugar Brix level 6.1%.

Shape is important in tomato production, but it is not always easy to produce perfectly shaped fruit as the weather plays a significant role. If grown inside a glasshouse, particularly one with heating during winter months, the production of high quality tomatoes is no problem. However, the total crop yield for a winter crop will be much lower than for a summer crop for most varieties. As far as marketable fruit is concerned, the winter crop yield may be only half to three quarters that of the summer crop for a mid-season variety. As an example, trials with Ultra Boy gave on the average a crop of 6.5 kg, made up of 48 marketable tomatoes, during late autumn and winter periods, whereas for the warmer periods a crop of 8.2 kg with 85 marketable fruit was achieved per plant.

With the majority of varieties, there is often a balance between yield and quality. As a general rule, tomatoes of the highest quality usually means relatively low yield and conversely a high yield usually means low quality. Good management allows the influencing of many characteristics of growth, so that the grower has some influence on the outcome of the final crop.

The availability of nutrients and moisture have an important influence on fruit size. When conditions have been highly favourable for pollination and the number of fruit set is high, the size of the individual fruits will be below an average size. To produce larger fruit, some of the fruit should be removed early to allow the remaining fruit to obtain more nutrients and water. Where the fruit is to be marketed, judicious thinning may lead to larger, better quality fruit and the possibility of an increased profit margin.

The most common deformities encountered among unmarketable fruit, are rough skins and misshapen fruit with skin that looks much like a peeled mandarin. They occur mostly during periods when night time or day time temperatures are low for extended periods. The peeled mandarin effect is likely to be caused by severe temperature fluctuations during a brief period at blossom set. Distortion of the flowers will be quite evident.

Another deformity is puffy fruit. The tomato has a large space between the wall and the central core of pulp and seeds. The fruit is usually lightweight, has prominent convolutions and in many cases is pointed. In most cases, this condition is the result of excessive nitrogen in the nutrient mixture, or improper use of hormone sprays, or conditions which cause poor pollen development, or inadequate pollination.

The gradual deterioration in firmness of tomato fruit with ripening, is due to the gradual 'solubilisation' of protopectin in the cell wall, to form pectin and several other products. The pectic substances are subject to degradation during the later stages of the ripening process and are accompanied by a loss of tissue cohesion.

Physiological disorders such as blotchy ripening, green shoulder, sunscald and blossom-end rot, also affect fruit quality, so reducing the marketable quantity.

Blotchy ripening exhibits an appearance of green, yellow, or translucent irregularly shaped patches of tissue, in most cases located in the vicinity of the calyx. Researchers have found that the incidence of blotchy ripening is associated with a number of factors, including a nutrient mixture containing high nitrogen and low potassium. It is considered that, although the nitrogen level may be adequate for the plant's needs, the nitrogen is not fully utilised, because protein synthesis is impaired by the potassium deficiency. Low light intensity and cool temperatures also contribute to the problem.

Green shoulder is frequently found on tomatoes grown in greenhouses, where there is a high light intensity combined with high temperature. Removal of leaves will aggravate the problem.

Sunscald occurs when the fruit shoulders are exposed to the sun and the internal cell contents have reached death point.

Because of their thick flesh, Roma tomatoes are widely used for bottling, sauce and tomato paste. During taste trials it usually finishes well down in the preferred list when assessed for salads and sandwiches. Connoisseurs say the solid flesh is dry and mealy compared with many other varieties.

Blossom end rot (BER) can be a major problem with hydroponically grown tomatoes in containers. While the direct cause of BER is a low supply of calcium in the fruit, the indirect cause is related to stress. The stress reduces the mobility of calcium within the plant, particularly to the fruit, resulting in tissue breakdown.

Orange or yellow colouring is a result of fruit maturing during temperatures above about 22°C. The colour may be in small areas near the stem but can also extend to cover at least 50% of the surface area in some cases. Fruit so effected softens fast and lacks taste. These samples are Red Gem varieties.

Fruits with various amounts of green shoulder. This disorder is associated with high temperature or high light intensity, but some research indicates insufficient potassium in the nutrient solution may be a contributing factor. Removal of leaves during summer may increase the number of fruit with green shoulder.

Misshapen fruit harvested in early October from several varieties including Grosse Lisse, Apollo, Magnifico and Mighty Red grown in an unheated glasshouse. Some varieties such as Sydney Giants, Worlds Largest and Ox Heart normally have grotesque or irregular shapes but it is rare with others which normally produce globe, oblate, round or pear shape fruit. Misshapen fruit is normally the result of inadequate pollination causing poor and uneven seed set within the fruit and happens mostly during the cold months.

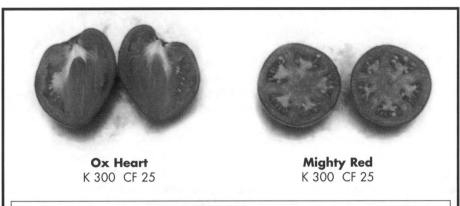

Ox Heart
K 300 CF 25

Mighty Red
K 300 CF 25

Samples of cross sections of Ox Heart and Mighty Red tomatoes at the red ripe colour stage. PLants were grown in medium 75% perlite, 20% scoria and 5% peat with potassium level 300ppm in the nutrient solution. The large core of the Ox Heart is evident. Ox Heart has a well balanced flavour with a pH of 4.7 and sugar Brix level of 6.5%. Mighty Red has an average pH of 4.4 and a sugar Brix level reading of 6.2%.

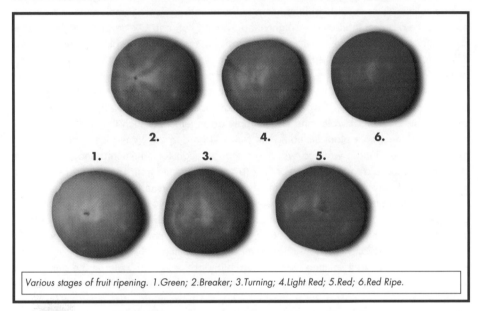

Various stages of fruit ripening. 1.Green; 2.Breaker; 3.Turning; 4.Light Red; 5.Red; 6.Red Ripe.

Blossom-end rot (BER) can be a serious problem with hydroponically grown tomatoes in containers. The grower needs to ensure good management practices are adopted, if the number of unmarketable fruit due to BER is kept to an absolute minimum.

One grower with three Red Cloud plants per polystyrene container, with vermiculite medium, had 18% crop rejection with BER when the timer of his nutrient feed system failed for 36 hours while he was away at a horticulture conference in mid summer. He had 200 plants with fruit on the first trusses when the supply was interrupted.

While the direct cause of blossom-end rot is a low supply of calcium in the fruit, the indirect cause is related to stress. The stress reduces the mobility of calcium within the plant, particularly to the fruit, resulting in tissue breakdown.

The extent of calcium uptake by the plant depends on a number of factors, including the ability of the root system to absorb it from the nutrient solution, the CF concentration of the solution, temperature of the solution in the root zone, and the degree of dissolved oxygen in the solution. Increasing the calcium content in the nutrient solution to an excessively high level will not prevent BER.

Trials indicate that aeration to improve the dissolved oxygen content has a major influence on BER. Inadequate solution aeration reduces element uptake, including calcium. In hot weather, when temperatures of the nutrient solution around the roots may rise, dissolved oxygen in the solution may be very low, reducing uptake and resulting in less calcium absorption and distribution by the plant. Also, in a high temperature situation where there is high leaf transpiration, transport of calcium to the critical area of fruit tissue would be reduced.

The extent of BER depends on the genetic derivation of the particular variety, the age of the fruit on the vine and the severity of the stress to which the plant is subjected.

Of several nutrient feed systems employed in container cultivation of tomatoes, only the static feed system showed a problem with BER, but it was relatively minor. Of 10 Mighty Red plants in 30 cm pots with a medium consisting of 50/50 perlite and small size gravel, only eight fruit out of about 280 exhibited BER in mid summer. As the solution was not aerated during the life of the trial, dissolved oxygen deficiency may have contributed to the problem.

Table 7.3 summarises the main physiological disorders or non-parasitic diseases experienced with tomatoes. All of these problems would result in unmarketable fruit. Good management is essential for the production of top quality fruit, but no grower can expect 100% marketable fruit from the crop. There will always be some that are below standard. Even an experienced hydroponic grower would be doing well if the crop resulted in 75% top grade tomatoes. The rest would probably be No 2 grade or culls.

Fruit splitting

Fruit splitting is of considerable concern to the tomato grower. Some varieties are more prone to the problem than others. Mighty Red, Moon Shot, and Ox Heart have given some concern in container culture, where in some crops, losses due to fruit splitting have reached 6%. Unfortunately, most fruit splitting occurs when the fruit is at the best stage, just prior to picking after having been carefully tended over a period of several weeks.

Pot cultivation will result in many such blemished fruit, unless the watering process is carefully controlled. When the bush is at an advanced stage of growth, it will absorb a considerable amount of water and if the supply arrangement is such that some drying out takes place, the whole plant including the fruit will harden up. When the irrigation cycle restarts and the plant is watered with more than enough for minimum need, there is an upsurge of sap and a rapid swelling of the previously restricted fruit. The swelling will cause the hard skin to crack. In some cases there may also be splits in the stem.

The problem can be minimised by ensuring that the roots always have an adequate supply of water, particularly during the hot days of summer when transpiration of water from the leaves is very high. A flow feed system with two cycles per day, or placing pots in a reservoir, will go a long way towards minimising fruit splitting.

Another cause of fruit splitting is the interruption of the flow of water in the stem. If the top of a large bush is cut off or heavy pruning takes place, there will be a tendency for the water in the stem to be diverted to the fruit. This can be minimised by extending the lopping or pruning over a number of days. One trial with Burnley Bounty revealed that the problem was worst when trusses 1 and 2 still carried large ripe fruit.

Hydroponicists have found some evidence of a relationship between fruit splitting and the strength of the nutrient solution during cool nights. Most varieties will crop satisfactorily with a CF of around 25, but when the higher trusses commence ripening during autumn, the conductivity should be increased to CF28 or even 30. This will minimise splitting during the cold nights, where the plants are grown outside or in an unheated glasshouse. Some recent work has indicated that the problem can be further reduced by running the conductivity at a lower level during the day than at night.

Storage

Storage of the crop is an ongoing problem with the commercial grower and suitable storage facilities are critical to efficient management. With the backyard grower, who may have less than 50 or so plants, storage problems may not reach major proportions if excess fruit is put to use as various preserves, relishes, chutneys and juice mixtures.

When the tomato is on the bush it receives food, vitamins and hormones made by the process of photosynthesis, and water supplied via the stem and root system. Since the fruit is a living entity, it requires a source of free energy. Sugars decomposed in respiration provide this vital energy.

Immediately the fruit is picked from the vine, the source of energy is removed. We are

Disorder	Effect	Likely cause
Radial cracking	Cracking occurs at stem end and radiates from centre of stem scar towards the shoulder.	Related to genetic make-up of individual varieties. High temperatures favour rapid expansion of fruit which causes cracking. Fluctuations in moisture availability in fruit and plant. Low level of potassium in fruit tissue.
Concentric cracking	Circular cracks and/or as zippering between the stem scar to below the fruit shoulder.	Related to genetic make-up of individual varieties. High temperatures favour rapid expansion of fruit which causes cracking. Fluctuations in moisture availability in plant and fruit. Low levels of potassium in fruit tissue.
Blotchy ripening	Parts of fruit remain yellow or orange and fail to ripen.	Result of only a single pigment, carotene, being produced in the fruit. Cause is usually too high temperature of fruit or insufficient potassium in the nutrient mixture.
Greenback	Green hard area around stalk. Fruit fails to fully ripen.	Too high level of sunlight or insufficient potassium in the nutrient mixture.
Blossom-end rot	Leathery dark coloured patch at bottom end of fruit.	Inadequate moisture control in root zone or shortage of calcium in nutrient mixture. Excessive salt levels, particularly potassium or magnesium.
Catface	Scarring of the blossom end of fruit. Excessive malformation.	Injury to flowers or faulty pollination. Susceptibility varies with variety.
Puffy fruit	Internal cavity between seed section and outer wall.	Faulty pollination resulting from environmental factors, including insufficient light, inadequate vibration with pollinator and low daytime temperature.
Sunscald	White to yellow hard patch on shoulder of fruit.	Exposure of fruit to direct sunlight.
Gray wall	Wall tissue is brown colour. Light brown blotches under skin.	Low light levels, low temperatures and root zone excessively wet.

Table 7.3 *Main physiological disorders or non-parasitic diseases of tomatoes.*

then concerned with the processes of respiration and transpiration. Stored food is hydrolyzed into soluble food, for example starch into glucose, and soluble food in the presence of oxygen in the air is oxidized to carbon dioxide and water. The water produced by respiration is given off by transpiration.

All living cells need a constant supply of energy, and since the respiration process liberates energy, the rate of respiration will be proportional to the available living cells. Thus two cartons of tomatoes will require more energy and produce significantly more carbon dioxide and liberate more heat, than one carton. As a general rule, the rate of respiration varies directly with water content of the product, so tomatoes fit into a class of vegetables which have high respiration.

Temperature has a major influence on the rate of respiration. Within the range 10° to 35°C, the higher the temperature the greater the rate of respiration, so that tomatoes should be stored in an environment at the bottom of this range, if reasonably good produce is to be maintained over an extended period.

In a stored condition, oxygen is absorbed from the air and carbon dioxide is given off, so that if the tomatoes are packed in an airtight container (e.g. a plastic container with a tight lid or in a sealed plastic bag), the available oxygen will be gradually used up, while the carbon dioxide surrounding the fruit will increase. This process decreases the rate of respiration. When concentration of the oxygen falls below a certain level, compounds in the form of alcohol and acetic acid will form. These are injurious to the tissues and protoplasm.

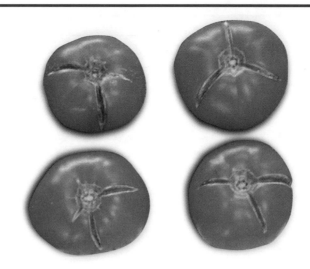

Split fruit from plants grown in 50% perlite/50% peat medium in 20cm diameter pots and irrigated by flow feed system daily at midday for one hour duration. Radial cracking is associated with water stresses within the plant particularly during periods of high temperature when the plants are under moisture stress due to high transpiration.

BURNLEY BOUNTY
K 400
P 60

BURNLEY BOUNTY
K 200
P 40

BURNLEY BOUNTY
K 300
P 50

Selection of seven best fruit from three groups of Burnley Bounty plants each grown in 30cm pots with 80% perlite/20% peat mixture over a 30mm scoria base. Each group comprised three plants making a total of nine plants in the trial. Each group was fed with Hoaglands mixture but modified for the potassium and phosphorus levels as shown. Solutions with the higher K/P ratios produced higher pH, higher sugar Brix levels and longer storage life.

It is evident therefore, that cartons, plastic bags or any other container, should have adequate ventilation holes or cut-outs to let in sufficient oxygen and let out some of the carbon dioxide. Experts recommend about half a dozen 6 mm diameter holes per package. Not only does inadequate ventilation result in off-flavour of tomatoes, but mature green fruit will not ripen.

As heat is liberated in the respiration process, storage containers should not contain excessive numbers of fruit. If they do, the temperature of the fruit in the centre will be much higher than those on the outside. The higher temperature induces a greater rate of transpiration and greater shrinkage of the fruit located in the middle.

A high humidity will tend to retard the rate of transpiration and is beneficial for storage. A good range is 70 to 80 per cent. It should not be too high, otherwise water will condense on the skin of the fruit and storage rot may develop. Ripening and colouring is controlled by the naturally occurring hormone ethylene. Mature green fruit which, for some reason, cannot be left on the vine to ripen naturally, may be ripened by spraying with an ethylene-releasing chemical available from the nurseryman. For best results moderate to high temperatures and humidity are desirable with the temperature being preferably above 18°C. Fruit can be harvested 10 to 14 days after application of the chemical.

However, ethylene is wasted on fruit already ripening in store. Fruit which has already started the ripening phase, will usually give off sufficient endogenous ethylene to ripen the other fruit in store.

When the fruit is picked from the plant, it should be handled carefully so that it is not bruised and the skin is not broken. Most damage is done when the fruit is pulled away from the bush. The calyx should be left in place on the fruit and the stem bent at the knee, just above the calyx, so that it breaks away cleanly. The method is illustrated in *Figure 7.3*.

It is the practice with many hydroponic growers in Australia and in England to market the fruit with the calyx attached to the tomato. Fruit is frequently sent to market in cartons containing two layers of fruit, to minimise puncturing of the fruit. However, cherry tomatoes are usually packed in small plastic containers, similar to containers used for strawberries, and calyces sometimes removed.

Trials with Grosse Lisse, Apollo and Jubilee showed a 7.5% increase in shelf life for fruit with calyces attached. The presence of volatile compounds contribute to the typical aroma associated with freshly picked red ripe tomatoes and also to their flavour. Some of the aroma appears to be associated with the calyx and is lost before the tomato reaches the consumer via the market, if the calyx is removed.

Damaged fruit is unmarketable for the fresh fruit market and careful handling will result in greater financial return from the crop. The main mechanical damage encountered in commercial growing of tomatoes, is bruising or skin breakage caused by impact, compression or vibration. Impact damage occurs when fruit is dropped or dumped from picking baskets into bulk crates.

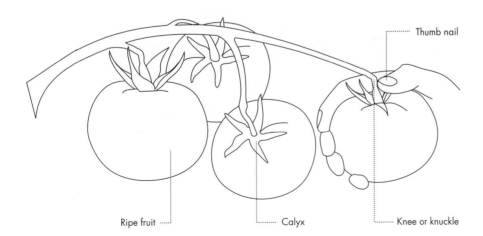

Thumb nail

Ripe fruit   Calyx   Knee or knuckle

Figure 7.3 *Correct method of picking tomatoes.*

Hot, ripe fruit is easily damaged, so extreme care is necessary if harvesting is carried out during hot weather. Compression bruising occurs if containers or crates are too deep. It also occurs when packing in standard shipping boxes, if fruit are forced into spaces that are too small. Many growers who market top quality hydroponically grown tomatoes, restrict packing to two layers and use a soft cardboard dividing tray between the layers. Vibration bruising occurs when the fruit is not properly packed, or transport trucks travel over rough roads for long distances.

If fruit is to be packed for sale, unmarketable fruit should be discarded and removed from the growing area. The best time to harvest is during the cool of the early morning. Fruit should be placed in a cool room, to reduce losses caused by over-maturity and 'boiling'. If a hot day is expected, picking should preferably be carried out before 9 a.m.

The best temperature for ripening tomatoes after they have been picked, is between 15°C and 22°C. This range results in the fruit being firm, of good colour and best flavour. If the temperature is much below 13°C, the fruit will seldom reach full colour for the particular variety. It will have a dry skin and be of poor taste. Tomatoes should not be stored in a domestic refrigerator. It is too cold. If the temperature is above 25°C during the ripening process, the colour will be pale, with red varieties being close to yellow, and they will be soft and of inferior flavour.

For storage however, a much lower temperature is required than for ripening. For green fruit, a storage temperature of about 12°C is recommended, with a relative humidity of 85 to 90 per cent. Under these conditions, a maximum storage life of two to four weeks is possible. For ripe fruit storage, the temperature should be about 10°C with a relative humidity of 85 to 90 per cent. Maximum storage life is up to 10 days.

In some cases, commercial growers may wish to manipulate the maturity of processing tomatoes to fit in with harvesting schedules. The growth regulant ethephon is used for this purpose. Ethephon breaks down to liberate ethylene, when applied to plant tissue. This results in more rapid and uniform ripening of immature and mature green fruit. Frequently the harvest date can be advanced up to 12 days, with an increase in ripe fruit yield over the optimum potential of the normal ripening rate. However, care must be exercised in its application. Application during high temperatures often causes defoliation and fruit loss, particularly when used at concentrations above the recommended level.

High contrast type hand held refractometer for measuring sugar levels with Brix scale 0 - 32% made by Shibuya Optical Co., Ltd, Japan. A temperature compensation table is provided to allow for correction of measurements outside the 20°C standard temperature range.

Grading

For the fresh market, tomatoes should be graded to uniform colour. Fruit of mixed maturity are not always easy to sell. Fully ripe tomatoes are only wanted in the home or at a processing factory. Tomatoes have three basic colour grades. These are immature, semi-ripe and ripe. Immature fruit is green and ripens unevenly. They find little demand in the market. Semi-ripe fruit are ideal for the market. Fruit with this colour grade have a slight pink colour (first pink) on the skin at the blossom end. Ripe fruit (forward colour) have more than two thirds colour. They ripen quickly, especially in warm weather and precooling may be necessary.

Markets have established minimum standards for fruit size, maturity and blemish. They vary slightly between States, but typically they may be cocktail (less than 45 mm diameter), small (45 mm or greater diameter but less than 60 mm), medium (60 mm or greater diameter but less than 80 mm) and large (greater than 80 mm in diameter).

To qualify for the best grade, no more than 10% of the fruit in a package should have superficial blemishes exceeding 5 mm on tomatoes of diameter less than 80 mm, or 10 mm on tomatoes larger than 80 mm. Lower grades may have superficial blemishes malformations, sunscald and healed growth cracks which do not affect the soundness of the fruit.

Large and very small size fruit may be welcome by the home gardener but are rarely stocked by major fruit and vegetable retailers. Research by some retailers has shown that Australian shoppers prefer medium size fruit graded in the 60 - 80 mm diameter range, whereas reports from overseas show that Americans prefer the large 'beefsteak' varieties and Europeans prefer much smaller tomatoes, in the 47 - 57 mm diameter range.

Shoppers prefer the 60 - 80mm grade size because the fruit is more convenient for sandwiches, salads and grills. Restauranteurs and hotel chefs also find the medium size best for dishes such as stuffed tomatoes, baked tomatoes, tomato topknots, poached egg in tomato etc.

The manager of one large fruit and vegetable market found that where customers were given a choice of fruit separately graded as small, medium and large, and offered at the same price per kilogram and of similar ripeness and firmness, the medium grade (60 - 80 mm) outsold the other grades 2.5:1 during summer/autumn months, but only 2:1 during winter/spring months. Apparently, the reason for the greater sale of small and large fruit in winter, compared with the medium size, may be because most were used for stews and soups, where the fruit was cut into small pieces prior to cooking and the original size was of little consideration in the final dish presentation. Frequently, small and large fruit are discounted in order to shift them from the shelf.

On this evidence, there would be some advantage for the grower if all marketable fruit could be harvested from the vine as medium size grade.

In a trial conducted in New South Wales during the months mid May to end August, with an average maximum temperature of 19°C, it was found that this target could be closely achieved by controlling the number of stems on the plant for at least one popular variety. The trial involved 12 Grosse Lisse variety plants arranged in three groups of four plants, comprising four pruned to single stems, four pruned to three stems and four pruned to five stems. Results are shown in Tables 7.4, 7.5 and 7.6. These results are for the plant of each group with the highest total weight yield. However, they are representative of other plants in the same group, with all results being within 6% of those shown in the Tables.

All plants were restricted to four trusses per stem and four fruit per truss. Plants were grown in 150 mm square rockwool blocks and fed with a nutrient solution maintained at EC 3.0 mS/cm and pH 6.0, with irrigation cycles being maintained at three cycles per day of 20 minute periods.

Although some problems had been experienced with similar trials with Grosse Lisse plants during summer months, when there was a problem with flowers dropping from the first truss, no trouble was experienced with this winter trial.

As a result of earlier experience in growing plants during winter time, the trial commenced with the nutrient solution having a ratio of N1: K1.6 and changed to N1: K2.5 about 21 days before the estimated date of commencement of harvesting. It was retained at this level until termination of the trial.

A 400 litre nutrient solution tank had an automatic water top-up facility and conductivity was adjusted as necessary, following daily reading of conductivity and pH. The solution was completely replaced at three weekly intervals during the trial period to prevent any major imbalance in the nutrient solution.

All stems were tied to separate drop cables, spaced in line and sufficiently apart, to ensure uniform light exposure to all stems and leaves. No leaves were removed during the trial.

Factors examined included fruit weight on an individual basis; average diameter measured cheek-to-cheek from three diameters of each fruit; average Brix %, measured with a hand refractometer and zeroed with distilled water, determined from three readings using fruit at orange/red coloration and placed in a juicer and liquid filtered before being measured; and pH level using the same liquid prepared for the Brix measurement.

	Fruit wt gm	Fruit dia. mm	Brix %	pH
Truss 1	135	67	6.1	4.34
	248	85		
	210	80		
	265	87		
Truss 2	132	66	6.1	4.33
	330	95		
	540	112		
	250	85		
Truss 3	255	86	6.0	4.24
	625	120		
	362	98		
	390	103		
Truss 4	135	67	5.9	4.20
	170	73		
	305	92		
	360	98		

Table 7.4 *Single Stem - Total Yield 4.712 kg.*

Single Stem
Av. 336g

Five best fruit picked on same day from a single stem plant

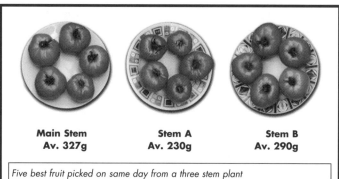

Main Stem
Av. 327g

Stem A
Av. 230g

Stem B
Av. 290g

Five best fruit picked on same day from a three stem plant

	Main Stem				Stem A				Stem B			
	Fruit wt gm	Fruit dia. mm	Brix %	pH	Fruit wt gm	Fruit dia. mm	Brix %	pH	Fruit wt gm	Fruit dia. mm	Brix %	pH
Truss 1	105	63	5.8	4.26	74	56	5.8	4.25	102	62	5.7	4.25
	115	64			80	58			120	65		
	205	77			53	50			-	-		
	-	-			-	-			52	50		
Truss 2	152	70	5.8	4.24	166	72	5.7	4.23	80	58	5.6	4.22
	52	50			55	51			60	52		
	-	-			110	63			77	58		
	75	57			-	-			-	-		
Truss 3	50	49	5.7	4.23	202	78	5.6	4.23	55	51	5.6	4.20
	-	-			85	59			110	63		
	102	62			90	61			99	62		
	72	55			-	-			-	-		
Truss 4	74	56	5.6	4.20	88	60	5.6	4.22	158	71	5.5	4.20
	-	-			-	-			120	65		
	90	61			45	47			85	59		
	77	58			65	53			-	-		

Table 7.6 *Five Stems - Total Yield 5.084 kg.*   (continued p163)

	Main Stem				Stem A				Stem B			
	Fruit wt gm	Fruit dia. mm	Brix %	pH	Fruit wt gm	Fruit dia. mm	Brix %	pH	Fruit wt gm	Fruit dia. mm	Brix %	pH
Truss 1	205	79	6.0	4.30	105	62	5.9	4.22	86	59	5.9	4.21
	145	69			210	80			105	62		
	135	67			85	57			202	79		
	152	70			150	70			95	61		
Truss 2	180	77	5.9	4.25	144	68	5.9	4.22	-	-	5.7	4.20
	-	-			102	62			150	70		
	230	83			-	-			110	63		
	190	78			65	53			190	78		
Truss 3	280	90	5.8	4.23	86	59	5.7	4.20	130	67	5.6	4.20
	-	-			202	79			145	69		
	115	63			-	-			-	-		
	75	55			95	61			122	65		
Truss 4	106	62	5.7	4.20	135	67	5.6	4.18	152	70	5.5	4.19
	-	-			85	58			65	54		
	220	82			-	-			-	-		
	85	57			102	62			95	61		

Table 7.5 *Three Stems - Total Yield 5.331 kg.*

Stem C				Stem D			
Fruit wt gm	Fruit dia. mm	Brix %	pH	Fruit wt gm	Fruit dia. mm	Brix %	pH
85	59	5.7	4.26	95	62	5.6	4.20
92	61			86	59		
110	63			75	57		
-	-			-	-		
58	52	5.7	4.19	55	51	5.5	4.20
72	55			110	63		
-	-			45	47		
-	-			-	-		
45	47	5.5	4.20	90	61	5.4	4.19
98	62			52	50		
75	57			-	-		
-	-			-	-		
102	62	5.3	4.19	75	57	5.2	4.18
-	-			45	47		
74	56			60	52		
-	-			85	59		

(Table 7.6 continued from p162)

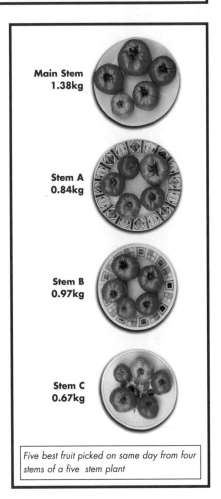

Main Stem
1.38kg

Stem A
0.84kg

Stem B
0.97kg

Stem C
0.67kg

Five best fruit picked on same day from four stems of a five stem plant

The results of the trial indicated the following:

- Best total weight yields were 4.712 kg for a single stem plant; 5.331 kg for a three stem plant; and 5.084 kg for a five stem plant.

- For the single stem plant, fruit diameter varied from 66 mm to 120mm, with 11 of the 16 fruit being above the limit of 80 mm for medium grade fruit.

- For the three stem plant, all of the 39 fruit produced, except 9, were within the 60-80 mm medium grade range.

- For the five stem plant, of the 58 fruit produced, only 24, or less than 50%, were within the 60-80 mm medium grade range.

- For the single stem plant, Brix levels varied from 6.1% for first truss fruit to 5.9% for fourth truss fruit. The pH was in the range 4.34 to 4.20.

- For the three stem plant, the Brix level ranged from 6.0% to 5.5% and pH from 4.30 to 4.18.

- For the five stem plant, the Brix level ranged from 5.8% to 5.2% and pH from 4.26 to 4.18.

- From observations of fruit on the first truss of each stem, it was noted that ripening from breaker stage to full red stage occurred at 7 - 9 days for fruit on all main stems, 8 - 10 days for fruit on all first laterals, and 9 - 12 days for fruit on second laterals.

It is likely that other indeterminate varieties with good growth and yield characteristics such as Burnley Bounty, Mighty Red, College Challenger and others may produce results similar to Grosse Lisse, when pruned to multi-stem growth. However, varieties such as Kelstar and Potentate would most likely produce unsatisfactory yields on multi-stem plants compared with single stem plants.

Packaging

Not many commercial growers accurately grade tomatoes into various sizes and then place them by hand in the container to form a pattern pack. Labour is too costly for such practice today. Instead, most prefer to volume fill the container, which may be constructed from wood, plastic, fibreboard or polystyrene. Net weight is usually about 10 kg.

However, hydroponically grown tomatoes often are of better overall quality and command a higher price than soil grown types. They are frequently supplied direct to high class hotels and restaurants and consequently, growers find it good business to give more attention to grading and packaging, than they otherwise would. Many growers label the highest quality fruit with individual stickers with the words "Hydroponically grown" or something similar.

Customers like to inspect fresh tomatoes before purchase and attractively presented fruit in clean, clearly labelled and well filled cartons will always have a market advantage over fruit poorly packed and presented.

If the hydroponicist wishes to obtain premium prices for the tomatoes, attention must be paid to the container, the labelling, to pattern packaging, and individual selection of fruit for each case or package. Some growers pack their tomatoes in two layer fibreboard boxes, containing about 8 kg of fruit. The two layers are separated by a thin clean cardboard sheet. Another package arrangement contains four, six or ten tomatoes. The purpose of the small package is to provide minimum need for produce counter handling.

A mini survey of three supermarkets over a two week period during late 1997 showed soil grown tomatoes as retailing at AUD $2.6 per kg, whereas hydroponically grown tomatoes with calyx on the fruit, and fruit individually labelled 'hydroponically grown' retailed at AUD $5.45 per kg. All three Managers of the Fruit and Vegetable Sections commented that sales were good, shelf life was longer, and there were fewer rejects of unmarketable fruit compared with the soil grown tomatoes.

Chapter 8. VARIETIES AND TYPES

Chapter 8. VARIETIES AND TYPES

Shapes and sizes

No other plant has had more attention from both amateur and professional plant breeders than the tomato. Many hundreds of varieties or cultivars, as they are known in the horticultural and research business, have been selected and developed by crossbreeding to produce a large range of shapes, sizes, colours and types suitable for the home gardener, the fresh market grower and the tomato processor.

With regard to shape, they are categorised as plum, pear, banana and cherry tomatoes, because their shapes are similar to these fruits. Other words used to indicate shape include globe, oblate and oxheart. In addition to the usual round, oblong and oval shapes, there is a so called 'square shape' with a thick skin, bred specifically for mechanical harvesting and more efficient packaging. Breeders estimate that this shape will replace other

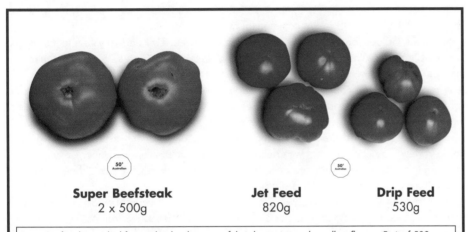

Super Beefsteak
2 x 500g

Jet Feed
820g

Drip Feed
530g

Super Beefsteak are ideal for sandwiches because of their large size and excellent flavour. Fruit of 500g are typical from first and second trusses. A nutrient solution provided three times daily by jet feed will produce fruit at least 285g averaged over all fruit to the sixth truss and at least 243g for drip feed arrangement. The photograph shows three fruit selected from fifth truss of one plant.

Pixie
CF 22

Pixie is ideal for pot cultivation requiring only a relatively small wireframe anchored to the lip of the pot to provide support. Grid dimensions should be large enough to enable fruit to be harvested from the side of the bush. A good yield is produced with a nutrient solution of concentration CF20 to CF23. Fruit size is typically 20-30mm in diameter and if medium is not kept too wet the taste and texture are of high order.

Variety	Size Range mm	Av. Diameter mm	Av. fruit per 250 g punnet	Av. sugar Brix %	Average pH
Yellow Baby (yellow)	19-22 dia. 25-30 length	20	50	7.4	4.2
Sweetie (red)	23-27	25	38	4.1	4.05
Unknown (orange/red)	23-33	28.5	16	4.0	4.0
Unknown (dark red)	36-43	38.5	11	5.0	4.15

Table 8.1 *Characteristics of cherry tomatoes as selected from Supermarket.*

shapes by the year 2000 in the commercial market.

Sizes of tomatoes range from cherry size, such as Sweet 100 and Tiny Tim, to the giants such as Ultra Boy, Whopper and World's Largest. In between these extremes are the medium sizes, such as Grosse Lisse, Burnley Bounty and many others.

In recent times, the cherry tomato has become very popular with the buying public. A spot check in 1996 at a large Supermarket store in country New South Wales, revealed that six, 1 metre square compartments were stocked with tomatoes. Two compartments stocked field grown red Gem variety tomatoes; one compartment displayed field grown Roma variety; one compartment was devoted to tomatoes labelled 'hydroponically grown', but variety not identified; and two compartments were stocked with four different types of cherry tomatoes, packed in 250 g plastic cartons.

The cherry types came from growers in South Australia, Victoria, New South Wales and Bowen in North Queensland. Only one of the growers labelled the fruit as 'hydroponically grown'. The four classes comprised an unknown variety of dark red colour, with fruit of average diameter 38.5 mm; an unknown variety of orange/red colour with average diameter 28.5 mm; Sweetie, a small bright red coloured tomato of average diameter 25 mm; and Yellow Baby, a small yellow coloured pear-shaped fruit of average diameter 20 mm and average length 27 mm.

The store management supplied sample cartons for analysis, with results being shown in *Table 8.1*. The Yellow Baby variety had a superb taste and recorded a sugar Brix level reading of 7.4%, compared with 4.1% for the red Sweetie fruit of about the same volume. Yellow Baby also registered a higher pH than Sweetie, being 4.2 compared with 4.05. The unknown orange/red coloured tomato registered a sugar Brix level reading of 4.0% and pH 4.0.

Colour and taste

The most popular colour with the consumer is red, which has a range from rich red/purple to a fiery red/orange colour. Other colours include pinks (at the fully ripe stage), yellow and pale yellow - sometimes referred to as white tomatoes. The colour is determined by the proportions of various carotene pigments.

Many people hold the view that the colour of a tomato has an important bearing on the flavour or taste, which is linked with the acid content of the fruit. According to laboratory measurements, some yellow- and white-coloured fruits are just as acid as reds and pinks. They taste milder because the varieties possessing these particular colours frequently have a high proportion of flesh to seeds and gel. Psychology and expectations also play tricks on our taste buds. Notwithstanding, measurements with Yellow Baby, a small pear-shaped yellow tomato, gave an average sugar Brix level reading of 7.4%, compared with 4.1% for a red variety of the same size.

There are orange-coloured varieties e.g. Carorich which has practically no lycopene (no nutritional value) but is high in ß-carotene (pro Vitamin A). However, they are not popular with many buyers because of their colour.

Seasonal cropping

Varieties of tomatoes available to the grower allow crops to be grown throughout the whole year in some parts of Australia. Tomatoes can also be grown to provide a continuous supply of tasty red ripe fruit in the colder areas of Victoria and South Australia, but require a glasshouse or polyhouse to give protection from frosts, hail and cold winds during part of the winter period. Heating is not essential, but for high yield commercial production these facilities may be a worthwhile investment.

The year round cultivation of tomatoes is helped by the availability of types classified as early, mid-season or main crop and late varieties. Many of the late crop varieties take up to 90 days to ripen after transplant, whereas the mid-season varieties can be ready for the table in 70 days. Some of the early varieties are even faster in maturing, with the average

Red Gem, a privately bred variety recently introduced to supply the commercial table market. It crops over a long periods with yields varying from 10.1kg in the cool months. A large percentage of the fruit is in the range 260-275 g with diameters 82-85mm. It is mild flavoured tomato with excellent shelf life.

These tomatoes were grown by an elderly gentleman who referred to them as Yellow Boy variety which had been grown by him for many years using his own seed. The fruit were from a plant in a small hydroponics installation comprising an assortment of containers mainly old kerosene tins about 20 litre size and filled with a mixture of gravel and sawdust. He mixed his own nutrient solution from fertilisers purchased from agricultural suppliers and applied the solution by watering can in the morning and late afternoon. The Yellow Boy fruit had a mild sweet taste with measurements indicating a pH of 4.3 and sugar Brix level of 5.10.

Roma
CF 22-24

Roma
CF 35

Roma produces a high yield of fruit and requires a good nutrient supply and preferably in the concentration range CF22 to CF24. The root zone should keep moist at all times as Roma is very susceptible to blossom end rot if roots are allowed to dry out for a short period. Commercial growers have incurred large losses when insufficient moisture was provided during hot weather. If fed with a solution of high concentration such as CF35, average fruit size will be 50g weight and 36mm average diameter compared with 100g average weight and 48mm average diameter for solution in range CF22 to CF24.

time being 60 days. The time taken to reach maturity is influenced by the weather conditions at the time and the feeding arrangement. Long periods of heavy cloud cover or prolonged cold spells, will extend the maturation period sometimes by as much as 30%.

Type selection

An important decision the grower has to make is whether to grow indeterminate or determinate types. One will require staking or supporting, whereas the other does not. This is a particularly critical decision where mass pot cultivation is practiced. In the case of the indeterminate type, the branches of the plant keep growing and produce fruit until frost kills the plant, or the grower cuts back the growing points. The plants will easily reach 3 m in length if grown under good conditions. They have a long production season and yields for most varieties are high. However, the maturity date is later than for most determinates.

With the determinate type, the branches stop growing and producing fruit after reaching a length of about 1fi m. This means that this type may be left to lie on the ground, or hang over the side of the pot. Fruit clusters are usually concentrated at the ends of short branches, exposing them to direct sunlight and the possibility of sunscald. The harvest duration of some early determinate plants is only about three weeks.

For the home gardener, who is often more concerned with having plants bearing over an extended period of time, the indeterminates may be preferred. However, if the housekeeper is also interested in having a large crop with a short production life, in order to can or preserve, then a determinate type may be preferred.

In theory, all indeterminate plant types are perennials, whereas all determinate types are annuals. In extended trials with Grosse Lisse and Burnley Bounty (both indeterminates), both were still producing good crops after two years when the trial was terminated.

Maturity periods

Earliness of ripening is a characteristic which needs to be taken into consideration, especially in areas where there is a short growing season, or in highland areas where summer temperatures are frequently much lower than on the lowlands or plains. Maturity periods (e.g. 60 day), are usually indicated on the seed packet or in catalogues. The dates shown are only rough averages of the time span from seedling plant-out stage, to the date when the first ripe tomato is produced, assuming good growing conditions.

In practice, maturity periods vary from about 60 days for some early varieties, to 135 days for late varieties. With hydroponics, experience has shown that maturity is frequently reached sooner than for a plant grown in soil.

Resistance to disease

Ability to resist tomato diseases may be a critical issue for soil grown tomatoes, but if good hygiene is practiced it is usually not a great problem in hydroponics.

The grower has to be continually on guard for disease introduction into the installation. The two major trouble makers are verticillium and fusarium wilt. These can be accidentally brought to the pot or growing bed area from an infected source. Growing varieties which are known to have good resistance to these and other diseases, will be a wise precaution in minimising the possibility of an outbreak of disease.

Preserving heirlooms

The exact number of tomato varieties available in Australia today is not known. One Australian nurseryman who has been associated with the growing of tomato seedlings for over four decades, estimates that there would be at least one thousand varieties. However, difficulty would be experienced in obtaining many of them. An encyclopaedia referring to the subject, gives a count of over 4000 throughout the world.

For those enthusiasts wishing to acquire seeds of the 'old timers', the situation has been complicated because of changes in names. Research shows that some old varieties were known by different synonyms in different parts of Australia and to different generations of growers. In some countries, there are clubs or societies whose principal aim is to keep alive many of the heirloom varieties of tomatoes, as well as other vegetables.

In Australia we are fortunate in having the Seed Savers Network (SSN), whose aims are to preserve the vegetable heritage by increasing the quantity of seed of traditional varieties through members, and to collect endangered commercial varieties and family heirloom varieties before they disappear.

Some of the little known tomato varieties which have been preserved by SSN members include Money Maker, a prolific tomato but rather tasteless, Micado Violettror a dark fruit variety with potato like leaf, Perfection with smooth thick fruit ideal for canning, Porter a good tasting variety with a pink plum colour, Sequoya a prolific oblate rich red tomato, Traveller with large pink flesh fruit, Urbana a long bearing type with red oblate fruit, Matura a rugged plant with round orange coloured fruit of medium size, Lutschis a very tasty tomato when fully ripe, Mackinley with pink colour fruit and potato like leaves, Golden Sunrise with yellow round fruit of medium size, Faddy a low bush bearing plum shaped fruit, Early Tan a prolific bearer of good quality fruit, Ace Royal a red tasty variety with fruit up to 8 cm diameter, Aranaylma a yellow flesh variety but of inferior taste, Beste von Allen a banana shaped fruit of large size and good for cooking, Cherokee a prolific bearer variety yielding rich red fruit, Cherry o' Pink a small pink fruit good for salads, Big Mexican a tasty variety of squarish shape excellent for a dish of baked tomatoes, and many other varieties.

The SSN recently acquired a collection of 100 different varieties from the seed collection of the Hungarian Botanical Gardens. The Network successfully grew plants and produced seeds for members from the collection. There are now varieties of tomatoes with such long names as Kecskemeti Uveghazi, Holger Suhrs Markt and Leningradski Skorospelyi. The Hungarian Botanic Gardens had, over a period going back many years, collected the seeds from USSR, Czechoslovakia, German Democratic Republic, Hungary and USA. Coming as many did from cold climates, these tomatoes would probably do well in southern States of Australia.

To preserve an heirloom variety requires the grower to be dedicated to the work. A major problem is to ensure that there is no cross-pollination with other varieties. This is difficult to achieve in the typical suburban garden, where many different varieties may be grown in close proximity.

There are many differences of opinion when it comes to recommending safe distances to keep varieties pure. Because tomatoes are self-pollinated, the problem is not as great as for say pumpkins. If grown side by side, there may be a crossing resulting from transfer of pollen by high wind or insects, but many growers claim that crossing will be reduced to almost zero where separation between plants is four metres or more. Many professional plant breeders separate older varieties by at least 20m, because their longer style increases the probability of cross pollination.

One dedicated grower living in the country, has kept a Yellow Pear variety going for over 40 years. However, his family claims that they are sick of eating only yellow tomatoes!

A number of growers have expressed concern with legislation introduced by the Australian Government regarding plant variety rights. Plant variety rights (PVR) means that if a plant breeder develops a new strain, it can be patented. If any tomato grower wants to exploit that variety of plant, royalties must be paid. However, as with other forms of patent, the plant breeder will first have to persuade a registrar of PVR that what has been developed is new.

PVR schemes exist in many countries, including Great Britain, USA and USSR, but the Australian authorities took some 16 years to formally approve the scheme.

Critics fear that small Australian seed firms will be taken over or wiped out by multinational firms, seeking to control the worlds food resources. They support their case by claiming that many seed varieties developed by multi-national firms are sterile or at best, produce a mutated offspring.

Burnley Bounty will crop over an extended period if well fed and given adequate room to grow. This plant grown in an unheated polyhouse produced this crop 20 months after seedling planted-out. At the time the vine was nearly 5 metres long.

Hybrids and standards

Up to about the Second World War, horticulturists had developed many strains of tomatoes for the specific needs of both the home grower and the commercial producer. In more recent times they have introduced hybrids which are the result of crossing two parent varieties. They can be repeated year after year by employing the same parental strains.

Hybrids have a number of advantages. They are improvements over the parents, possess a high degree of uniformity of plant habit, have high productivity and many types have high resistance to diseases and problems such as nematodes, *verticillium* and *fusarium* wilt, skin cracking etc, all of which are of great concern to the tomato grower. Hybrid varieties can also be developed to produce extra large fruit.

Hybrid seeds are much more expensive than standard types, because the horticulturist has to produce them through a hand pollination process. The pollen producing anther is removed from the flower by hand and the pollen of another plant deposited by hand on the stigma of the flower. The process is labour intensive and is the reason why the seed is so expensive. However, if the operation is properly performed, the resultant fruit will have all the characteristics of both parents at least for the first generation. First generation hybrids are identified on the seed packet as F1 hybrids.

Hybrid varieties perform very well in pots and other containers. They can take a lot of abuse, such as hot pots, erratic watering and inconsistency in nutrient formulation. This is mainly because a hybrid plant exhibits more favourable growth than either of its parents. This property is called "hybrid vigour".

Although hybrids may have high resistance to a number of common diseases which affect tomatoes, because of inherited properties from parents, they may be less resistant to other diseases. Hence their growth has to be carefully watched, so that suitable control action may be taken at the first sign of likely trouble.

Standard varieties are the non-hybrid types and the origin of some can be traced back a long way. Although hybrid types seem to be very popular among home gardeners, they have not entirely replaced. the standard types. In fact, many growers using pots and specialising in the production of top quality tomatoes prefer the standard types, as certain varieties have been found to be more resistant to some local diseases than newer hybrids. Standards can also produce good yields on nutrient mixtures of low strength, whereas many hybrids are gross feeders and conductivity needs to be maintained at a high level for a good yield.

Many tomato growers who still follow the old school traditions, claim that all the cross-breeding in recent years has resulted in the deterioration of the most important characteristic of the fruit - the taste. Many of the early standard varieties are still available, but just because they have been around for a long time does not mean that they all possess that delicious taste that most people imagine to be the hallmark of the ideal tomato. The reason so many have disappeared from the seed racks, is simply because, for a number of reasons, they have lost favour with many growers.

Grafted tomatoes

Various diseases and disorders are of major concern to tomato growers. It is an extreme disappointment to find advanced, apparently healthy plants suddenly affected by *verticillum* or *fusarium* wilt, nematodes or other problems.

Horticulturists have succeeded in raising disease-free stocks which have vigorous root systems and which have good resistance to some of the widespread diseases. The hybrid stock is not itself satisfactory for good fruit production, but the problem is overcome by grafting a good fruiting variety onto the stem.

There are a number of root stocks available, including one which is resistant to nematodes and root rot, a second which is resistant to root rot, *fusarium* and *verticillium*, and a third which is resistant to all four of these problems. In addition to these important factors, some grafted varieties are said to have longer life, greater yield and superior fruit setting and ripening properties at low temperatures, compared with ungrafted types. Some nurserymen claim crops up to 40 kg are typical for grafted varieties, but in practice this is seldom achieved, particularly in hydroponic installations.

Several hydroponicists have reported no significant increase in total weight yields for grafted plants, but tests with some varieties revealed a small increase in total soluble solids and fruit pH compared with non grafted types.

To produce a grafted plant, the hybrid root stock and the selected variety are planted so that at the time of grafting, both seedlings are about the same size. Since the hybrid root stock seed is somewhat harder and takes longer to germinate, it is usual practice to plant these seeds five or six days earlier.

Grafting is carried out when the seedlings have firm stems and plants are about 10 to 12 cm in height. Nurserymen have their own particular grafting techniques, but one

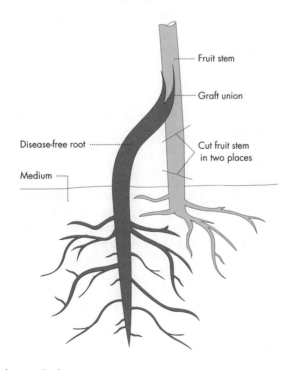

Fruit stem

Graft union

Cut fruit stem in two places

Disease-free root

Medium

Figure 8.1 *Grafting method.*

method is to lift the plant from the growing tray, cut off the top of the root stock, leaving one or two leaves, then make a downward cut with a very sharp pruning knife or razor blade, so that the cut does not go quite half way through the stem. The plant selected for cropping is then given an upward cut, with care being taken not to cut off the top of the plant. The two stems are then fixed together by placing the cut lips neatly into each other. They are then firmly but gently held together by a tape, or miniature soft plastic clip or peg. The pair of plants joined together are then potted as one plant and left to grow in the normal way until the wound has properly healed. The plant should be supported by a small stick during the healing stage and kept away from wind, so that there is no movement of the stem.

When the plant has been put into its final growing place, the root of the fruiting plant is cut away. Normal practice is to make the cut in two stages. First a razor blade cut is made about half way through the stem. After 4 or 5 days, the cut is taken right through the stem and another complete cut made about 10 mm away, so that there is no chance of the stem bridging and healing over the cut. Details are shown in *Figure 8.1*.

The reason the fruiting plant root system is completely isolated, is to ensure that disease cannot be transmitted into the stem by bypassing the resistant root stock. Typical fruit stocks used include Grosse Lisse, Carmelo, Estrella and Florabon. The root system and growth of the grafted plant are enormous if given good conditions. A well developed plant will take up room equal to four or five non-grafted plants, so this has to be taken into account when selecting a growing spot for the plant.

Grafted plants are heavy feeders and for good results in container culture, plants should be fed by a drip system three times for one hour cycles on a hot day, or irrigated at least three times a day with a flow system. If grown in pots, the pot size should have a minimum diameter of 30 cm and height of 30 cm. Experience has shown that pots smaller than this are too restrictive for effective root growth and the crop would be very much below average. If the plant is not fed at regular short intervals during hot weather, the pot should stand in a reservoir of about 50 mm of well aerated nutrients.

Because of the heavy growth of grafted plants, a large lattice support is preferred, but if it is desired to use a wire cage surrounding a pot, then the cage needs to be of solid construction. The cage should be about 0.5 m diameter and 1.5 m high and be solidly anchored at the base, or fixed to a solid post or wall. The vine should be pruned to three or four leaders which can be trained around the mesh. An advantage of the cage is that it is easy to protect the vine during cold spells, by simply covering it with plastic.

Some hydroponicists have not been pleased with the performance of grafted varieties grown in pots. There have been a number of reports that whilst fruit numbers are large, the average size is smaller than that of many of the non-grafted varieties.

Because of the high cost of a grafted plant compared with a single potted seedling variety, they are not widely grown by home gardeners. Some growers consider it is not a practical way of growing tomatoes in Australia, because the climate allows a relatively long growing season. In Europe however, where the growing season is short and much of the production takes place in glasshouses, grafted varieties are used to a much greater extent to ensure vigorous growth and cropping.

Popular varieties

Most people have their favourite variety of tomato. Some prefer large beefsteak varieties because of their convenience in sandwich making, others prefer the small cherry types for salads, while some have a strong preference for so called 'low acid' types. Surveys indicate that most choices concern a matter of personal preference.

The tomato varieties currently available either through normal nursery sources, or through clubs whose members are involved in the preservation of old varieties, are such that almost everyone can be satisfied in regard to taste, texture, size, colour and resistance to disease.

Climate has a major influence on the overall performance of the plant and the fruit quality, so that whilst one particular variety may be popular in one district, it may not be favoured in another with different climatic conditions.

A large number of table varieties have been grown successfully in pots using hydroponics techniques. Most are generally available either as seeds or seedlings from the local nurseryman.

Some do much better than others in different States, so the advice of local growers should be sought in selecting the best varieties for a particular district.

So called 'processing varieties' are of interest to commercial growers, but of little interest to the fresh market or home gardener. Processing types include Pacesetter 882, UC 82B, UC 134, Roma, K 10, UC 204B, Peto 95 and many others. They are used for pulp products and whole peeled tomatoes, and most are suitable for mechanical harvesting.

Other varieties grown commercially include Burnley Surecrop, Daydream, Delta Contender, ES 58, Flora Dade, Floradel, Grosse Lisse No 45, Hayslip, Manapal, Napoli, Rouge de Marmande, Rumsey Cross, Salad Special, Tiny Tim, Tropic, VF 36, and Walter. Among the F1 hybrids, there are Big Berry 131, Patio Prize, Rumseys Red, Sunny, Super Sweet 130, Sweet Bite and Tempo. The seeds of many of these varieties are only available in bulk quantities in minimum size packs of 50 g. However, F1 hybrid seeds are very expensive and some varieties are available in 5 g packs. Prices range from about $25 to $350 per 50 gram pack, depending on the variety.

Desirable characteristics

There are many desirable characteristics of a good tomato. Some are more important for the home grower, others more important for the fresh market grower, while still others are important for the process market. These may be listed as:

- Smooth fruit of globe shape and 60 mm to 100 mm diameter.
- Deep red exterior or flesh colour, unless some other colour is preferred for a particular market.
- Good flavour.
- High resistance to diseases which commonly affect tomatoes e.g. *fusarium* and *verticillium* wilt, tomato mosaic virus etc.
- High resistance to physiological disorders e.g. blossom-end rot, blotchy ripening, greenback, fruit cracking, catfacing and roughness.
- Short internodes.
- Good fruit setting under a wide range of environmental conditions.
- Good crop yield when grown hydroponically.
- Good handling capability - will not bruise easily.
- Looks, smells and tastes like a real tomato.
- Breaks away easily at the knuckle when ripe.

It would be too much to expect all varieties to chalk up top marks for all these characteristics, but a few go very close to it. When disease resistance is claimed, it has to be considered that there are often many strains of each disease organism and while a particular variety may be resistant to some strains, it may be susceptible to others. The identification of various strains is a job for the laboratory and a commercial grower needs to determine quickly the exact type of a disease at the first indication of trouble, so that steps can be taken to prevent spread throughout the installation. This is particularly important with recirculating hydroponics systems.

Yield characteristics in containers

Generally speaking, yields from the most popular tomato varieties will average 6 to 7.5 kg of marketable fruit per plant, but this will vary considerably with the growing environment. *Figure 8.2* shows the result of trials with Burnley Bounty, Grosse Lisse and Mighty Red, grown under identical feed conditions using a nutrient mixture of CF25 to CF28, with a pH around 6.0. Fruit was picked during the cold months of April to the end of July.

The volume of medium per plant will have an influence on yield, as indicated in *Figure 8.3* with the variety Ultra Boy. Two plants were grown in a 25 litre lay-flat bag, giving 12.5 litres of medium per plant, a little over that provided for the 30 cm diameter pot.

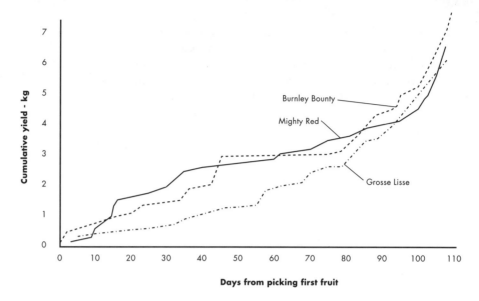

Figure 8.2 *Marketable yield from three varieties*

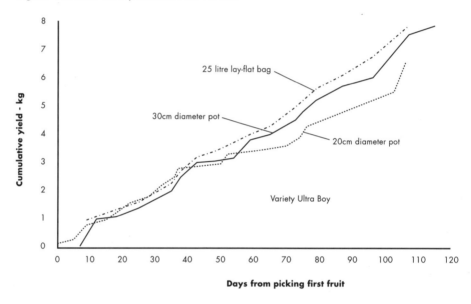

Figure 8.3 *Yield comparison 30cm & 20cm pots & lay - flat bag.*

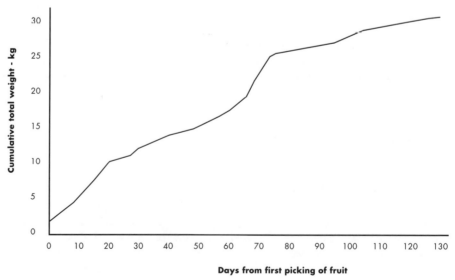

Figure 8.4 *Celebrity - total yield.*

Average total yield for the plants in the lay-flat bag was slightly higher than that from the plant in the 30cm pot, but both were better than the yield from the plant in the 20 cm pot.

The yields shown in the figures were for top (No.1 Grade or Grade A) quality marketable fruit. The total fruit yield was considerably higher, with No.2 Grade taking up about 25% and culls about 5%. This resulted in only 60% of the crop being included in the graphed yield figures. The No.1 Grade yield varies somewhat for different varieties, experience of the grower, the season, disease and physiological factors, but it is rare for the No.1 Grade to exceed 80% of the total fruit harvested.

Figure 8.4 shows the total crop yield (including unmarketable fruit) of the variety Celebrity, a prolific bearer under the right conditions. It was grown in a hydroponic poly-house by Mr Ray Rogers of Hydroponic Sales & Service in South Australia. The plant was planted as a seedling in mid September, and the fruit harvested over the period from early January to early May. it was grown in a polystyrene container, using about 40 litres of perlite. A 50 mm reservoir of nutrient solution was maintained to provide capillary feed, ensuring adequate moisture throughout the container medium.

The conductivity of the nutrient solution has a major influence on the yield of top quality fruit. *Table 8.2* shows the effects of different conductivity levels on the production of marketable fruit from three popular tomato varieties. The trials were carried out with pots immersed in reservoirs 50 mm deep, with the solution level automatically maintained by a valve.

Only fruit of Grade A or No.1 marketable quality was included in the yield figures - all others were rejected. As a general rule, rejected percentages were highest for the lowest and highest nutrient concentrations. A major proportion of rejects resulted from blossom-end rot of fruit. Others included small size, split fruit, misshapen fruit and greenback.

Variety	Conductivity Factor - CF	Av. fruit weight g	Av. marketable yield - kg	Reject %
Alicante	15 - 18	120	4.8	31
	20 - 26	128	6.9	25
	30 - 35	132	6.3	26
	40 - 50	102	4.2	38
Burnley Bounty	15 - 18	150	6.2	30
	20 - 26	228	7.5	24
	30 - 35	230	7.45	27
	40 - 50	170	5.9	26
Kelstar	15 - 18	192	6.1	29
	20 - 26	271	8.8	22
	30 - 35	280	8.5	20
	40 - 50	183	6.1	37

Table 8.2 *Yield variations from first six trusses of plants fed with different nutrient levels.*

Chapter 9. PESTS AND DISEASES

Chapter 9. PESTS AND DISEASES

Soilless culture not immune

Although there are many advantages in growing tomatoes hydroponically, the grower is still faced with the problem of dealing with a number of diseases, which can be encountered even in the absence of soil. Also, the majority of pests do not distinguish between soil grown and soilless grown crops.

The principal end result of attack by disease or insect, is a loss of productivity and whilst this may not be of great concern for the small home gardener, it may in severe cases mean financial disaster for a commercial grower.

The environmental conditions in which the tomatoes are grown, play a significant role in the incidence and severity of pests. The plants are susceptible to infection by air borne pests, such as aphids, mites and fungal pathogens, and such situations as high humidity and stagnant air favour a number of diseases, particularly powdery mildew. Powdery mildew is seldom encountered with tomatoes grown in a field in well drained soil, but is frequently a problem with tomatoes grown hydroponically in a polyhouse or glasshouse.

The wise manager will watch the plants and fruit for any sign of disease. A spray program should be implemented immediately the first indications of disease appear and be continued until fresh outbreaks cease. Spraying before a disease is evident may be costly and unnecessary, particularly if the weather conditions are not suitable for sustaining the disease.

At best, pesticides may stop further damage, but they cannot return a crop to its previous healthy and unblemished condition. If a bug has attacked a fruit, then that fruit is unmarketable in most cases.

Management

Pests and diseases can be introduced into an installation by a number of methods. Some can be introduced when air-borne spores land on a plant or are carried by insects or workers. Others may enter via the root system being introduced, by seed, cutting, water supply, or the media. The management of air-borne pests is no different from soil cultivation techniques, but management to control root pathogens requires a different approach.

A high degree of cleanliness is essential to minimise the spread of pests and diseases. Infected and infested plants should not be thrown on the ground or the floor, when removed from the growing area. They should be placed immediately in a bucket, or preferably in a plastic bag and the top tied. Pruning tools and other instruments should be sterilized by dipping them in a bucket of suitable sterilizer. Workers' hands should be thoroughly soaped and scrubbed. If this is not done, it may be extremely difficult to prevent the spread to other areas of the crop.

The container and medium used with any plant identified as having a disease should, without question, be thoroughly sterilized using sodium hypochlorite at the approved strength. Methyl bromide/chloropicrin is also effective. The reuse of the medium has economic advantages, but only if it does not result in the transfer of disease to the following crop. Sterilization is therefore essential for commercial crops.

Most public water supply systems are suitable for hydroponics, without any further chemical treatment. The heavy dosing of public water supplies with chlorine takes care of a lot of the micro-organisms which otherwise could be of concern to the grower. Some work has been done on the sterilization of water using ultra-violet light, but the provision of a suitable installation could perhaps only be justified for large scale commercial operations, where there is an identified problem with the water.

Seeds and seedlings

It is important to buy tomato seeds from a reliable source, as seeds can carry fungal or virus diseases and certain pests. A number of *fusarium* wilt diseases can be carried by seed, as some growers have found out to their disappointment. When seedlings emerge, they should be carefully examined so that any diseased or abnormal material can be removed immediately.

Seedlings which have been grown in soil should have all traces of soil removed, by washing the roots in flowing water. Some growers suggest the use of tepid water, while others prefer cold water. Those in favour of cold water treatment maintain that the cold water has an effect similar to an anaesthetic, and the seedling suffers less shock in being transferred to a new growing environment.

Dipping the roots in a fungicide, before transplanting to the hydroponics installation, will minimise the risk of fungal disease spread. However, if the seedling has a virus, the fungicide will not be effective.

Tomato seeds are in the 3-5 mm size range, have a silky appearance and will retain viability for a long time, even up to 10 years, with 90% germination if seeds are stored under cool dry conditions.

Pests

The most common insects encountered in the cultivation of tomatoes in containers, are red spiders, aphids, caterpillars, mites and white flies. No dedicated gardener likes using insecticides. The gardener's best friends, such as ladybirds, bees and wasps are nearing extinction in some areas because of the indiscriminate use of insecticides. With little threat from predators, the more robust and cunning villains of the pest world have only one goal, and that is to feed off the most accessible crop.

When trouble strikes, the local nurseryman or Department of Agriculture staff are happy to advise on measures to be taken and types of chemicals to be used, if this course is necessary. Two widely used chemicals are maldison and carbaryl. Maldison is effective against insects which feed on the leaf sap e.g. aphids and red spiders, while carbaryl is useful where insects eat the whole leaf tissue, e.g. caterpillars. When applying these materials the underside of the leaf should be treated as well as the top.

• Aphids
Aphids are small, soft bodied, green, grey or black insects with thin spidery legs. They may be winged or wingless and are usually slow moving. The insects cluster on the tips of the shoots and by sucking the sap, reduce the vigour of the plant. These pests should be closely controlled, as they are carriers of virus diseases which can seriously reduce crop yield.

They are most commonly seen in spring and autumn, when the weather is mild and humid.

• Looper caterpillars
These are voracious feeders of tomato plant leaves. They are soft bodied caterpillars, usually green with bright coloured bands on either side of the body, and are about 4 cm long when fully grown. They move about with a distinct looping action. Their presence is easily observed by the stripped foliage and tell-tale droppings.

They are at their peak of activity during summer and although they mostly attack foliage leaving large holes, they may attack fruit and flowers.

• Budworms
Budworms are caterpillars coloured brown, reddish or green and about 4 cm long when fully grown. They have irregular dark stripes on their back and a light stripe on each side of the body. Their action is to climb the plant and bore holes in the fruit. These pests are hard to kill and it is essential that any infestation be tackled early in the season, before the fruit becomes vulnerable to attack. Most problems are experienced in early and late summer.

• Thrips
Thrips are small, yellow, green, grey or black torpedo-shaped insects with or without wings. They have stylet type mouth parts, which slit the surface and withdraw sap from the leaves, fruit and flowers.

Although their injury to tomatoes is not great, they are carriers of spotted wilt virus disease, which seriously affects tomato plants.

One thrip species which has recently received considerable publicity in horticultural publications is the Western Flower Thrip (WFT). It has been a pest overseas for at least 12 years and about four years ago was detected in Western Australia. It has now spread to all states.

Although not yet a major problem with hydroponically grown tomatoes, it may spread viruses should it become established, particularly in a glasshouse environment.

A major problem is that the pest has become resistant to a wide range of chemicals and may be difficult to control should it become established in a growing area.

Thrips are very small but with the aid of a microscope can be distinguished from other thrip species by long black spines on the front edges of the shoulders.

• White fly

These are tiny white, leaf sucking pests that attach themselves to the underside of leaves. When disturbed, they float around like white dust or snow if the plant is heavily infested. For effective control, the undersides of the leaves need to be well saturated with spray.

The white fly (nymphs) appear as small, clear or opaque, pale green egg-like structures on the leaves. White fly is the most common pest in glasshouse tomato crops. The tiny insects, in sucking sap from the leaves, cause discolouration, leaf drop and stunting. They secrete a sticky substance, sometimes called honeydew, making it necessary to clean any affected fruit before marketing or using it on the table.

Some growers have publicised their experience in eliminating or controlling white fly. They range from planting marigolds, nasturtiums, garlic or basil close to the tomato bushes, to increasing the level of magnesium in the nutrient feed mixture. However, many growers who have tried these methods are of the firm opinion that they have no effect in control. *Figure 9.1* shows the life cycle of the greenhouse white fly.

Coloured sticky traps have been used by hydroponicists with varying degrees of success, to trap not only white fly, but some other insects.

Yellow coloured traps are the most widely employed for capturing white fly, although they may also trap aphids and thrips.

Traps are usually made by the hydroponicist and consist of flat boards, cylinders or spheres, painted a yellow or corio sand colour and coated with a sticky substance. One Adelaide grower found greater numbers of fly on spheres than any other shapes. He used 15 cm diameter plastic play balls.

Substances used to trap the insect include petroleum jelly, axle grease, honey and a number of commercially available substances. The substance should be applied very thinly, so that it does not black out the background yellow colour. Frequent cleaning of traps

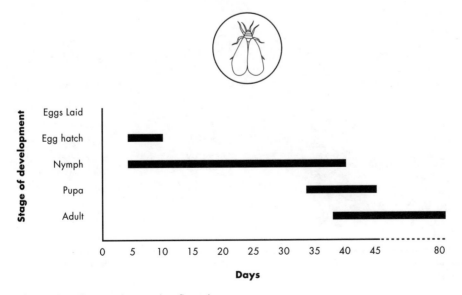

Figure 9.1 *The greenhouse white fly cycle.*

One of the most common pests in tomato greenhouse crops is whitefly. The insect secretes a sticky substance on the fruit making it necessary to clean the fruit before marketing. A number of non chemical devices are available to deal with the problem. One is the use of sticky fly paper or sticky substance applied to a sheet of metal painted yellow or orange colour.

is essential, together with renewal of the sticky substance.

To minimise the time consuming work of removal and cleaning of traps, one grower employed a flat yellow painted steel plate (about 30 cm square) for each trap, as a permanent attracting background, and used small disposable plates (about 10 cm by 20 cm) cut from plastic milk bottles and coated with the sticky substance. They were fixed to the main plate by a small piece of double-sided tape. The disposable plates were renewed on a monthly basis, until flies appeared on the traps. They were then replaced. at fortnightly intervals. Over a five year period, he did not use any chemical treatment specifically for control of the white fly.

Sticky traps have a number of advantages. They:

• Reduce the use of chemicals and encourage beneficial predators to migrate to the growing area.

• Provide an early warning of pests in the growing area.

• Are compatible with biological control techniques.

• Can indicate the effect of any control measure which may be implemented.

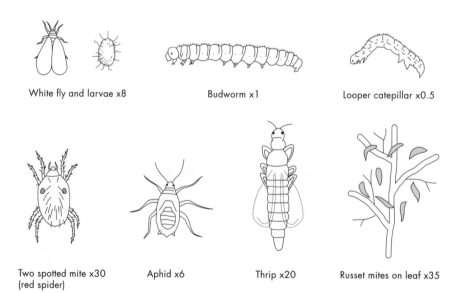

Figure 9.2 Typical tomato pests (indicating magnification).

- **Two spotted mite**

This is a serious summer pest for tomato growers. They are usually first noticed by the appearance of the leaves, which begin to look scorched, russety and dry. The undersides of affected leaves usually have fine webs, under which are hundreds of green to red mites and pearly eggs. The mites suck the sap of the leaves and when infestation becomes severe in warm weather, they are extremely difficult to control. They are not easy to remove, as they are resistant to many sprays commonly used.

- **Russet mite**

Russet mites are most severe in the autumn and are much smaller than two spotted mites. They are cream and torpedo-shaped, but are difficult to see with the unaided eye. However, the damage they cause is easily identified. The stems of the plant becomes bronzed and the lower leaves wither and die. The skin of the fruit becomes leathery and the flavour is affected. The fruit has a corky appearance. In severe cases the plant will die.

Figure 9.2 illustrates the appearance of typical pests encountered in growing tomatoes.

Intergrated pest management (IPM) using predators as biocontrol agents has been gaining some support in recent times, particularly in dealing with two spotted mites. The predatory mites can be used with a range of insecticides.

Diseases

Good disease control is essential for successful tomato growing. Most fungus diseases are difficult to deal with once they are firmly established. Problems should be anticipated and one of the fungicides recommended for tomatoes applied as a preventative measure. Prevention is the only defence against virus diseases. Once a plant is infected with a virus disease, nothing can be done to save it.

Diseases are difficult to identify, even for the seasoned grower. To identify which strain or type of disease has affected a plant is no job for the amateur. It requires a skilled and trained worker with suitable laboratory equipment.

Diseases are caused by pathogenic micro-organisms, which find their way to the plant via the hands of the workers, the air, water, carrier insects, or infected media. The categories of pathogenic microbes which cause diseases in container culture include viruses, bacteria and fungi. If soil is introduced, for example with seedlings, another category called nematodes may be found..

Viruses are minute organisms for which there is no cure. First signs of trouble usually show up as colour changes in leaves, or in some cases as curling or puckering of the leaf. A plant affected by a virus will be stunted, it will produce poor quality fruit and frequently the plant will die prematurely.

Bacteria are unicellular or multicellular organisms. Pathogenic bacteria can cause rotting or decay of leaves, stems and other parts of the plant. They also cause blockage of the vascular

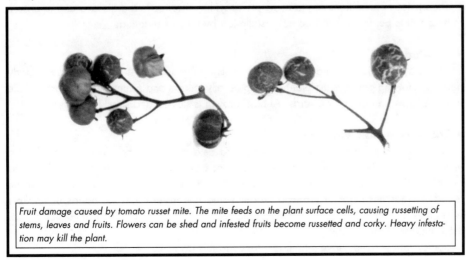

Fruit damage caused by tomato russet mite. The mite feeds on the plant surface cells, causing russetting of stems, leaves and fruits. Flowers can be shed and infested fruits become russetted and corky. Heavy infestation may kill the plant.

system, so preventing the movement of water and nutrients.

Fungi are multicellular complex organisms, which spread rapidly in an environment of cool temperature and high moisture. Those most encountered include powdery mildew, root rot, botrytis, fusarium and verticillium.

Crop sanitation practice is very important to prevent the introduction of pathogens into the system. These include:

- Use of disease-free seedlings.

- Removal of root residues from previous plants.

- Disinfection of the entire system, including growing containers, tanks and feed lines.

- Chlorination of water if derived from local sources.

- The entire system, particularly containers, should be clear of soil to prevent contamination.

- Ultra-violet irradiation of the nutrient solution as it leaves the pump system.

There are more than 30 diseases which affect tomatoes in Australia, but some appear to be confined to specific areas or districts. Those most commonly seen include:

- ## Fusarium wilt

Fusarium wilt is caused by a particular fungus which affects tomatoes. It is normally soil-borne and infects roots. It then grows through the water-conducting tissues in the plant stem. Plants become infected by growing in contaminated soil or medium, but the disease can be spread to new pots or media by transplanting infected seedlings. It may also spread to other pots or areas by contaminated nutrient solution.

When a plant is infected, the leaves yellow and wilt from the base of the plant upwards. Sometimes only one branch of the plant, or one side of a leaf, may show definite symptoms. In other cases the entire plant may wilt and die.

Fusarium wilt can be identified by cutting the stem of an affected plant length-wise. The woody part of the interior will show dark discolouration.

The most common form of *fusarium* wilt is known as Race 1, to distinguish it from other species of the disease. In recent years, breeders have developed plants with resistance to the second most common species, known as Race 2.

Resistant cultivars may become infected, but the disease will usually not be as severe as with susceptible cultivars and a reasonable crop yield should still be obtained.

- ## Verticillium wilt

Symptoms of this disease are similar to *fusarium* wilt, but the lower leaves tend to wither and dry without preliminary yellowing. Withering and wilting progress from the bottom up. Generally, the disease moves slower than *fusarium* wilt, causing stunting rather than plant death. Plants will continue to produce fruit, but they will be small and frequently unmarketable. The disease spreads in the same way as *fusarium* wilt.

The obvious precautions are to grow plants with resistance to the disease and to ensure that no soil is put in the hydroponics installation by way of seedlings.

- ## Spotted wilt

This is a virus disease and causes black spots on tomato leaves and stems, particularly near the growing points of the plant. Wilting usually follows and sometimes the plant will die from the growing point downwards. At best, growth is stunted and small fruit is produced.

- ## Tobacco mosaic virus

This causes a yellow to brown mottling on leaves and stems. Ripe fruit may also show a yellow mottling. Besides affecting the appearance of fruit, the virus reduces yield by as much as 20%. The virus is extremely infectious and is easily spread by workers. It can be found in cigarettes or other tobacco products and is transferred to the hands of smokers when they touch the tobacco. Washing hands with a laundry detergent gives better control than plain soap and water.

Some plant varieties have inbuilt resistance to this particular virus.

Component	Symptom	Likely causes	Action
Leaves	grey furry patches	grey mould	apply fungicide
	yellow between veins	manganese deficiency	apply foliar spray
	blue tinged	environment too cold	correct environment
	papery patches	too much sun	fit shade cloth
	brown areas on edges	blight	no cure
	yellow/brown patches	leaf mould	apply spray
	distorted or discoloured leaves	mosaic virus	no cure
	silky webbing on leaves	red spider mite	apply spray
	rolled leaf	wide temperature variations	correct environment
	leaf shrivel	virus	no cure
	wilted	root or stem rot or various wilt diseases	no cure
	dark tan spots	bacterial spot	apply fungicide
	greenfly infestation	aphids	apply spray
	sticky surface	whitefly	apply spray
	bronzing of foilage	russet mite	apply spray
	holed leaves	caterpillars	apply spray or dust
Roots	brown, corky	root rot	no cure
	swellings on roots	nematodes	no cure
Stem	brown canker at base	stem rot	no cure
	tunnelled	caterpillars	spray or dust
	grey mouldy patches	grey mould	apply fungicide
Fruit	blossom drop	not pollinated	tap plants
	dry set	not pollinated	tap plants
	sticky	whitefly	apply spray
	rotten	blight	apply spray
	dark patch on bottom	blossom end rot	keep well watered
	blotchy ripening	fails to ripen fully	check potassium level
	papery skin	sunscald	shield from sun
	hollow	several causes	check environment etc
	split fruit	excessive water	adjust
	greenback	too much sun or potassium deficiency	check shading/nutrients
	brown rings	buckeye rot	no cure

Table 9.1 Typical symptoms and causes

Table 9.1 shows a check list of typical symptoms and causes.

Figure 9.3 summarises the main means by which plant pathogens may find their way into a hydroponic installation and *Figure 9.4* illustrates in chart form, typical action in dealing with a pest or disease problem.

The introduction of pathogens into the crop, particularly with a recirculating nutrient solution, can have serious consequences on the final crop yield.

Not withstanding precautions in terms of housekeeping, some growers have experienced major problems from some media used in pot installations. One grower traced the problem to river sand medium and another traced the problem to peat medium.

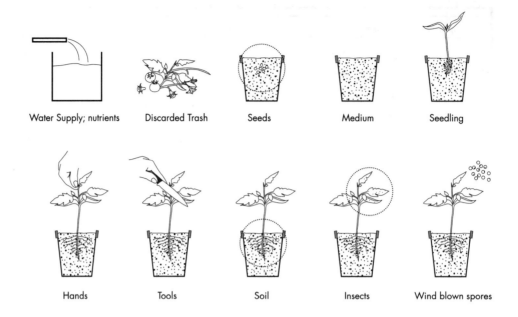

Figure 9.3 *Entry points of diseases into hydroponic system.*

River sand, even though well washed, often contains many plant pathogens. *Pythium* species in particular have been identified in hydroponic installations. Peat, by its very nature, can be a major source in the introduction of plant pathogens. Overseas growers who have used peat on a large scale from a variety of sources, have reported problems with *Fusarium* and *Pythium* species. Once introduced, a root infecting pathogen will spread rapidly throughout the installation. Control is frequently difficult.

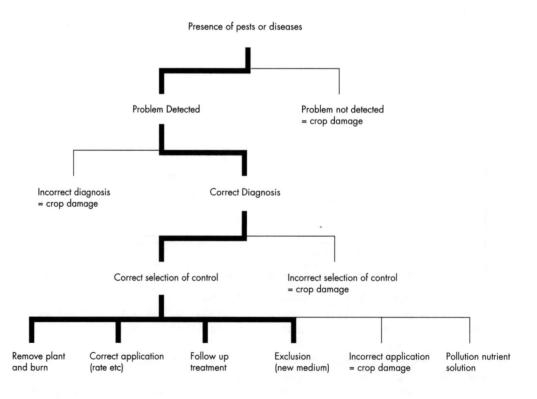

Figure 9.4 *Action for pest and disease eradication.*

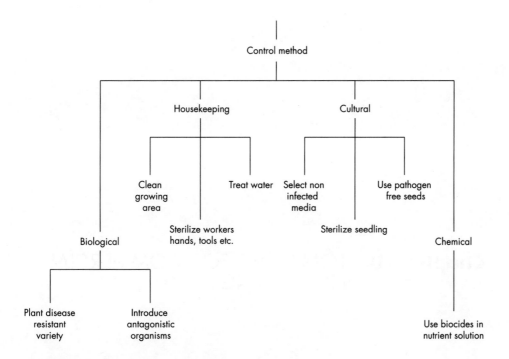

Figure 9.5 *Typical pathogen control methods.*

Figure 9.5 illustrates in chart form some control methods which may be appropriate in minimising the problem.

There are a number of techniques which can be employed to control the spread of water-borne plant pathogens in a hydroponic system. They include heat treatment, UV irradiation, ozonisation and slow sand filtration.

Chapter 10. TOMATOES FOR COMMERCIAL PROCESSING

Chapter 10. TOMATOES FOR COMMERCIAL PROCESSING

Production

Tomatoes grown for processing purposes are cultivated in enormous quantities and to date there has not been any significant swing to the use of hydroponics in Australia, to meet the huge demand of the processors. In some areas of the world however, the areas under cultivation for processing requirements have been increasing and growers using mechanical harvesting methods have selected sites of almost total sand, and use drip irrigation feeding standard hydroponic nutrients.

In typical field installations, plants are grown either as singles or in groups of three, surrounded by a strip of plastic 30 to 70 cm in diameter and walls about 30 cm deep. This prevents the nutrient solution from spreading out sidewards and causes it to sink below, where the roots follow. This ensures that roots are kept well down from the hot surface of the sand.

Varieties grown for commercial processing are usually chosen to obtain the best economic return. Local conditions and experience will have considerable influence on the variety selected. Not all varieties perform consistently well in all areas every year. Major physiological problems encountered may include blotchy ripening, cracking and green back or shoulder.

The major processors in Australia obtain their tomatoes from contract growers. The H.J.Heinz Company for example, purchases some 30-35,000 tonnes of tomatoes each year, which is the production output of about 1000 hectares. To produce this quantity by hydroponics would require very large scale installations, but in the future, should many of the present field areas become no longer suitable for various reasons, then growers may have to consider meeting the demand by standard or modified hydroponic techniques.

Under the present field cultivation arrangements, the basic needs of the processing company and growers to produce an economic crop are:

Tomato research facility by a leading processing company with plants being grown in an environmentally controlled greenhouse. Each plant is isolated from the others by growing in a terracotta pot with the pot standing in a terracotta saucer to eliminate transfer of water or soil borne pathogens from one plant to another. Each year the H J Heinz Company alone creates and examines many hundreds of new varieties for potential commercial use.

- The grower's ability to prepare land for and subsequently to manage and harvest a large area of raw crop. This means access to, or ownership of, a full range of equipment needed to plough and cultivate land and develop irrigation channels.
- The grower must have an adequate area of land of the correct soil type, with irrigation water rights sufficient to produce a satisfactory crop of tomatoes under normal conditions.
- In the case of hand picked crops, sufficient labour must be available for picking at harvest.
- In the case of mechanically harvested crops, the necessary equipment for harvesting the crop must be available.
- During the development of the crop after planting, the grower must be able to carry out weed control measures and fertiliser application to ensure crop success.
- The grower must be willing to co-operate with the Agricultural Officers employed by the company.

Tomatoes are either picked by hand or by machine and filled into wooden bins, each containing about 400 kg. Bins are loaded onto semi-trailers, about 32 to each load, and transported to the processing factory. The total size of the Australian canned tomato industry is about 200,000 tonnes annually.

Typically, field crops are grown in 16 ha plots, with growers having an average of 5 to 8 such plots. No area is planted more than two years in a row. One hectare of tomatoes will accommodate about 50,000 to 150,000 plants and an average yield is 35 tonne. However, yield varies considerably from district to district.

The processors have their growers plant plots in different climatic areas at different times, so that each day a different area is ready for harvest, ensuring a continual supply. On those plots where harvesting is carried out manually, the picking rate is 2 to 5 tonnes per person daily, whereas a machine harvester will easily handle 200 tonnes per day.

Agronomy extension service

The large processing companies offer tomato growers an agronomy extension service, backed by a tomato breeding program. In the case of H.J.Heinz Company, its Agricultural Field Officers plan with contract tomato growers a planting, management and harvesting schedule. Regular visits by field staff ensure crops are managed to achieve top yields of the best quality tomatoes. Approximately thirty growers are supervised by four qualified agricultural staff.

Among new technologies used in the tomato growing industry are laser land levelling, trickle irrigation, tissue testing, electronic colour sorters and harvesters.

The Heinz organisation conducts an extensive plant breeding program. It commenced prior to 1950, and has developed Big Red and many descendants. Big Red, developed in the days of hand harvesting, has now been superseded by a new group of varieties suitable for machine harvesting - The Big Red Family. They show excellent characteristics for machine harvesting and processing, but the size and shape make them unsuitable for the fresh market.

The Australian Heinz tomato program is supported by Heinz International team in USA, Canada and Portugal. Each year, over one thousand new varieties are created and examined in Australia for commercial use. Before a variety is accepted into the Big Red Family, it needs to be identified as a superior selection.

Desirable properties

Tomatoes grown for the commercial processing industry, require some qualities which differ significantly from those destined for the fresh fruit market. The processors require their tomatoes for sale as whole peeled tomatoes, tomato sauce, tomato paste and pulp for addition to soups, baked beans, spaghetti etc. In the case of the whole peeled tomato, the market requires that particular attention be paid to fruit size, shape and colour. The capability to hold together after peeling, is also a factor of considerable importance. Other attributes include small stem attachment, absence of white core tissue and good skin separation.

Although individual companies look for different overall attributes in raw tomatoes and plants, depending on the product lines to be manufactured, there is a high degree on commonality. Typical desirable qualities are:

- Good rich red fruit colour.
- Good carrying qualities.
- Resistance to mould development.
- Resistance to splitting.
- High soluble and insoluble solids content.
- Good pectin content.
- Good vine storage.
- Compact bushes.
- Sufficient leaf cover to minimise sunscald.
- High yield.
- Early maturity.
- Tolerance to low and high temperatures.
- Resistance to shattering, if harvested mechanically.
- Resistance to rain-induced cracking.
- Absence of calyx in harvested fruit.
- Uniform ripening characteristics.
- Resistance to diseases.
- Adaptable to a range of root environments.
- Acid content should not be too low.

In addition, processors require that the ripe fruit have some specific characteristics. These include:

- Acceptable tomato flavour.
- Rich red colour.
- Absence of white tissue or green jelly.
- pH in the range 4.1 to 4.3.
- Total solids preferably above 6%.
- Ascorbic acid above 18 mg per 100 g of puree.
- Acidity between 5.5 and 7.0.

Good tomato colour is present in most varieties being cultivated for processing purposes, but emphasis is now being placed by plant breeders on the development of varieties with greater total solids and with greater resistance to the unreliable climatic conditions frequently experienced in many of the growing areas.

Although processors prefer tomatoes with total soluble solids (TSS) of at least 6%, many soil grown commercial varieties are in the range 3.8% to 5.5%. The site has considerable influence on the TSS. For example, at one site in New South Wales, TSS figures were Flora-Dade, 4.0%; Redlands, 3.83%; and Summertaste, 4.33%. But at another site, results obtained were Flora-Dade, 4.93%; Redlands, 5.63%; and, Summertaste 5.92%. There was also significant variations in pH levels.

Sugars, which include glucose, fructose and sucrose account for about 65% of the total TSS, while organic acids and amino acids such as citric, malic and others make up the balance.

Sugars constitute 1.5-5.0% of the fresh weight of the fruit and have an important effect on taste. Reducing sugars for many varieties range from 2.9 to 3.3 (g/100 ml), with typical sugar/acid ratios varying from 0.3 to 4.4.

Tests reveal that there is a decline in the sugar content of ripe fruit after harvest, when the fruit is stored at room temperature. Other factors which have an adverse effect on the sugar level include shading of fruit by dense leaves, reduced light from the use of shade-cloth, removal of leaves from the plant and too high a nitrogen level in the nutrient solution.

Acids in the fruit play an important part in the taste component and in the processing of tomatoes. Processors look for acidity in the range 5.5 to 7.0.

Maximum acidity in the fruit coincides with the first appearance of pink colour. Malic acid concentration, which for Flora-Dade is about 0.15 and Grosse Lisse 0.21 (%w/v), falls as the fruit ripens, while citric acid, which for Flora-Dade is about 0.63 and Grosse Lisse 0.42 (%w/v), increases to the green/yellow ripeness stage and then levels out.

To achieve a better balance between sweetness and acidity, it is believed that sugar content of the fruit should be increased. This can be achieved by raising the TSS. Varieties can be bred to provide higher TSS, but this is a long process. There is some evidence in hydroponic trials that TSS can be increased with some varieties by increasing the CF level of the nutrient solution. However, with some varieties, total weight yield falls if the CF is taken above about 35, and more research needs to be done in this area.

Processing

The processing technique is much the same for most large companies, but the following procedure used by Edgell-Birds Eye is typical:

- The semi trailers arrive at the factory with loads of up to 300 boxes.

- The tomatoes are unpacked from the bulk boxes, which are then scrubbed, sterilized and returned to the growers, ready to crate the next consignment of ripe fruit.

- The tomatoes are first washed with high pressure jet sprays, as they pass through water channels and gently rotating drums, from which they are collected directly on to moving conveyors. They are quality graded and weighed, and separated into their various categories. This is because different varieties and conditions of fruit are used for each of the specific processes - in the solid packs of whole peeled tomatoes, tomato supreme, tomato puree, or the liquid products such as tomato juice and tomato soup.

- Fruit selected for the whole peeled tomato pack, are carried on conveyor belts through a steam blanching tunnel, where the tomatoes are subjected to high temperature live steam for about 1fi minutes, followed at once by a direct jet cold spray of water. The application of these extremes of temperature loosens the skin from the flesh, and it is then easily removed. The peeled tomatoes are then carried to a semi-automatic hand pack filler, where they are systematically packed into correctly sized cans, by highly qualified operators.

- Simultaneously, tomatoes for the liquid packs undergo a different process, in which they are pressed through specially designed juice extractors, which squeeze all the juice from the fruit. A quantity of this sieved juice is drawn off, prepared with salt and sugar, and added to the cans of whole peeled tomatoes.

- On completion of the filling process, the cans proceed immediately to the closing machines for hermetic sealing.

- In the next step, the cans are packed into crates, and pressure cooked at very high temperature, in order that all the food value and flavour are retained in the product. The crates are then rapidly cooled, the cans removed from the crates and stacked on pallets in the warehouse.

- After a short period of time, the products settle down. Technical checks are made and finally the cans are labelled, packed into outer cartons suitable for either overseas or home markets and despatched en route to their point of sale.

- The further processing of the other tomato products, such as tomato puree, tomato juice and tomato soup, operates on a liquid flow system. These are prepared in stainless steel steam vessels according to the required formulation (or recipe), then canned, pressure cooked, labelled and cartoned for despatch in precisely the same manner as the whole peeled tomatoes.

- Tomato pulp is processed from ripe tomatoes. It is sieved, flash-sterilized, and sealed in large cans for use continually throughout the year, as an ingredient in a wide variety of products requiring tomato as a liquid flavouring medium.

Appendix: SELECTION OF TOMATO VARIETIES FOR HYDROPONIC PRODUCTION

A selection of twenty popular varieties which have been successfully grown in containers employing hydroponic techniques. Details are provided of their characteristics, yields, recommended nutrient concentrations, and growing media.

Apollo

- Early to midseason
- Hybrid
- Indeterminate

Apollo is a superb F_1 hybrid staking variety that has been popular with home gardeners, particularly hydroponicists since its introduction some years ago. It performs well in pot culture with very loose or coarse medium. A nutrient solution maintained around CF 25 will give best performance, with a large percentage of marketable fruit.

It produces a very good crop with phosphorus about 50 ppm and potassium about 250 ppm. However, it is important to keep the nitrogen/potassium ratio at 1.5 to 1 during the bright light and high temperature environment of summer. Weights up to 7.5kg per plant from six trusses, are typical with Apollo, with good management of the nutrient mixture and the pH level.

Apollo produces a good crop of large fruit over an extended period when fed by jet, flow or drip feed on a properly controlled basis. If feed cycles are irregular during very hot weather results may be disappointing, especially with fruit size. Given favourable weather conditions fruit of weight 120 to 150 g with five or six fruit per truss can be expected. The fruit is smooth and globular.

The variety exhibits good resistance to *verticillium* wilt, but is a wise precaution to thoroughly sterilize pots before planting a new crop.

Apollo is widely sought after for use with salads and sandwiches. It is delicious with a sprinkling of chopped up basil or a dash of cinnamon, if a spice is preferred. Average pH from an early season crop was 4.3.

Because the variety was unavailable for a period, Yates in 1994 introduced Improved Apollo, a vigorous grower with the same prize winning characteristics of Apollo.

Burnley Bounty

- Late
- Standard
- Indeterminate

A very popular variety which performs exceptionally well in pots with most media. If planted in late summer, it will produce a prolific crop well into spring, if protected from cold wind and frost. In an unheated greenhouse, large red ripe tomatoes can be picked well into August even in southern States. Crops of 7.5 kg per plant are typical for a six truss vine.

Burnley Bounty thrives on a strong nutrient mixture. Strengths in the range CF25 to 30 are ideal and will result in large numbers of fruit 175 to 280 g in weight. It responds well to increased phosphorus (to 60 ppm) and potassium to 400 ppm. However, with such a high level of potassium, the magnesium should be kept at about 75 ppm.

In mid winter when there may be long periods of cloud combined with low temperatures, best results will be obtained with a nitrogen/potassium ratio of N1 to K2. If this is not done, there may be a significant increase in the number of off-shaped fruit combined with a reduction in total yield.

Plants usually take 60 to 75 days to reach maturity from seedling stage. The fruit has a pleasantly sharp taste and is suitable for salads, grills, sandwiches and soups. They freeze well, but like all frozen tomatoes are only suitable for soups or stews when thawed out.

With Burnley Bounty, a high yield of well shaped fruit will be obtained if the stem is stopped one leaf from the top truss, after six or seven trusses have formed.

It will set fruit at temperatures much lower than for many other indeterminates and this makes it well sought after for extending a crop into the colder weather.

Average pH for tomatoes picked from six trusses in October was 4.45. With a nutrient solution of conductivity CF 25 and solution modified to provide P 60 ppm and K 400 ppm, the average sugar Brix level, for selected fruit picked in September was 4.6% and in December it was 6.2%.

Burnley Gem

- Early
- Standard
- Determinate

This variety was developed by the Victorian Department of Agriculture about 1968 and does well in most States, except in the very hot areas. It has the ability to set fruit at low temperatures and because of this is widely grown for an early crop. Fruit is highly coloured, frequently with dark green shoulders.

Burnley Gem is a dwarf bush variety which performs well in pots, but a wire frame is desirable to contain branches and fruit.

It produces a good crop of tomatoes when fed with nutrient solution in the range CF 25 to 30 and a pH of around 6.1. The bush is easily contained with a frame fitted to a 30 cm diameter pot and will produce a yield of medium sized fruit when fed with a jet or flow feed system providing 500 to 600 ml of nutrient per minute, for 10 minutes twice a day during hot weather. During cooler periods, or in the early growth stage, one feed per day is usually sufficient. For drip feed, irrigation should be provided at two hourly intervals during daytime and once about midnight. Each cycle should be for at least 15 mins duration. Fruit is smooth and round and of medium size.giving a delicious flavour if left on the bush till the fully ripe stage. It is ideal for grilling on a crumpet with a sprinkling of chopped chives. It also makes a supreme tomato soup, with a sprinkling of oregano or basil before serving.

Burnley Gem exhibits good resistance to *fusarium* wilt, one of the major diseases encountered by tomato growers. Modest truss thinning at early growing stage will improve the size of remaining fruit, as well as the yield of subsequent trusses.

In a trial with five plants in 20 cm pots with scoria medium, several of the fruit exhibited sunscald and blossom-end rot when harvested at the end of the trial, during early January.

Celebrity

- Midseason
- Hybrid
- Determinate

An F₁ hybrid which has vigorous growth characteristics if well fed with a balanced nutrient mixture. When grown in a pot, the bush should be secured inside a heavy gauge wireframe, anchored to the pot. Alternatively, it can be tied to a wire mesh frame supported by posts. The plant grows well with most media, provided there is good aeration. It will crop poorly if grown in vermiculite which has broken down, or in scoria which has too much fines.

A nutrient strength of CF 25 to 28 has been found to produce a heavy yield of medium sized tomatoes, with many in the range 200 to 220 g. The skin is thinner than many other hybrids, making it popular for salads and sandwiches. Chefs have described the flavour as being fairly robust.

Celebrity crops well with most feed methods, but produces slightly better with a flow system particularly when nearing the peak of the crop. Maturity is about 70 days from seedling transplant. One characteristic that has been noticed with Celebrity is that, whilst it can take a fair degree of high temperatures for an extended period, it shows a lot distress if subjected to hot winds. The leaves curl up and growing points droop. Blossom-end rot is much greater under this environment.

It is a very good variety where disease is a problem. It has resistance to *verticillium* wilt races 1 and 2, *fusarium* wilt and tobacco mosaic virus. It also exhibits resistance to nematodes, but this latter disease is seldom experienced in hydroponic installations if seedlings are not taken from areas where nematodes have been a problem.

With nutrient solution strength of CF25, measured average sugar Brix level for fruit on the first truss in October was 5.8%. With CF increased to 30, the sugar Brix level of fruit on the second truss was measured at 6.6% in January.

College Challenger

- Mid-late season
- Hybrid
- Indeterminate

This variety bred at Hawkesbury Agricultural College, in New South Wales, produces a large yield of globe shaped fruit similar in shape and size to Grosse Lisse, but ripens much earlier.

Although it reaches peak production fairly quickly, it will continue to produce good size fruit for many months after, even into early autumn, if given good conditions and fed with a nutrient solution in the range CF28-30. Several plants in a trial, fed with a solution of CF35 produced larger fruit of marketable quality, but fewer in number. Several had a BER problem.

The plant is a vigorous grower if well fed, and needs a lot of pruning attention to keep the vine under control. The nitrogen level needs to be kept under control, otherwise there will be excessive vegetative growth. Nevertheless, the nitrogen level should not fall much below 180 ppm, otherwise problems will be experienced with delayed fruit set and reduced total yield.

Ripening fruit of College Challenger can sometimes be severely affected under high temperature conditions. Trials with six plants growing in 30 cm pots, with 50/50 perlite/scoria medium, and irrigated with a flow-through system three times daily, resulted in a low yield following an extended period of temperature which exceeded 27°C for at least six days. The fruit turned yellow/orange, they were soft and lacked taste. Of 17 large fruit on the first four trusses, 7 were unmarketable. Another plant with 26 fruit of total weight 5.6 kg, produced 9 fruit which were rejected as being unmarketable class. Most of the fruit rejected were in the range 220 to 340 g.

Typical pH of samples harvested in mid summer was 4.2, with average sugar Brix level being 4.5%. Fruit were firm and had good shelf life after being harvested at the fully ripe stage. Maturity was reached about 60 days after plant out.

In addition to keeping a close watch on the nitrogen level with this variety, the potassium should also be kept under observation. A potassium level of at least 200 ppm will ensure firm fruit with a long shelf life.

First Prize

- Midseason
- Hybrid
- Bush

First Prize is a bush hybrid type, with a strong thick support stem. It is best grown with a wire frame attached to the pot rim, as this helps to support the fruit. It thrives in perlite or scoria and there is very little difference in crop yield using 30 cm or 20 cm diameter pots.

The plant does not produce a good leaf cover for the fruit and some screening from the sun is often necessary to minimise loss of marketable fruit from sunscald. The root system needs to be kept moist during hot weather, as this variety is subject to blossom-end rot of fruit.

A medium strength solution of CF 22 to 25, with a pH of about 6.2, has produced good results with flow and drip feed systems. With high strength solutions for extended periods, there is a tendency for fruit growth to slow down and mature more rapidly. The nitrogen/potassium should be carefully controlled, particularly if grown under partially shaded conditions. A ratio N1:K2 should be used.

When grown in pots, the bush will produce good quality medium sized fruit around 100 to 120 g, but the fruit takes much longer to ripen than most other varieties. If picked before full maturity, the fruit has poor flavour. A sprinkling of chopped basil leaves will enhance the flavour. Chives chopped into small pieces and sprinkled over a slice of tomato on wholemeal bread makes a delicious sandwich with First Prize. The fruit has a thin skin and this makes it popular with Chefs preparing salads.

Although a trial of six plants fed with a nutrient solution CF30 showed a higher sugar Brix level than those fed with a solution of CF20, there was an increase in fruit with blossom-end rot of about 10%.

Gardeners Delight

- Early
- Standard
- Determinate

Gardener's Delight is, according to many old timers, one of the few tomatoes readily available which possesses a delicious sweet taste, similar to many of the popular varieties grown by home gardeners in the early 1930's.

Fruit is only bite size, but is magnificient in salads and as mini slices on bread rolls. It adds that real tomato taste when added to a stew.

Pot culture indicates that it needs to be well watered, as it has a tendency to wilt when temperatures pass the 25°C mark. Gardener's Delight is a heavy feeder, and produces a good crop with a nutrient solution of CF23 to 26. Potassium in the range 300 to 400 ppm will ensure high quality fruit. The iron level should be watched with this variety, as the growing leaves tend to pale off quickly if the level drops too low. An iron level of 10 ppm will help growth, but when the first picking takes place the level should be dropped to about 5 ppm.

Fruit measuring 25 to 37mm are borne in clusters of 6 to 12 and usually ripen evenly on the stem. The fruit has good resistance to cracking and will take a fair amount of poor management in relation to erratic irrigation cycles. Temperatures have to be fairly high and the medium close to dry before any sign of wilt begins to show. This is one of the reasons why Gardener's Delight is so popular with growers who have only a patio or a balcony on which to place their pots.

Maturity time is about 65 days from seedling to harvest. This cherry tomato is frequently identified as 'Sugar Lump' in some seed catalogues.

In a taste test trial during 1993, it was ranked eighth, scoring 67 points out of a possible 100 when judged on flavour, colour and texture. Average pH reading for a sample of 10 fruit was 4.15 and sugar Brix level for the same sample was 5.1%.

Grosse Lisse

- Midseason
- Standard
- Indeterminate

A very popular high yielding variety, widely grown by hydroponicists. In pot culture it produces a good crop in the range 6.5 to 8kg for 30 cm pot and 6 to 7kg for 20 cm pot. Many fruit will be around 300 to 450g in weight for the first six trusses. Grosse Lisse is a heavy feeder and needs the nutrient mixture to be maintained in the region CF28 to 30, with phosphorus at 50 to 60 ppm and potassium 300 to 350 ppm. However, the nitrogen/potassium ratio should be adjusted for seasonal conditions. By keeping it to N1 to K2 during colder months, fruit will be well shaped and firm.

Calcium levels should be maintained above 100 ppm for Grosse Lisse. If allowed to fall to about 50 ppm, there will be considerable loss of marketable fruit due to blossom-end rot problems. Although basically a midseason variety, it will crop well into July and August if protected from frost and cold wind blasts. When ripe, fruit is a rich red colour.

Jet or flow feed at a rate of 500 to 600ml per minute, for 10 minutes, three times daily will produce a high yield of top quality fruit, if the nutrient mixture and pH are maintained at correct levels. Fruit will be ready for picking in about 95 days from plant out. The plant loses a lot of water because of the density of the leaves so the feed system needs to be closely monitored to ensure that the medium is always maintained at the optimum moisture condition. Blossom-end rot will be a problem if the watering system has been badly designed. The root system should have sufficient water during hot periods.

Good hygiene is very important with this variety. It is susceptible to *verticillium* and *fusarium* wilt, tobacco mosaic virus and target spot. Fruit frequently exhibit sunscald, so leaves should not be removed near the fruit during mid summer periods. Average pH level for a trial of eight plants was 4.25, with the plants being fed with nutrient solution of CF 30. The sugar Brix level varied from 6.0% at the first truss, to 5.8% at the sixth truss.

Jubilee

- Late
- Standard
- Indeterminate

This variety has been around for a very long time and is one of the most popular non-red colour tomatoes with the home gardener. It has an outstanding yellow-orange hue which gives it something of a novelty characteristic.

Connoisseurs claim it has a mild flavour and seems to be less acidic than many of the rich red varieties. It makes a delicious meal when grilled with some sweet basil leaves. The fruit seed cavities are irregular, rather than being symmetrical. This gives it a high flesh content. Fruit are large, round and smooth with no shoulders.

With a nutrient feed strength of CF23 to 26 and a nitrogen/potassium ratio at N1:K1.5 during the end of winter, yields of 4.5 to 6.5kg per plant are typical when grown in pots. Best results are obtained with a medium comprising 50/50 perlite and peat. Peat alone also gives good results, but not as good as a mixture including perlite. When the temperature drops below about 15°C, Jubilee take much longer to ripen compared with temperatures in the 20°C and above range. Experience has shown that this variety will react quickly if pH of the nutrient solution falls below 5.5, so care should be taken to regularly monitor the pH and make necessary adjustments as required. Potassium hydroxide added to the feed tank will raise the pH.

Not a lot is known of disease resistance characteristics of Jubilee, but trials with a group of 12 plants in 30 cm diameter pots over a period of about 15 months did not reveal any disease problems.

Jubilee will not take kindly to a low moisture medium. It wilts quickly and some shoots do not always fully recover after application of water. Plant yields in pots in a 2 cm reservoir out performed those in drip fed pots without a reservoir, by about 10%.

Magnifico

- Early
- Hybrid
- Indeterminate

This is a very early hybrid variety which produces a prolific crop of firm, smooth and sweet tasting fruit. Fruit is generally medium size, in the range 150 to 300g, but towards the end of the cropping season when temperatures tend to be high, fruit sizes drop considerably to around 100 - 180g in weight.

The plant has an extensive root system and does not like a cramped growing environment. It will do much better in a 30 cm diameter pot than a 20 cm one. Wet roots tend to retard growth of Magnifico, but it reacts quickly if the roots are deprived of moisture during warm weather. A reservoir system has been used with some success,.but the level should be kept to about 50 mm if a highly absorbent medium such as perlite is used. Tests with perlite, vermiculite, scoria and peat have given reasonably good results, but best yield has been obtained with a 50/50 mixture of perlite and scoria.

Magnifico does well with a nutrient strength of CF23 to 26 and a pH of around 6.3. Crop yields up to 7 kg are typical for six trusses under these conditions. Maturity is reached in 80 to 90 days after transplant.

A drip feed system produces a good crop if nutrient is applied regularly and at no greater intervals than two hours during sunlight periods. There should be sufficient feed to produce a waste of about 50 ml.

Some problems have been experienced with greenback with this variety when grown in pots. It is more evident in the warm sunny weather, but an increase in the potassium level will minimise the problem. Although disease problems are seldom encountered with Magnifico, bacterial spot has been experienced with some hydroponic installations

Mighty Red

- Early to late
- Hybrid
- Indeterminate

Mighty Red is a popular variety, particularly in South Australia, where it was released some years ago. It produces a good crop of medium to large size fruit over a long period, from summer to early winter. Taste is very good and it is widely used in salads, for sandwiches and in relish.

Solid high tripod stake system is one of the preferred support systems for pot culture. The fruit is heavy and it pays to support the loaded trusses with stocking or mesh as the stalk has a tendency to pinch and so restrict the flow of water to the fruit.

Mighty Red has a large root system and does well in a 30 cm pot, providing the roots are kept moist. The roots are tolerant of wet feet and a 50mm reservoir is a good means of ensuring adequate moisture is available during the hot days of summer.

A drip or flow system with nutrient strength CF25 to 30 will produce a high yield of top quality tomatoes. A drip feed setup should give irrigation at two hourly intervals during daylight hours and once at midnight during summer. Sufficient nutrient should be applied to give a waste of 50 ml. In a flow system, nutrient should be applied at a rate of about 600 ml per minute for 10 minutes three times daily.

With a flow arrangement, yields of 6 to 7.5kg are typical for six trusses, with individual fruit being in the range 250 to 400g and odd ones weighing 430g. Maximum productivity will be reached in 142 days. Mighty Red produces high yields in most media, but results with 70/30 perlite and peat gave the best results in a trial involving media of perlite, perlite and peat, coarse sand, vermiculite, scoria and 6 mm gravel.

The variety appears to be reasonably resistant to many diseases which affect tomatoes, but one test trial had to be abandoned, because of an outbreak of tobacco mosaic virus brought in with seedlings from an external source. Typical pH for first truss fruit in mid summer is 4.4. Sugar Brix levels vary with nutrient concentrations, but measurement of fruit on the first truss of one plant gave an average of 6.2%

Fruit are subject, to sunscald so care should be exercised when removing leaves near the fruit.

Ox Heart

- Late
- Standard
- Indeterminate

As its name implies, the fruit is shaped like a large heart. The variety has been popular with gardeners for about 70 years and is often advertised as being of low acid content.

Ox Heart is deep pink in colour, large, fleshy, of mild taste and has few seeds. Fruit weights are frequently 450 to 600g, with odd ones close to 1 kg each. To produce large fruit, this variety requires a nutrient strength of CF25 to 28, with potassium about 300 ppm. Nitrogen should be kept below 250ppm, otherwise side shoots and leaf growth will be excessive, resulting in reduced fruit size.

The plant is large and will take up a lot of water during a hot day. However, it prefers a pot environment that is not excessively wet for long periods. Water logged roots will produce large fruit, but they will be soft and watery. For firm solid fruit, most of the pot medium should be moist only. Scoria and fine gravel seem to provide the best growing conditions. A drip feed system gives good results as most of the medium, particularly near the top, is fairly dry. However, during hot periods of a summer day, dripping may have to be maintained without interruption.

Chefs find Ox Heart ideal for stuffing with chopped up and pre-cooked vegetables and also as a breakfast grill with a sprinkling of cinnamon spice.

Diseases are not a problem with this variety, although some growers have had crops ruined by Irish blight, particularly during cool and wet weather. However, the problem in most cases cleared up with return of fine weather.

Average pH readings of selected fruit picked from the first truss of six plants during mid December was 4.7. With a nutrient mixture of CF25, average sugar Brix level of fruit from the same fruit was 6.5%.

In a trial involving five plants in 30 cm pots and scoria/perlite medium, several fruit exhibited circumferential splitting during hot weather in mid December.

Pixie

- Early to late
- Hybrid
- Dwarf

Pixie is a small bush F_1 hybrid, ideal for pot cultivation. However, a wire cage securely tied to the rim of the pot is required. It can be successfully grown indoors if placed near a window where there is some sunlight, but it is also very popular with hydroponicists for the balcony or patio.

Pixie is an extremely fast cropper, being productive in 40 to 50 days from seedling stage. It is not unusual for 20 to 30 trusses to be carried by a single bush. Fruit size is up to 30 mm diameter, but it is very fleshy and its delicious flavour is similar to many of the large top quality tomatoes.

If protected from cold winds and frosts, Pixie will crop well into winter, but at this stage the nutrient solution should be adjusted to ensure a nitrogen/potassium ratio of N1 : K1.5. A strength in the range CF20 to 23 will result in a good yield. Some trials with this variety indicate that the flavour of winter grown fruit will be enhanced if the medium is kept just damp enough to meet the needs of the plant. A root system that is maintained in a very wet condition will result in the production of fruit which is watery and of poor taste.

Many cooks agree that Pixie makes a superb chutney and is ideal for incorporation in a stew, where a tangy tomato taste is required. Pixie trials indicate that it is only partially resistant to tobacco mosaic virus, so care needs to be taken to ensure that this disease is not introduced from infected sources.

When Pixie is fed with a nutrient solution of about CF30, the total weight yield will be reduced by about 12% compared with a plant fed with CF20 to 23. However, sugar Brix level will be increased by about 1.0%.

Ponderosa

- Late
- Standard
- Indeterminate

This beefsteak type tomato has been around for 100 years, but seeds have not always been easy to obtain. It is a deliciously flavoured tomato with a sweet taste and is highly prized for grills and sandwiches. The flesh is very firm with few seeds and a little gel. It has a taste which some experts class as a 'real old fashioned tomato taste'.

Pot culture with flow or jet feed arrangements reveals that Ponderosa does not have a yield as high as many of the new hybrid types. With a nutrient feed of CF26 to 30, fruit size averages 300 g, but there are frequently several in the range 350 - 400 g on the first and second trusses. Trusses usually carry only two to three fruit and because of the weight of the fruit, need support.

During hot sunshine weather, some protection may be required, as the foliage is not very dense. Sunscald has resulted in a lot of unmarketable fruit in some installations, so leaves should not be cut away unless they are diseased. The plant seems to be a high priority target for red spider mite and this aggravates the leaf shading problem.

Maturity takes longer than many other varieties, being 85 to 90 days from seedling transplant stage. Ponderosa grows well in most media but trials with perlite, scoria, sand, peat and small gravel indicate that a mixture of perlite and peat at 60/40 gives the best crop yield. The plant is capable of high yield with most feed systems. However, it requires a well aerated nutrient solution and this should be taken into account when setting up the feed arrangements. Also, it does not like wet roots, so a reservoir should not be provided.

Ponderosa appears to have a reasonably high resistance to tomato diseases, as very few cases of trouble are known among growers. Summer ripened fruit has a pH of 4.7 on the average, putting the tomato on the preferred list.by connoisseurs.

Roma

- Midseason to late.
- Standard
- Determinate

A medium sized bush that has been around for some 30 years. It produces egg-shaped fruit with a tough skin, thick flesh and few seeds. The fruit can be peeled quite easily and is ideal for bottling, sauce and tomato paste. Whilst it can be eaten fresh with salad, its solid thick flesh lacks flavour compared with many other varieties. It usually finishes well down the list in taste tests. The fruit is pear or egg shaped with a slight neck and will grow to 75 mm in length if well fed. It has a thick leaf cover which covers the large crop from the sun.

Blossom-end rot is a major problem with Roma and calcium should be maintained to at least 200 ppm with a good supply of water. A foliar spray may also be necessary to keep losses to a low level.

Roma produces well with most media, but care should be taken to ensure that the medium is well moistened throughout the growing season. Losses as high as 30% have been reported for plants grown in pots using vermiculite which received insufficient water during hot periods of the day. A mixture of peat/perlite at 30/70 gives good results when fed with flow or jet systems. The variety prefers a medium strength nutrient solution when grown in pots. A strength maintained in the range CF22 - 24 has produced good results with the pH maintained at 6.0. It does not like salt build-up and it pays to flush out the pots at intervals of about three weeks.

Breeders have recently produced an improved Roma called Super Roma with larger fruit, a bigger yield and improved disease resistance. The new tomato also has improved flavour and produces a high yield crop within 70 days of seedling transplant.

Tests on a selection of fruit in the 60-75 g range from a single bush gave an average pH of 4.5. Average sugar Brix level for three tomatoes from different plants was 4.8%.

Rouge de Marmande

- Early
- Standard
- Determinate

A very popular variety of tomato, producing medium to large flat, wrinkled or scalloped fruit with a delicious flavour. Originally a French import about 70 years ago, it has been described as 'the classic European taste master'. It has a reputation as a gourmet's tomato and although not widely available as fruit at the green grocer, it is sought out by serious cooks for its unequalled texture and flavour. It has few rivals for use in tomato soup.

In pot culture, good results have been obtained with a medium strength nutrient mixture of CF20 - 24 applied using a drip system, with levels of phosphorus at 50 ppm and potassium at 250 ppm. Maximum productivity will be reached in about 130 days. Some pot installations have produced an excessive number of unmarketable fruit as a result of blossom-end rot. It is important that the level of calcium be maintained at about 160 ppm.

A wire frame is one of the best methods of supporting this variety when grown in pots. Staking is not satisfactory due to the bushy nature of the growth. Whatever method is used to support the plant, it is essential to keep the leaves and particularly the fruit well clear of the top of the medium. They are grown when weather conditions are usually cold and wet and the medium is normally very damp. Disease spreads rapidly if allowed to occur and poor management could lead to a poor yield of top quality fruit. This variety is susceptible to tobacco mosaic virus and many crops have been ruined when the disease quickly spread throughout the crop. If there is any sign of TMV, pots should be washed in trisodium phosphate and gloves and tools should be cleaned in the solution.

Rouge de Marmande will set fruit in the cooler weather more readily than many other types, but if grown in a glasshouse, manual pollination of flowers will be necessary to produce a high yield.

Measurement of a selection of fruit ready for the table gave a pH reading of 4.1. There does not appear to be much change in sugar Brix level for fruit produced in nutrient solutions of CF20 - 24 and CF28 - 30. The yield from the CF28 - 30 solution was about 5% lower.

Super Beefsteak

- Midsummer to late
- Hybrid
- Indeterminate

This is a tomato with a rich flavour, which produces well in hot weather when many other varieties are struggling to produce top quality marketable fruit. However, it must be kept well fed with a high strength nutrient mixture.

Trials of 20 plants in 30cm diameter pots produced good yields during winter, when a solution of CF27 - 30 and pH 6.2 was applied, with phosphorus at 40 - 50ppm and potassium at 200 - 250ppm. The nitrogen/potassium ratio should be maintained at N1 : K1.5 for best results. If the potassium is not kept at a high level, there will most probably be a high percentage of greenback fruit.

Fruit size will average 300 g, with odd singles at 900g on lower trusses when grown in 30cm pots. With 20cm pots, the yield will be about 20% lower and the root system will be very restricted. Super Beefsteak grows quickly with a flow or jet system feed, providing about 600 ml of the feed solution is applied per minute, over a 10 minute period, twice daily during a hot day. The plant does not produce a good crop if grown in an environment where the roots are in stagnant water. If a reservoir is used, the solution should be kept well aerated.

A medium of perlite and peat will result in a high yield. A ratio of 60/40 perlite to peat produced slightly better results than a straight perlite medium. However, the total weight difference was small. During hot summer days, the plants exhibited less stress with the mixture which contained the peat. Some trials indicated a fruit setting problem when grown in glasshouses during summer but once the fruit had set, growth was rapid.

The fruit of this variety is large and contains a high level of water, so care should be taken to ensure that the plant is not subjected to wet/dry cycles during hot weather. If this occurs, there will be a large number of cracked fruit. Super Beefsteak exhibits good resistance to *verticillium* wilt and *fusarium* wilt. Maturity is reached about 80 days after transplant.

Sweet 100

- Early
- Hybrid
- Indeterminate

Sweet 100, also known as Sweet Bite, is a relatively tall growing hybrid that produces masses of fruit, sometimes 100 or more - hence its name. It will provide a good crop over many months. Fruit is small, with most being about 20 mm in diameter and hanging from the plant like bunches of grapes. It is a very popular tomato with hotel, restaurant and airline Chefs for use with salads.

The leaves do not provide good coverage of the fruit and it is frequently necessary to shade fruit during hot sunny days, to minimise fruit loss due to sunscald. The plant is a gross feeder and produces a top crop with a flow feed or jet feed system. If drip feed is employed in the hydroponic installation, feed cycles should be at intervals of no more than two hours during hot days.

A nutrient mixture of strength CF22 to 28 will produce a high yield of top quality fruit. Some commercial growers use a strength of CF30 during the early stage in order to promote flower production on the lower trusses. However, after setting of fruit on the first three or four trusses, they reduce the level to CF25.

Sweet 100 will produce good crops with almost all media normally used with hydroponics. Most people who grow this variety on balconies or patios in pots use a perlite/peat mixture, as it retains moisture for periods longer than straight perlite. Many commercial growers using pots, use a very coarse sand mixed with 5mm gravel and feed with a drip system, which provides a continuous nutrient feed throughout the day and two periods during the night. Fruit will split if over watered for a long period. Maturity is reached at 60 to 70 days after seedling plant out.

Typical pH for well ripened fruit is 4.3, with sugar Brix level being in the range 4.8 to 5.1% for fruit ripened on the vine during October/November.

Tiny Tim

- Early
- Standard
- Dwarf

This is a true mini tomato, bearing fruit that are popular with Chefs for specialist salads. It is quite fleshy, with a rich fruity flavour.

The bush is usually less than 40 cm in height and does not require support if kept out of the wind. However if grown on the balcony, or out of doors where wind is likely to be encountered, a small wire frame tied to the lip of the pot should be provided. This is particularly important if perlite or vermiculite is used as medium.

Crops are in the form of masses of small light red fruit, about 20mm in diameter .The plant has a small root system and will dry out quickly during hot weather, unless water is applied regularly. A growing medium which includes a high percentage of peat will help to minimise drying out. A perlite/peat mixture of 30/70 has been used by a number of growers, using pots kept out of doors.

Because of the small size of the bush, hand watering is the most widely used method of applying the nutrient solution. However, where large numbers are grown, drip feeding is often used. The nutrient mixture should not be too high in strength,.as the plant tends to produce few fruit. A strength of CF20 to 23 has proved to be satisfactory. The pot should be regularly flushed with clean water, as the plant reacts quickly to accumulated salts. Maturity is reached in 50 to 60 days from seedling plant out.

Tiny Tim does not appear to be susceptible to most of the common diseases which affect tomatoes, but one grower reported problems with nematodes in half a dozen pots. The seedlings had been grown in soil and although the soil had been well washed off, it is likely that the disease originated in the soil rather than in the hydroponics installation.

Average pH measured from six fruit was 4.25, with sugar Brix level being in the range 5.0 to 5.2 % for vine ripened fruit.

Ultra Boy

- Midseason
- Hybrid
- Indeterminate

This relatively new F_1 hybrid out performs many other hybrids, in terms of crop yield, flavour and resistance to disease. The flesh is fine grained and solid with skin having a bright crimson colour. Fruit is smooth and globular in shape.

Ultra Boy produces a rich, sweet tasting fruit, with crops up to 8.2kg per plant when grown under good conditions in 30cm diameter pots. Many individual fruits are in the range 400 to 500g. If the tomato is to be peeled, the skin comes away easily. This variety is a gross feeder, requiring a strong nutrient solution to about CF 27 to 30, with phosphorus 40 to 50 ppm and potassium 250 to 300 ppm.

Most media are suitable but a mixture of perlite and scoria in the ratio 60/40 will result in a top quality crop of high yield. It does not mind wet roots and in fact, if pots stand in a reservoir, the roots will quickly grow out of the pot drainage holes and spread out into the solution. A reservoir depth of 50mm, containing well aerated solution, will benefit the plant during summer. Jet and flow feed systems give good results, but feeding should extend over a period of at least 10 minutes when the plant is at an advanced stage of growth. A lot of water is taken up by the roots during hot weather. Care must be taken to ensure that roots are not allowed to dry out to the stage where wilting occurs, as the plant is susceptible to high fruit loss due to blossom-end rot. Also, some fruit cracking has been observed with erratic feed cycles.

Harvesting time in pot culture is a little longer than many other hybrids. It usually takes 65 to 70 days before first fruit is ready for picking, but the magnificent taste when grown hydroponically is well worth the extra waiting time. Best eating time is about one week after picking from the vine at the full red stage.

This variety did not show any disease problems with several pot trials conducted throughout a full 12 month period. In a recent taste test involving some 30 varieties, Ultra Boy was placed second.

REFERENCES

1. *Fundamentals of Horticulture.* Edmond J.B., et al, Tata McGraw Hill Publishing Co. Ltd, New Delhi, 1977.
2. *Advanced Guide to Hydroponics.* Douglas J.S., Pelham Books Ltd, London, 1976.
3. *Hydroponic Food Production.* Resh H.M., Woodbridge Press Publishing Co., Santa Barbara, 1981.
4. *Tomato Colour Guides.* SA Dept of Agriculture Fact Sheet No 39/81.
5. *Terrific Tomatoes.* Editors of Organic Gardening and Farming Magazine, Rodale Press, Pennsylvania, 1975.
6. *The Total Tomato.* Du Bose F., Harper Colophon Books, New York, 1985.
7. *Food From Your Greenhouse.* Witham-Fogg H.G., John Bartholomew and Son Ltd, Bromley, 1978.
8. *Hydroponics-Gardening Without Soil.* Harris D., Hydroponics Sales and Service, Daw Park, 1986.
9. *Perlite-Technical Information.* Australian Perlite Pty Ltd, Botany.
10. *Horticultural Perlite for Commercial Growers.* The Perlite Institute, New York, 1978.
11. *The ABC of NFT.* Cooper A., Casper Publications Pty Ltd, Sydney, 1996.
12. *Hydroponics - The Bengal System.* Douglas J.S., Oxford University Press, New Delhi, 1959.
13. *Hydroponic Gardening.* Dalton L. and Smith R., Lothian Publishing Co Pty Ltd, Port Melbourne, 1984.
14. *Hydroponics Plus.* Bentley M., O'Connor Printers, Sth Dakota, 1974.
15. *Tomatoes for Everyone.* Allerton F.W., Faber and Faber, London 1968.
16. *Proceedings Fifth International Congress on Soilless Culture.* ISOSC, Wageningen, 1980.
17. *Proceedings Sixth International Congress on Soilless Culture.* ISOSC, Wageningen, 1984.
18. *The ABC's of Hydroponics.* Schubert M. and Blaicher W., Sterling Publishing Co, New York, 1984.
19. *Hydroponics - Plants Without Soil.* Weir R.N., WA Dept of Agriculture, Farm Note 128/84.
20. *Plant Cultivation Without Soil.* World Farming Jan/Feb, 1980.
21. *Growing Tomatoes in WA.* Hawson M.G., WA Dept of Agriculture, Farm Note 71/84.
22. *Hydroponics: Disorders, Pests, Diseases and Their Management,* Price T.V., Proceedings Symposium Burnley College, Melbourne, 1982.
23. *Fungal Wilt Diseases of Tomatoes.* Carter E.M., WA Dept of Agriculture, Farm Note 48/84.
24. *Tomato Pests and Their Control.* Sproul A.N., WA Dept of Agriculture, Farm Note 113/84.
25. *Growing Tomatoes at Home.* Philp B., SA Dept of Agriculture, Fact Sheet, 114/76.
26. *Grow More Nutritious Vegetables Without Soil.* Taylor J., Parkside Press Publishing Co, California, 1983.
27. *Metric Tables of Composition of Australian Food.* Thomas S., Cordon M., Commonwealth Dept of Health, Canberra.
28. *Nutrition Information.* Australian Nutrition Foundation, Adelaide.
29. Various Information Pamphlets. Health Promotion Branch, Public Health Service, Adelaide.
30. *Soilless Culture.* Sattnby T., Collingridge Ltd, London, 1953.
31. *Temperatures for Tomatoes.* McGlasson W.B., NSW Dept of Agriculture, Ag Facts Sheet 262/65.
32. *Hydroponic Gardening in Australia.* Romer J., Reed Books Pty Ltd, Frenchs Forest, 1986.
33. *The Seed Saver.* Newsletter of the Seed Savers Network, Nimbun, 1986/8.
34. *The Effects of Aeration on Growth of the Tomato in Nutrient Solution.* Durrell W.D., Plant Physiology, April, 1941.
35. *Vegetable Growing Handbook.* Irrigation Research and Extension Committee, Griffith, 1985.
36. *Evaluation of New Cultivars of Fresh Market Tomatoes for Coastal Areas of NSW 1984-85.* Nguyen V.Q. et al, Food Technology in Australia, May, 1986.
37. *Determination of Sensory Quality in Fresh Market Tomatoes.* Kavanagh E.E. and McGlasson W.B., CSIRO Food Res. Q. 43, 1983.
38. *Harvest Maturity and Acceptability of Flora-Dade Tomatoes.* Kavanagh E.E. et al, Journal Amer. Soc. Hort. Sc., III(1), 1986.
39. *Response to Nitrogen and Potassium of Tomatoes Grown in Sand Culture.* Huett D.O. Aust. Journal Exp. Agr. 26, 1986.
40. McGlasson W.B. Personal Correspondence, 1986.
41. Newsletters, Hydroponic Society of America, Concord, California, Various issues, 1986-97.
42. *Hydroponics for Everyone.* Sutherland S.K., Hyland House, Melbourne, 1986.
43. *Hydroponics for Schools and the Home Grower.* Victorian Schools Nursery, Melbourne, 1986.
44. *Introducing Horticulture.* Idczak R., Editor AE Press, Melbourne, 1986.
45. Edgell-Birds Eye, Various company leaflets, Crows Nest, NSW.
46. H.J.Heinz Co. Aust. Ltd, Various company leaflets, Dandenong,   Vic.
47. SPC Ltd. Various company leaflets, Melbourne, Vic.
48. *The Development of Hydroponic Culture in Scotland.* Hall D.A. and Wilson G.C.S. Research and Development in Agriculture 3,2, 1986.

49. *Hydroponics. A guide to Soilless Culture Systems.* University of California, leaflet 2949, 1980.

50. *Greenhouse Tomato Production.* University of California Leaflet 2806, 1975.

51. *Proceedings of Processing Tomato Workshop.* CSIRO, North Ryde 1-2 June, 1976.

52. *Product brochures, various.* TPS Pty Ltd, Brisbane 1986-95.

53. *Hydroponics - Effective Growing Techniques.* Eighth Annual Conference Proceedings, Hydroponic Society of America, 1987.

54. *Hydroponics - The Evolving Art - The Evolving Science.* Proceedings Seventh Annual Conference, Hydroponic Society of America, 1986.

55. *Tomato Diseases and Disorders.* Co-operative Extension Service, Iowa State University, Ames, Iowa, 1987.

56. *Iowa Commercial Vegetable Production.* Co-operative Extension Service, Iowa State University, Ames, Iowa, 1987.

57. *Iowa Commercial Vegetable Production - Fresh Market Tomatoes.* Taber H.G., et al, Iowa State University, Ames, Iowa, 1987.

58. *Master Guide to Planning Profitable Hydroponic Greenhouse Operations.* Savage A.J., International Centre for Special Studies, Honolulu, 1987.

59. *Soilless Culture. Vol. 3 No 2,* ISOSC, Wageningen, 1987.

60. *Growing Greenhouse Tomatoes in the Nutrient Film Hydroponic System.* Wilcox G.E., Yard and Garden, Purdue University, West Lafayette, 1981.

61. *Growing Grafted Tomatoes.* Stephen D., Organic Growing, Summer, 1987.

62. *Tomato Production. Hydroponic Growing Systems.* Ministry of Agriculture, Fisheries and Food Booklet, 2249, 1984.

63. *The Influence of Withholding Oxygen Supply to Roots by Day and Night on Blossom End Rot of Tomatoes in Water Culture.* Tachibana S., Soilless Culture, No I, 1988.

64. Hydroponics Workshop, 16-18 March, 1987, Dept of Agriculture NSW.

65. Hydroponics Workshop, 29-31 March, 1988, Dept of Agriculture NSW.

66. *Commercial Hydroponics.* Mason John, Kangaroo Press Pty Ltd, Kenthurst, 1990.

67. *The Aussie Tomato Book.* Smith Keith and Irene, Viking Penguin Books Aust., Ltd, Ringwood, 1994.

68. *Growing Greenhouse Tomatoes in Soil and in Soilless Media.* Papadopoulos A.P., Agriculture Canada Publication 1865/E, 1991.

69. *Hydroponic Tomatoes for the Home Gardener.* Resh, Howard M., Woodbridge Press Publishing Co., Santa Barbara, 1993.

70. *Tomato Varieties.* Jack Ross, Practical Hydroponics, May/June, 1992.

71. *The Importance of Aeration in Tomato Production.* Jack Ross, Practical Hydroponics, September/October, 1992.

72. *The Biochemistry of Fruits and Their Products.* Hulme A.C. Editor, Academic Press, London, 1971.

73. *Salinity Meters, A Pandora's Box.* Steven Carruthers, Practical Hydroponics & Greenhouses, March/April, 1996.

74. *Sewage Effluent, A Hydroponics Nutrient Solution for Crops.* Loveridge Robert F and Butler John E, Proceedings 8th International Congress on Soilless Culture, ISOSC, Wageningen, 1993.

75. *Proceedings South Pacific Hydroponics Conference,* Surfers Paradise, 6-8 August 1990, Australian Hydroponics Association Inc.

76. Australian Hydroponic Conference, Warwick Farm, 17-19 July, 1995, Australian Hydroponic Association Inc.

77. *Hydroponic Gardening,* Carruthers Steven, Lothian Publishing Co., Pty Ltd, Port Melbourne, 1993.

78. *Hydroponics Made Easy, A Useful Guide for Novice and Intermediate Users of Hydroponics,* Fah Jim, Agromatic Corp & Greenhouses Pty Ltd, Melbourne, 1996.

79. *Hydroponic Fruit Quality Testing.* Dr Lynette Morgan, Practical Hydroponics & Greenhouses, May/June, 1997.

80. *Hot Tomatoes,* Roger Fox, Practical Hydroponics & Greenhouses, November/December, 1997.

GENERAL INDEX

TOMATO VARIETY INDEX